IMAGES of America

Kayenta and Monument Valley

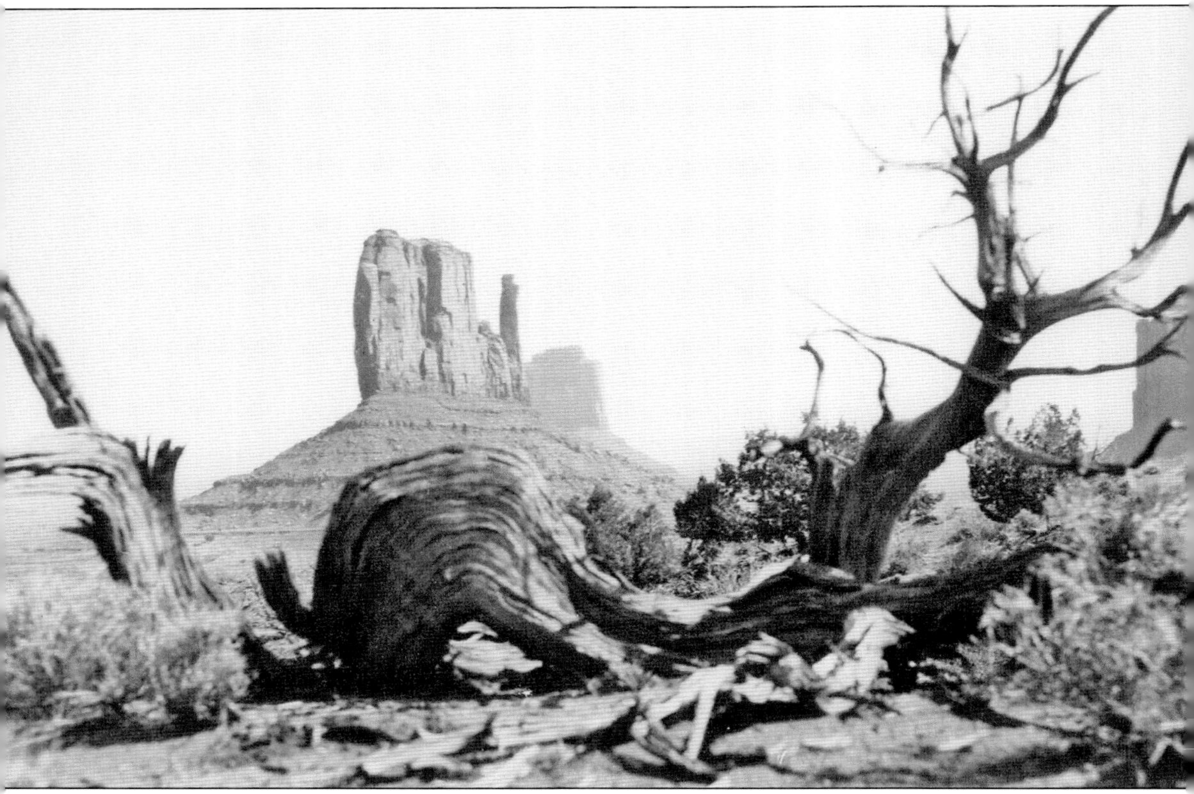

Monument Valley is part of the Colorado Plateau, which runs from southern Utah to northeastern Arizona and east to west-central New Mexico. Eons ago, earth sediments were compressed, and about 65 million years ago, the land of the plateau began to rise. As the sediment layers were exposed to water and wind, the layers of strata began to erode and form the stunning buttes, towers, and monoliths that are seen today in Monument Valley. (Authors' collections.)

On the Cover: Three men visit at the gasoline pump at the Kayenta Trading Post in 1936. The Anglo man at left is thought to be one of the scientists involved with the Rainbow Bridge/Monument Valley Expedition. The Navajo man on the right with the bandana is Hall Burns, and his younger brother John is standing behind the gasoline hose. (Authors' collections.)

IMAGES
of America

Kayenta and Monument Valley

Carolyn O'Bagy Davis and Harvey Leake
Foreword by Richard Paul Mike

ARCADIA
PUBLISHING

ISBN 978-0-7385-8630-4

Published by Arcadia Publishing
Charleston, South Carolina

Printed in the United States of America

Library of Congress Control Number: 2010926124

For all general information, please contact Arcadia Publishing:
Telephone 843-853-2070
Fax 843-853-0044
E-mail sales@arcadiapublishing.com
For customer service and orders:
Toll-Free 1-888-313-2665

Visit us on the Internet at www.arcadiapublishing.com

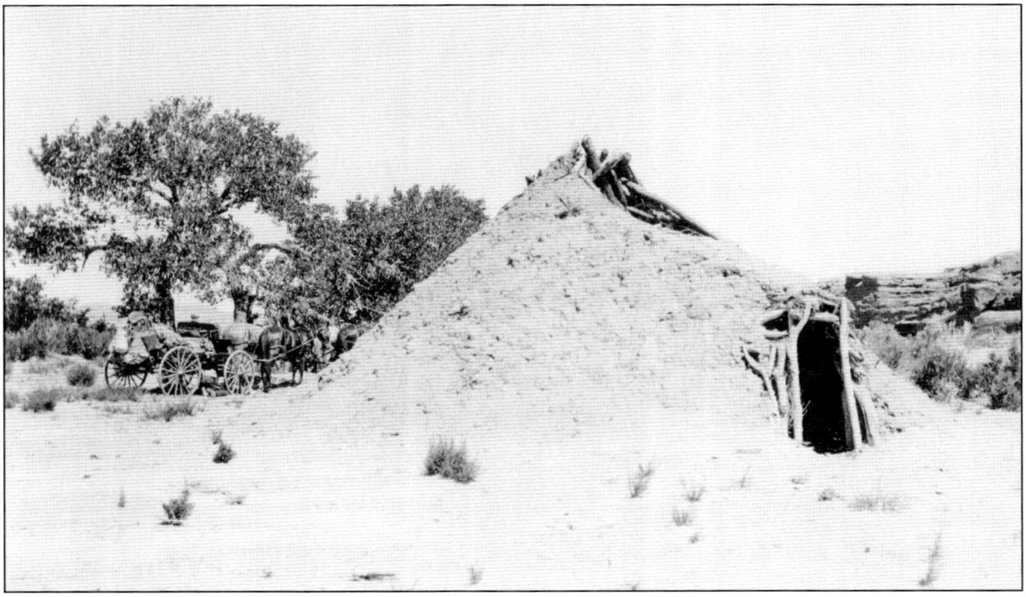

This old-style hogan was built with forked poles interlocked at the top to form a cone or beehive shape. Smaller logs and sticks fill in the space between the larger poles, and the whole exterior is covered with mud plaster. The door, always facing toward the east, is the only opening in the hogan, with the exception of a smoke hole at the top of the structure. (Authors' collections.)

CONTENTS

FOREWORD

Before Hawaii and Alaska joined the union, Kayenta was known as the furthest town from a railroad in the continental United States. Because we were mere human beings at the mercy of the elements and our machines, having patience and sufferance was a requirement of all who lived on the Navajo Reservation. Many a tale was told about births that took place in the worst of storms or how a wedding delay prompted a mother-in-law's loss of temper, making her the brunt of laughter and jokes for months thereafter. Another value, inherited by automobile owners in the 1940s, was to help your stranded brothers and sisters or pick them up if they were hitchhiking, lest you be the one praying for deliverance with your pickup truck stuck in the sand, or trudging down the road with an empty five-gallon gasoline can, or under the hood of your car looking at an engine you knew absolutely nothing about, hoping and praying for an automobile—that day! Paved roads through Kayenta in 1960 ushered in an epoch of stores, pickup trucks, television, telephones, and modern Navajo life. Babies were born in clinics or hospitals, and hitchhikers and broken automobiles were barely seen as drivers whizzed past them down the highways.

The mail truck went puttering to Kayenta once a week, weather permitting. Even at a young age, I preferred the road to Flagstaff, Arizona, over the one to New Mexico, Kayenta being at midpoint. The dirt road to Shiprock was strewn with endless cataclysmic upheavals and deformations of sandstone rocks, breaking into "river" rocks as you approached Teec Nos Pos. The route to Flagstaff had long stretches of sand dunes with an occasional expanse of clay. In the event of rain, I considered the 5 miles before the Elephant's Feet the gooiest, stickiest red clay ever to beset a tire. Those old automobiles without independent suspension would slip off the road and could not get back on the road. Meanwhile, the Navajos would smirk as they rode their horses past the tourists. Some of these tourists would literally be stuck for two or three days until the road dried a little or a team of Navajo horses pulled them out for a fee.

Samuel Holiday, a young U.S. Marine recruit, told me the story of how he went with my father, King Mike, to visit my mother, who lived with her mother, Anna Blackwater, and her sisters at a place we called Blackwater. There my grandmother had orchards of apple, peach, and apricot trees, a farm, a sheep corral, and a cluster of seven hogans located 50 miles northeast of Kayenta. Samuel said that he and my father were granted their 30-day pass after completing their Navajo code talker training course at Camp Pendleton, California. They took the train to Flagstaff, Arizona. There they transferred to the mail truck that left for Kayenta on Tuesdays. Upon their arrival in Kayenta, they discovered that they missed the mail truck from Farmington, which had departed an hour earlier. Samuel was from the Monument Valley area, so he found some relatives to board and feed them. "The next day, we started hitchhiking to your grandmother's place," he said. "We walked all day and not a car came by. We walked to Baby Rocks that day." Baby Rocks was 15 miles from Kayenta. The Navajo people back in those days always carried a canteen of water, mutton jerky, and tortillas. Samuel said, "We found another clan relative who boarded and fed us at Baby Rocks so we didn't have to sleep on the open ground. The next day, only one car came by and picked us up." The automobile carried its passengers to the old Mexican Water Trading Post.

From the Mexican Water Trading Post, it was only 9 miles to Blackwater. So Samuel and my father, King Mike, trudged the last 9 miles to Blackwater and arrived there at 2:00 p.m.. I can imagine the surprise my aunts and my grandmother had seeing my father arriving at their home unannounced. Samuel said, "Your mother was herding sheep, so they had to send one of your aunts to fetch her. The other aunts all started cooking for me and your father, and they all wanted to hear every detail of Marine training and of our trip to get here. Your father was talking and I wanted to smoke, so I went outside of the main hogan and lit up a cigarette. Your mother came into camp on the back of a grey donkey, so I stayed out of sight behind the main hogan. Her hair was unkempt and her blouse was a patchwork of rags, as was her squaw dress. Her face was a little sunburned, and to tell you the truth, your mother didn't look so good. I went back into the hogan, talked a little, and had several smokes outside, but I never saw your mother. Your father did most of the talking; we finished the meal hours ago, and your aunts had already washed the dishes and put away all the pots and pans. About two or three hours later while we were still talking, your mother finally came into the Hogan. Wow! She was the most beautiful woman I had ever seen. Her hair was washed. Her fingernails were red, she had on new clothes and perfume. She had on lipstick and make-up.

"I stayed at Blackwater for a couple of days and decided to return to my folks, who lived between Oljato and Monument Valley. One of your uncles and I went by horseback, and we galloped to Mexican Water Trading Post, and it only took two hours to cover 9 miles. At the trading post I caught the mail truck to Kayenta, and your uncle took my horse back to Blackwater.

"I was supposed to meet your father several weeks later so we could catch the mail truck together back to Flagstaff, but your father didn't show up and I got worried because I knew that the mail truck wouldn't return for another week. My tensions went away at Tuba City when your father boarded the mail truck. King Mike told me that he bought a house in Tuba City because your mother wanted to live near a post office so she could write and receive letters from him. This made sense to me because it took us a hard day's walk for two days to reach Blackwater from Kayenta. Kayenta only received mail once a week, whereas Tuba City got mail three days a week. Your father said that the house was only partly finished, so he and a couple of my mother's brothers went to Tuba City and finished it."

And now, the reservation has changed to the Navajo Nation. Kayenta has grown and is its own local township. Kayenta built a new post office, and mail is distributed five days a week. The Navajo code talkers are passing into history and with them memories from what has been called the "Greatest Generation." It was an ordinary thing for the people of the Greatest Generation, like my mother, to pack up all her belongings and move to Tuba City to raise three children all by herself. My mother, clinging to one infant with one hand and her other hand clutching a toddler, would walk to the Tuba City Trading Post down a dirt pathway a mile from our house to receive letters from my father three days a week instead of one. As for me, I was the oldest at four years old, so I could walk independently away from my mother and two sisters down the path to the trading post.

—Richard Paul Mike

ACKNOWLEDGMENTS

Many people generously loaned photographs and shared information for this project. The authors wish to thank Malcolm Benally, Luke Blair, Dan Cassidy, Andrew L. Christenson, Cynthia Cobb, Shonie De La Rosa, Mario Dominguez, Ken Douthitt, Tom Hanks, Ed Mell, Dennis Preisser, Andrew Singer, Lillian Smith, and Charlie Smith. Joe McNeill identified the actors from photographs in the 1928 silent film *Kit Carson*. Kenneth W. Milano searched for Kayenta records at the Presbyterian Historical Archives in Philadelphia, Pennsylvania. Nathan LaFont and Ronnie Baird at Goulding's Monument Valley Lodge shared photographs and valuable historic background, and photographer Kenji Kawano loaned pictures of the Navajo code talkers. Billy Crawley's stories and photograph collections brought to life the marvelous years in the development of the Navajo Tribal Park at Monument Valley, exploring and touring that magnificent country. And finally, our deepest thanks to Samuel Tom Holiday for an unforgettable day listening to the tales of his early life in a hogan in Monument Valley and his experiences as a code talker in World War II. That day we were honored to meet a true American hero, one of the many remarkable people we met in Kayenta and Monument Valley in the course of compiling this book. It has truly been a privilege.

We also wish to give a heartfelt thank-you to Richard Paul Mike, who has generously given his time and enthusiastic support for this book. He took the authors to places that were relevant to the Kayenta story; he made important introductions with Kayenta people, and he was always there to help. We know that Kayenta is a very special place to Richard Paul Mike, and through his valuable assistance, we have been able to share the unique story of his home.

Unless otherwise noted, the photographs in this volume are from the collections of the authors.

INTRODUCTION

Kayenta is a gateway, like Tibet, to the Unknown. It is a frontier, perhaps the last real frontier in the States. Only Paiutes and Navajos brave the stupendous beyond.

—Winifred Hawkridge Dixon, *Westward Hoboes*, 1921

Located at the northern base of Black Mesa, Kayenta has been called "a lonely sentinel in an arid land." Until fairly recent times, Kayenta has been remote and isolated because of the surrounding topographical features. To the north are the San Juan and Colorado Rivers, barriers to most travel. The land in between is unwelcoming, with jagged sandstone formations that loom forbiddingly in an arid country cut with deep canyons. Landmarks with names such as Wildcat and Cobra Head Canyons and Skeleton Mesa comprise the wild country of Tsegi Canyon (pronounced "Se gee"). To the east is Comb Ridge, and to the north is the dramatic country of Monument Valley, a land of monoliths and mesas. Kayenta has long been a destination on travel routes, essentially the only passage in northeastern Arizona. From the south, access was through Marsh Pass following Laguna Creek, a sandy trail subject to floods from the waters in the distant mountains. The imposing black spire of Agathla Peak, also known as El Capitan, looms in the distance. To the northwest, Rainbow Bridge—Nonnezoshe—is one of the largest natural stone arches in the world. Additionally, it was one of the last discovered natural wonders in North America.

Ruins of stone dwellings on benches and mesa tops and cliff dwellings in the rocky canyons give evidence of early occupation. Caves and rock shelters dot the area. West of Kayenta are the immense cliff dwellings of Keet Seel, Betatakin, and Inscription House, which today comprise Navajo National Monument. These early dwellers, called Anasazi or Ancestral Puebloans, are the ancestors of the modern pueblo people. Although they were early inhabitants of the area, they eventually migrated to the area of the Hopi villages on the southern edges of Black Mesa and the New Mexico pueblos to the east.

The next group to inhabit the region was a band of Southern Paiutes, whose presence near Navajo Mountain was first documented in 1776, when Frs. Silvestre Vélez de Escalante and Francisco Atanasio Domínguez encountered them during an expedition to find a route to California.

By the 1500s, groups of Navajos were coming into the area around Kayenta and Monument Valley. These nomadic people left few traces of their presence, although there is archaeological evidence of early inhabitation from tree-ring dates taken from Navajo hogans—the round shelters constructed of logs with mud mortar. The language of the Navajos has Athabascan roots that can be traced far to the north and the many native peoples of western Canada. Navajos are desert dwellers. The name by which they are known, *Diné*, means "the People."

By the early 1800s, the Spanish were exerting increasing control over the land in northern New Mexico and Arizona as they sought to enlarge their holdings of livestock and grazing land. Conflict between the Spanish and Navajos escalated until 1823, when New Mexico governor Jose

Antonio Vizcarra led a force of 1,500 men west from Santa Fe to the Hopi villages and north into the country around Kayenta and Oljato (pronounced "Ol jay toe") with the objective of subduing the Navajos in that little-known area. Thirty-two Navajos were killed during this encounter, as well as five Paiutes. Relations between Navajos, Spanish, and Anglos continued to be contentious, and sometimes violent, through the following decades.

In 1855, Ethan Pettit led a group of Mormons to explore and trade with the Navajos in the Marsh Pass area, and in 1859, on an exploratory mission, Capt. J. G. Walker led a group of soldiers from Fort Defiance over Black Mesa. A Mormon exploring party passed through the area in 1879, traveling by wagon from Tuba City through Marsh Pass to Aneth, Utah. However, other than prospectors and a few wandering traders, for most of the 19th century the Kayenta and Monument Valley area was seldom visited by outsiders.

In the winter of 1863, Col. Christopher "Kit" Carson was given orders to capture every living Navajo and take them to Fort Sumner, 180 miles southeast of Santa Fe, New Mexico. The U.S. government adopted a plan of relocation to solve the problem of conflict between Anglos and Navajos after years of trouble. Carson and his soldiers stormed through traditional Navajo lands, killing Navajo livestock, burning crops, and cutting down fruit trees. Starvation forced the surrender of almost 8,000 Navajos, who were made to walk 300 miles to Fort Sumner, where they would remain until 1868. Hundreds died during the "Long Walk," and there were more deaths at Fort Sumner because of poor food and miserable conditions.

There were a few isolated bands of Navajos who were never captured. One group was a band led by the famous chief Hoskininni of the Tachinii, or Red Streak Clan. For four years, during the unrelenting pursuit of the soldiers, Hoskininni and his people hid in the rugged country near Navajo Mountain, existing on wild foods, seeds and grasses, and piñon nuts. They posted sentinels to watch for soldiers and moved constantly. They traveled across the sandstone rock to hide their trails, building camps near the base of craggy canyon walls that funneled the campfire smoke upwards and hid the source from the dreaded Ute army scouts (traditional enemies of the Navajo, Ute scouts were employed by the government in campaigns against the Navajos). Hoskininni was a wise and crafty leader, but he was also aided during those years by the wild and forbidding country where the Navajos took shelter from the soldiers.

After four years of living in hiding from the government soldiers and facing constant starvation, the Navajos of the Kayenta area had a well-founded fear and aversion of Anglos and any newcomers to their land around Monument Valley. Prospectors came into the Navajo country searching for precious metals. Many of these men were never heard from again, and it was assumed that the Navajos were accountable for their disappearances.

In the early years of the 20th century, the only inhabitants of the isolated country on the northern edge of Black Mesa were Paiutes and nomadic Navajo families tending to their flocks of sheep and planting small plots of corn in the arid, high-desert country of today's northeastern Arizona. The Navajos who lived in the Kayenta area were a hardy, resourceful people with understandable suspicion of the white men who were coming to their lands in increasing numbers. From early times, the lands of Kayenta and Monument Valley sheltered and gave life to the Navajos, a brave and enduring people who continue to abide in that beautiful country to this day.

One

Red Canyons and Purple Sage

The northern border country of Arizona near Monument Valley was a frontier wilderness until the early 1900s. Even though Anglos and Spanish settlers were moving north and west into Arizona Territory, this wild expanse was unsurveyed and barely explored, its adventurers turned back by sheer cliffs, steep and rocky trails, scarcity of water, extreme temperatures, and wind-swept sand dunes. Cliff dwellings and stone walls give evidence of early inhabitation by a people who by 1300 AD had moved on.

Descendants of the bands of traditional Navajos who had evaded capture by Kit Carson's soldiers and incarceration at Fort Sumner in 1863 were living in the nether region of Navajo Mountain and Monument Valley. This band of Navajos was led by the famous medicine man and leader Hoskininni. In this inaccessible terrain, they maintained their nomadic way of life, herding horses and large flocks of sheep and moving seasonally to follow the grazing.

Many early explorers and settlers in the area considered the desert country to be ugly. With only a sparse covering of cedar and piñon trees, the unbroken expanse of sand and stone was unwelcoming to the eyes of those from the south and east. The isolated region was also nearly inaccessible. The Colorado and San Juan Rivers blocked travel from the north and west, and deep canyons and narrow passes, along with deep sand or clinging mud, kept most people away. Even the dramatic vistas of Monument Valley were unappealing to settlers looking for land to settle on. Scant rain made farming impossible, and lack of grass made the country unwelcome for ranching. Few outsiders visited the area; almost none settled there. But the very harshness of the landscape has preserved its unique beauty into the 21st century, and today the Kayenta and Monument Valley area is a destination for hundreds of thousands of visitors.

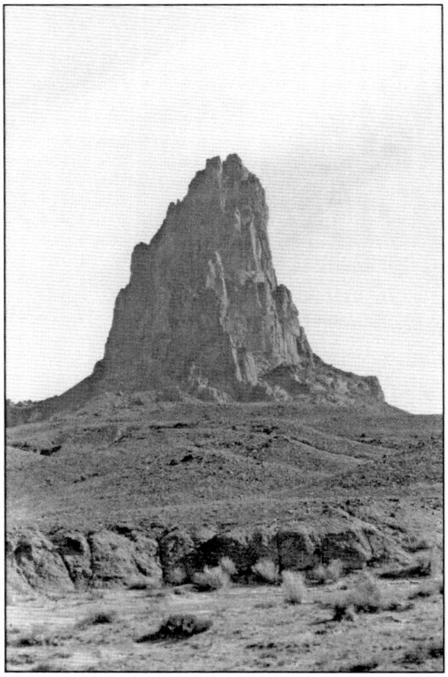

The dark, volcanic monolith of Agathla Peak rises 1,500 feet above the valley floor about 8 miles north of Kayenta. Also known as El Capitan, the sheer and imposing landmark has spiritual significance to the Navajo people. According to historian Laurance Linford, Agathla is spoken of in the Bead Chant, which tells of Navajo clan migrations. The name translates as "Much Wool" or "Much Fur," references to the processing of deer hides, in which the skins were scraped across the rock to remove the hair. Later visitors to the area compared the jagged stone peak to a Gothic cathedral.

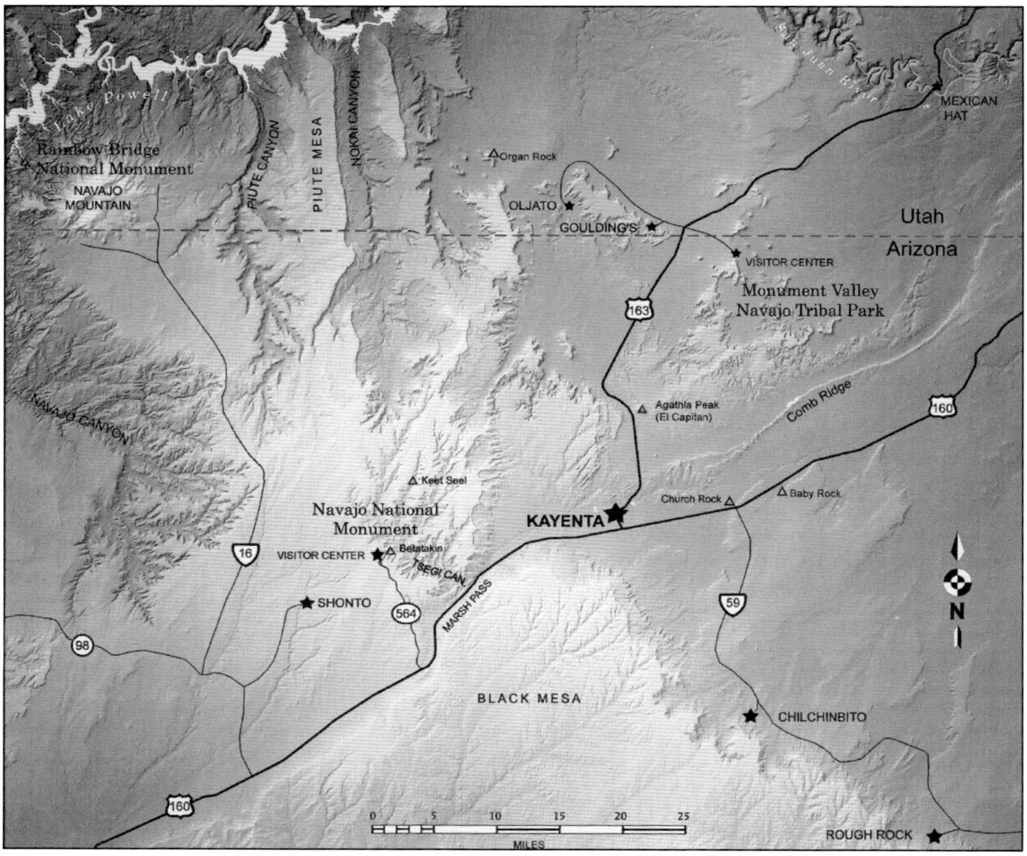

The dramatic buttes and monoliths in Monument Valley have been sculpted by wind and water over millions of years. Early people, the Anasazi, lived here hundreds of years ago, and today only fragments of their lives can be found in the rock art, pottery shards, and some rock walls throughout the country. Today Monument Valley is the homeland of the Diné, the Navajo people. The Totem Pole is one of the dramatic spires in the valley. It rises 450 feet above the valley floor.

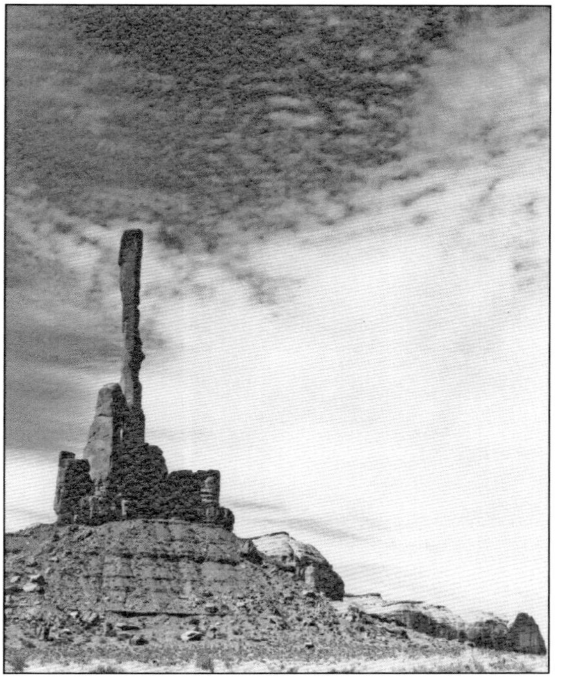

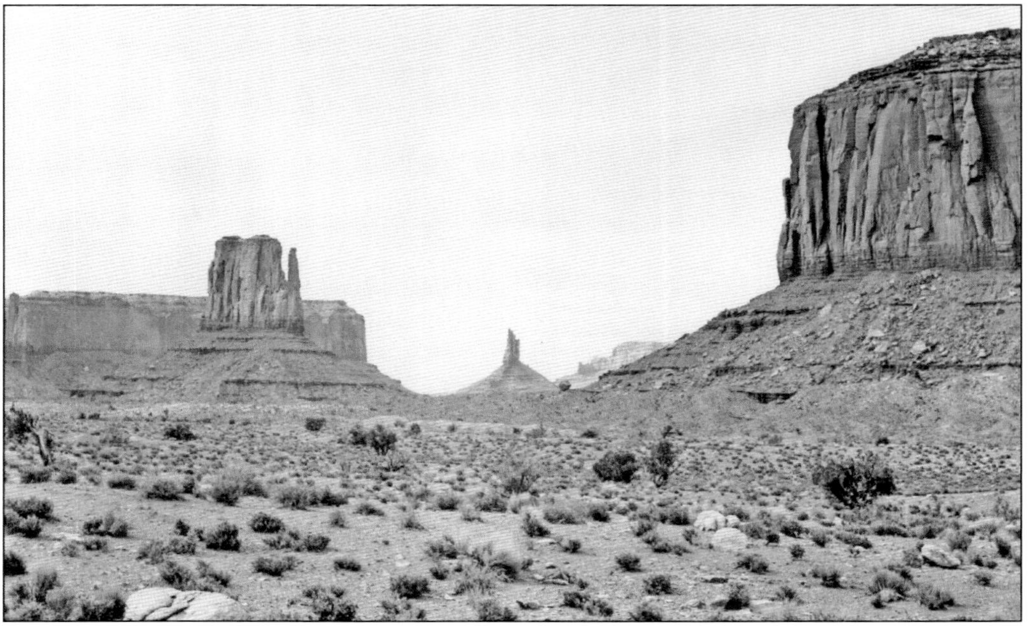

Merrick Butte, on the right, was named for James Merrick, the Anglo prospector who was killed, along with his partner Ernest Mitchell, in 1880 in the Monument Valley area. Navajos in the area were suspected to have killed the two prospectors, but it was later learned that they were robbed and killed by a band of Utes. Merrick and Mitchell were reputed to have discovered a valuable mine that was reported to assay at $800 a ton. Decades of searchers have never found their diggings. There were other killings in this lonely and dangerous land, where the nearest law enforcement was miles to the east in Durango, Colorado.

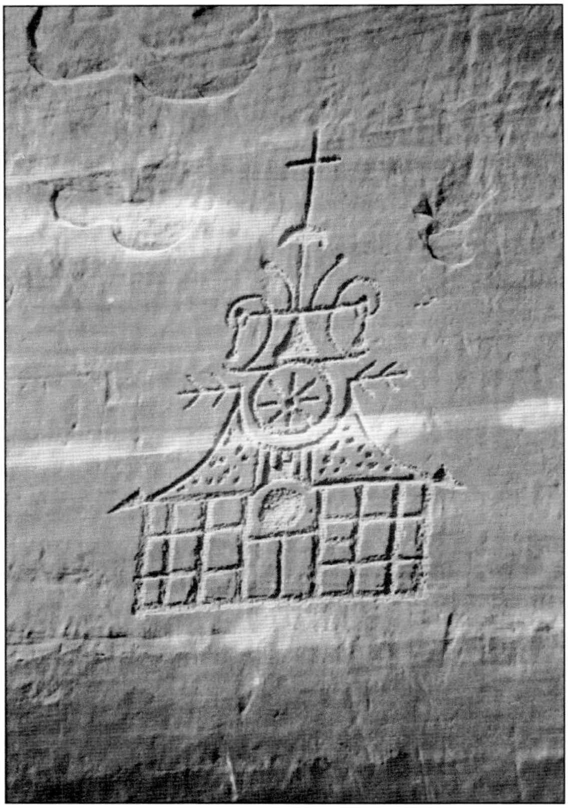

Spanish explorers passed south of Kayenta in 1823, when a detachment led by Col. Francisco Salazar traveled from the Hopi mesas east to the Chinle Valley. Petroglyphs believed to have been inscribed by early Spanish explorers can be found on stone canyon walls 35 miles east of the Kayenta valley. (Courtesy of Billy Crawley.)

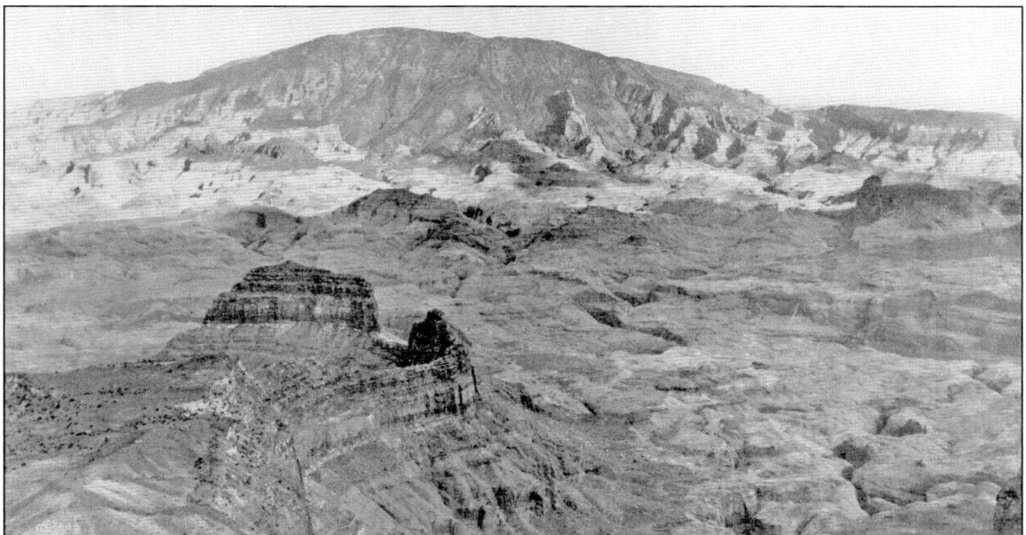

The rugged country north of Navajo Mountain is cut with deep slots. The arid landscape is hostile to plant and human life alike. Travel is difficult and hazardous. Much of the country surrounding Kayenta is rugged and forbidding, and few people venture into the area where deep canyons and sheer sandstone walls make travel nearly impossible.

Organ Rock is located just north of Oljato. The area is sometimes called the "other Monument Valley." It is on the route down to Copper Canyon on the way to the San Juan River.

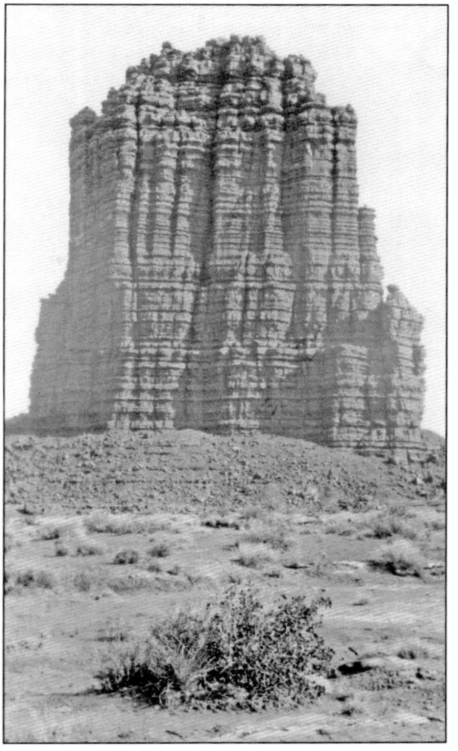

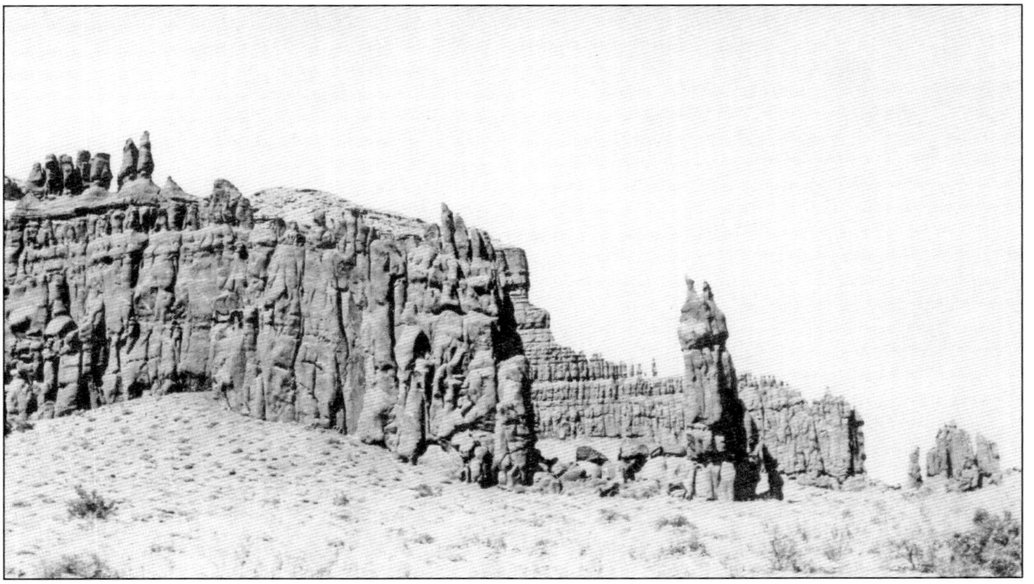

The stacked rocks that make up the Baby Rocks landform on the low mesa are located about 11 miles east of Kayenta. In the early 1900s, settlers came to the area from Kayenta to farm on the banks of Laguna Creek, but numerous floods washed out the fields, and the people moved east to Dinnehotso. Baby Rocks Trading Post was built here in the early 1960s. The post was built in the form of a figure eight—two hogans touching—from local stone. Nothing is left of the trading post today.

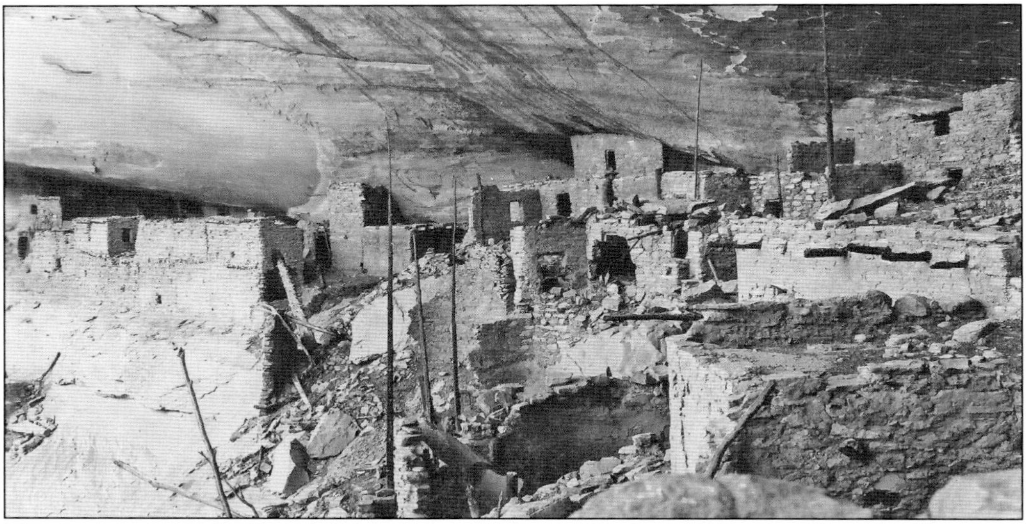

The dramatic cliff dwelling known as Keet Seel was discovered by Richard Wetherill in 1895, and the name, loosely translated from Navajo, means "Broken Pottery." The ruin is located in a branch of Tsegi Canyon, and with 160 rooms, it is the largest cliff dwelling in Arizona. It was occupied around 1250 AD and then abandoned by 1300 AD.

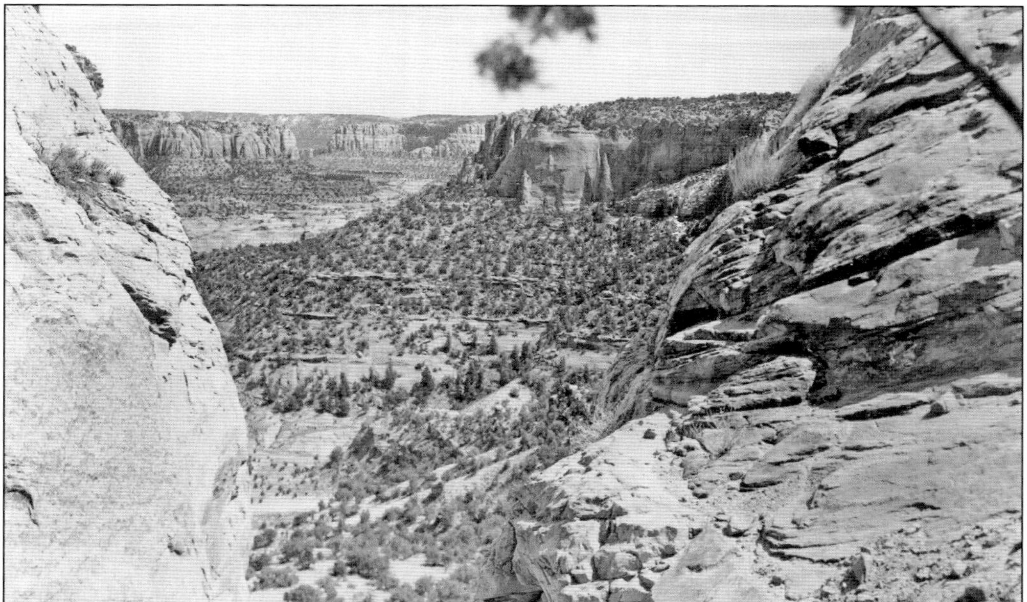

Tsegi Canyon is a deep and winding slash in the landscape; the translation from Navajo means "in between the rocks." The majestic canyon was also home to early inhabitants. Ruins and cliff dwellings are scattered along the length of the canyon, located between Skeleton and Zilnez Mesas. S. H. Babington, a 1934 visitor, wrote of the area, "Most of the canyon walls were brilliant red. However, some of them had patches of turquoise green, copper blue, golden yellow, or chalky white, depending upon the type of lichen growing on their faces. Juniper and piñon were growing on the banks of the washes and on the gentle slopes of the canyon walls, and an occasional spruce or ponderosa pine rose from the southern heights."

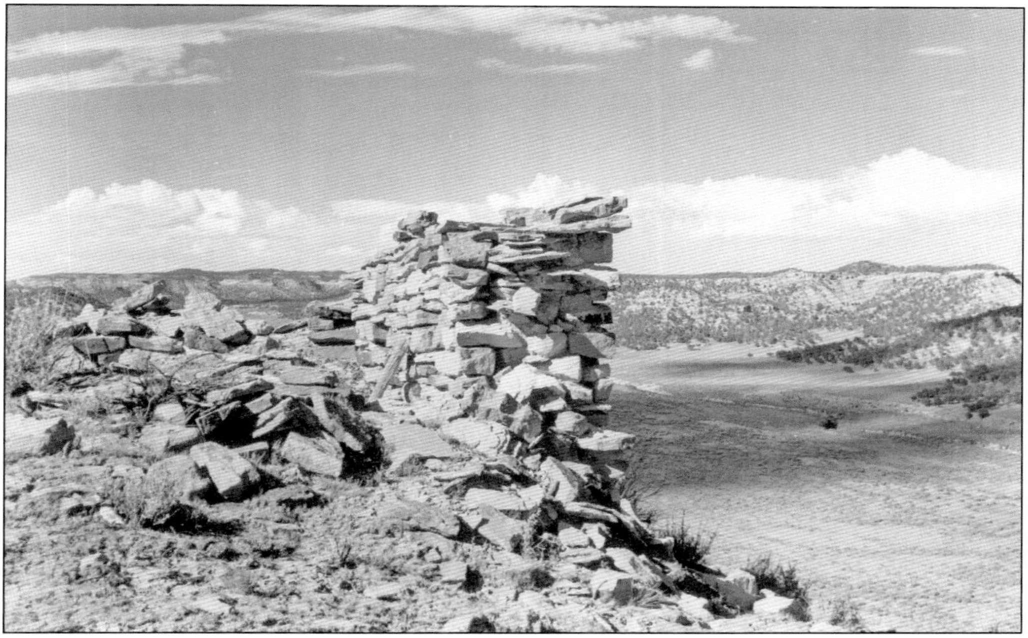

Stone walls on the mesa tops and ledges give evidence of early inhabitation in the country north of Black Mesa.

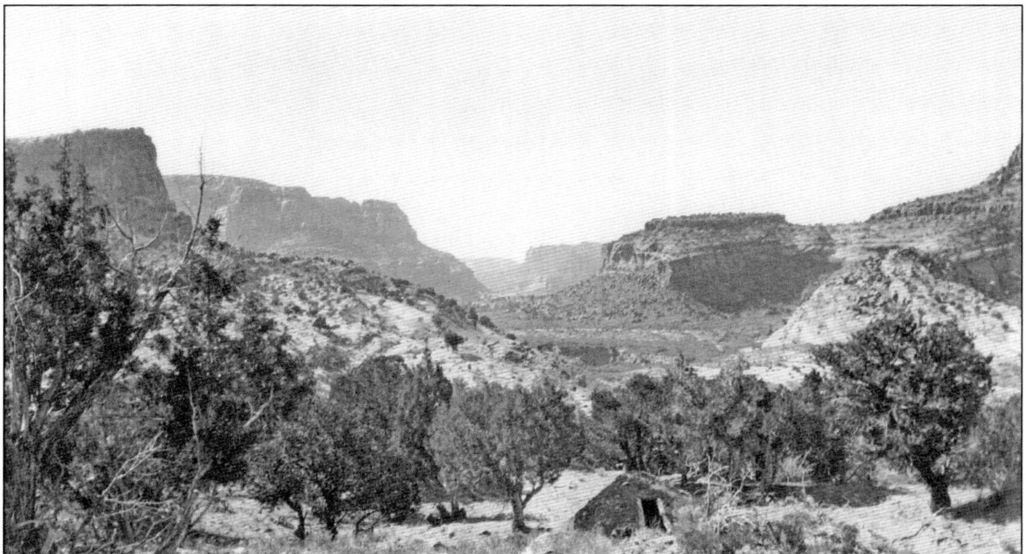

Early Spanish explorers called Marsh Pass "Puerta de las Lemitas" after the three-leaved sumac that grows in the area. Americans mistook the name Lemita with *limita* in the mistaken belief that Marsh Pass was the limit beyond which the Navajos would not retreat, or that the country to the north and west was too rugged for survival. Marsh Pass is the narrow valley formed by Laguna Creek between Black Mesa to the south and Tsegi Canyon to the north. It provides the only access to Kayenta from the west. Of Marsh Pass a visitor wrote, "The deep blue narrow ribbon of sky with jagged borders above us was spattered with vivid clusters of milky white clouds in the shape of immense monsters."

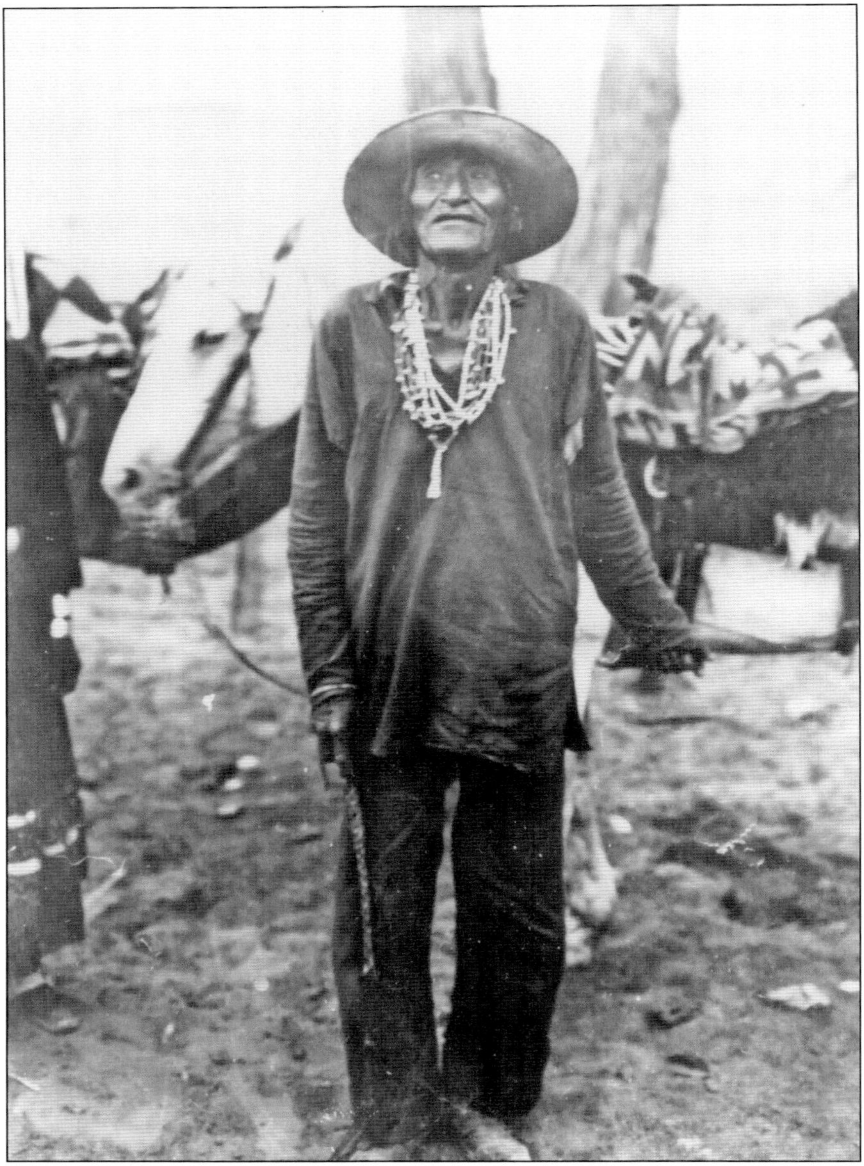

Hoskininni was born in the 1820s, about 4 miles northwest of the present-day town of Kayenta at Kée agodi ("Short Foot"). He became a famous medicine man and chief, and when Kit Carson's soldiers were hunting Navajos during the forced relocation to Fort Sumner in 1863, Hoskininni led his people to safety in the rugged country near Navajo Mountain. When the treaty was signed in 1868, Hoskininni returned to the Oljato and Monument Valley country. After years of conflict, he regarded white people with suspicion and distrust, but he befriended the owners of the first trading post in the area, John and Louisa Wetherill. When Hoskininni died in the fall of 1909, his hogan was burned, according to Navajo custom. Archaeologist Neil Judd, who met the famous leader the summer he died, wrote that this photograph and others taken at the same time were blamed for his death just a few weeks later. Hoskininni was buried about 3 miles north of Kayenta at Standing Black Rock. Two horses were killed over his grave to carry him on his journey to the land of peace and summer.

Two

Moonlight Water

On March 17, 1906, John Wetherill, his trading partner Clyde Colville, and his brother-in-law John Wade arrived at Oljato, "Moonlight Water," where the water from the spring glowed in the moonlight and the tall cottonwoods were framed by the red cliffs. They had been warned against entering the distant country, where other white men had been murdered or had simply disappeared, never to be seen again. John and Louisa Wetherill had been trading at Chaco Canyon in northwestern New Mexico when they decided to build a new trading post among the western Navajos. At first the newcomers were not welcomed. The son of Hoskininni, who always rode with four armed men, met Wetherill, Wade, and Colville at Oljato and told the men to leave. Hoskininni Begay said, "We want no white men here." But John Wetherill talked of the advantage of having a trading post at Oljato, where local Navajos could purchase flour and coffee and sell their silver jewelry and rugs. After days of talks and a feast of rabbit stew and coffee provided by John Wetherill, Hoskininni and his son Hoskininni Begay invited them to stay and build a new store. The nearest post at that time was at Round Rock, 70 miles away. A trading post at Oljato would provide a much closer place to trade turquoise and wool for flour, coffee, and other necessities.

John Wetherill returned to Chaco Canyon for his family—son Benjamin, daughter Georgia Ida, and wife Louisa. As the Wetherill family traveled west to Oljato, they were warned at every trading post and Navajo community not to continue, because they would be killed by the hostile Navajos at Oljato. But the Wetherills persisted, traveling across the unmarked, trackless desert to the place of the moonlight water. Here they established their home and lived among the Navajo people for the rest of their lives. Louisa already spoke fluent Navajo and came to be known as Hoskininni's granddaughter. Called Asthon Sosi—"Slim Woman"—by the Navajos, she became the liaison between the Diné and the white soldiers and government officers, trusted by the Navajo people to be their spokesperson.

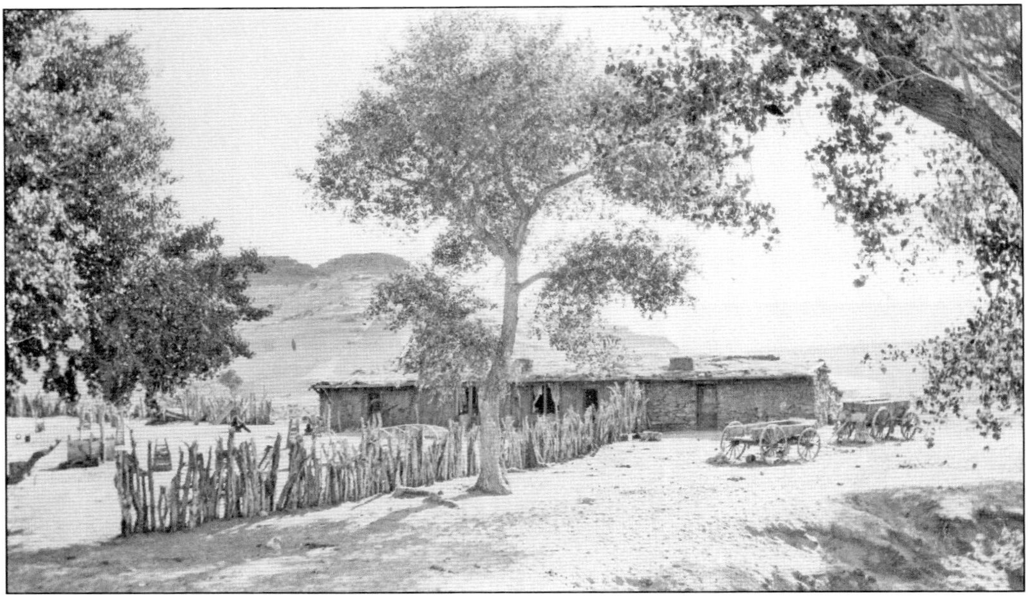

John and Louisa Wetherill and Clyde Colville began trading at Oljato in a tent with a plank laid across two wooden Arbuckles Coffee crates. John later built a house of vertical logs and mud with a dirt roof, with another stone room adjoining it for the trading post. A fence of cedar posts separated the yard of the house from the trading post. In this photograph, taken about 1908, the trading post is the building to the right, and the attached Wetherill home is on the left.

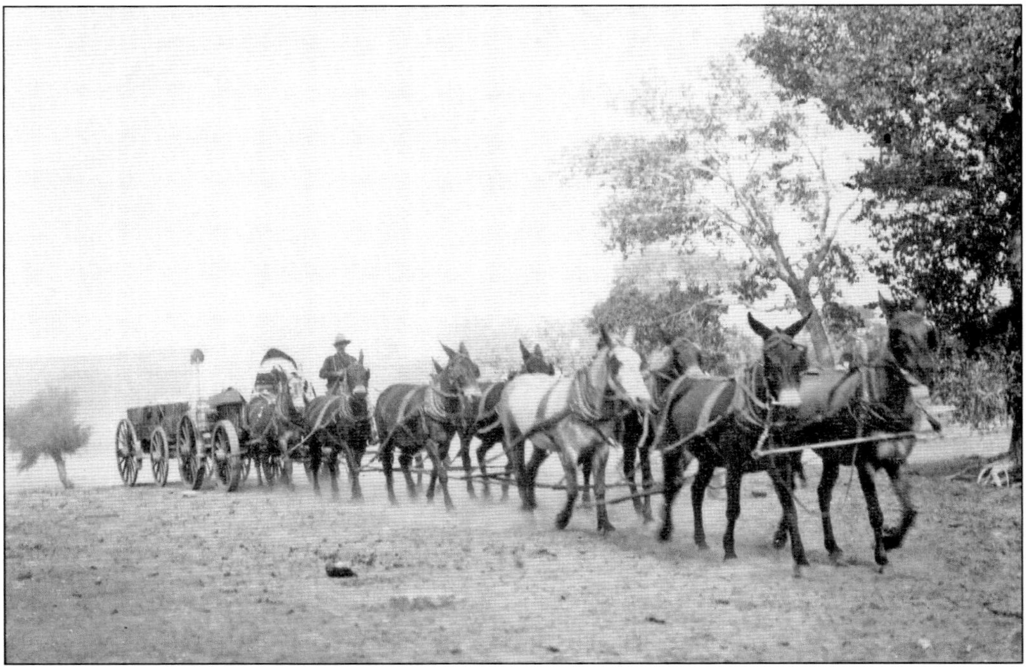

Merchandise for the trading post had to be freighted for miles from Gallup, New Mexico, with the heavily loaded wagons roped together and pulled by teams of 8 to 10 horses. Advancing only 5 miles a day, the journey could take more than a month.

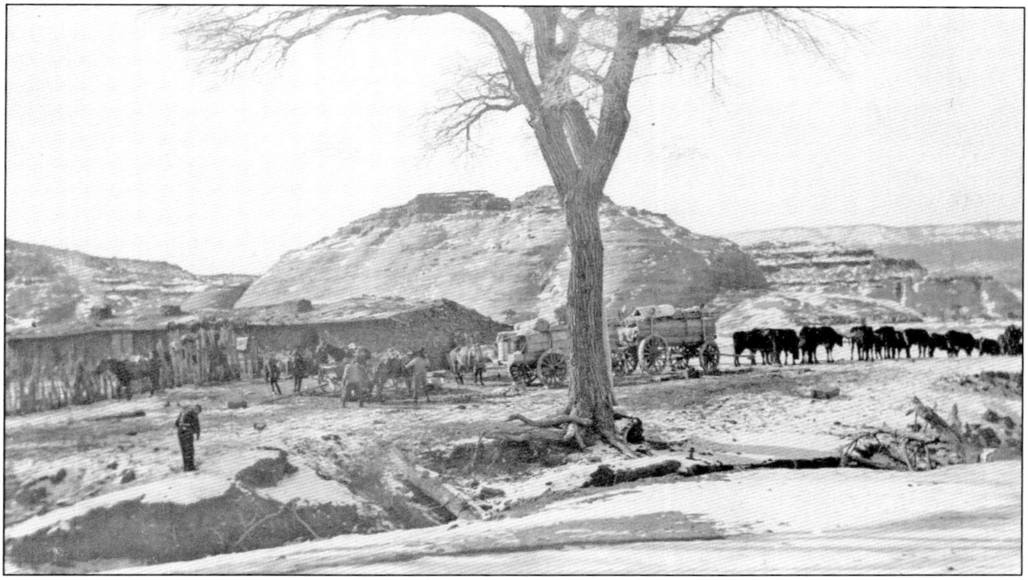

A double freight wagon is preparing to leave Oljato Trading Post in the 1909 photograph above. Two of the wagons are hitched together, and the string of oxen pulling them extends far beyond the limits of the frame. Oljato Wash, covered with snow, runs in front of the trading post and Wetherill home. In the 1907 photograph below, Georgia Ida Wetherill and an unidentified Navajo stand in front of the Wetherill house with the trading post in the attached room behind the fence. The gate behind Georgia Ida is constructed with Arbuckles Coffee boxes. In spite of the danger most whites faced in the region, the Wetherills lived in peace founded on mutual respect with the local Navajos. Georgia Ida, known as Etai Yazi ("Little Girl") to the Navajos, grew up at the remote trading post.

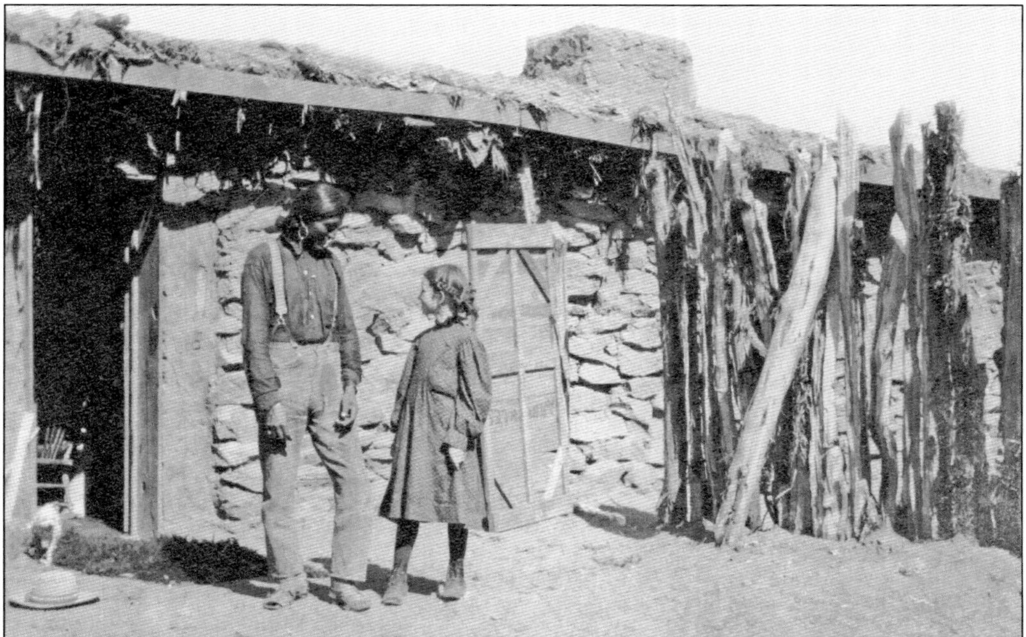

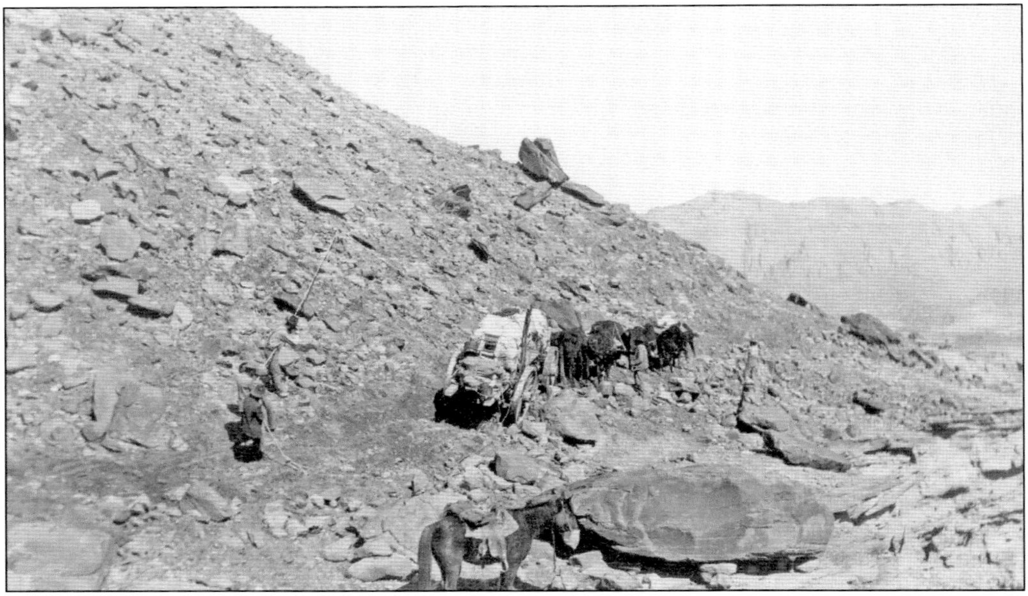

Charles H. Spencer was a mining entrepreneur in the San Juan area. He is most well known for commissioning the construction of a steamboat in San Francisco in 1911 to bring coal down the Colorado River to his gold mine. In the 1909 photograph above, three men at the left pull on a rope looped around a rock in an effort to prevent the ore wagon from tipping over and falling into the ravine. Below, also in 1909, Spencer's huge freighting wagons are loaded with provisions from the trading post. Pictured from left to right are Charles H. Spencer, W. M. Reid, unidentified, R. W. Stevenson, John H. Marks, George Keplinger, John Wetherill, Louisa Wetherill, Preston Apperson, George Peterson, Clyde Colville, Mr. Twitty, J. DeJarld, Henry King, Harry Ashenhurst, and Georgia Ida Wetherill standing in the wagon bed.

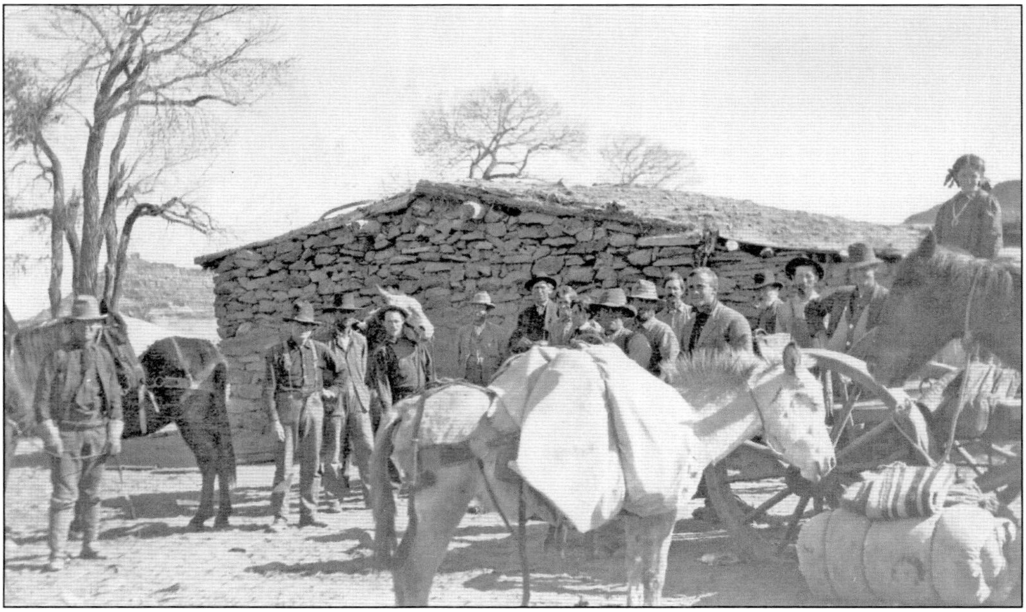

A visitor to the Wetherill's trading post wrote, "This John Wetherill is, himself, one of the scenic and natural wonders of the southwest." John was a Quaker and always a gentleman. Another wrote, "Hosteen John was tough. He was one of those guys who could do anything. . . . It was a privilege to have met him." Even though there was still hostility between Anglos and Navajos when the Wetherills arrived at Oljato, John never carried a gun. He was one of the five Wetherill brothers from Mancos, Colorado, responsible for the discovery of many of the famous cliff dwelling ruins in what was to become Mesa Verde National Park. The boy at the right in this 1909 photograph is Malcolm Cummings, son of a Utah archaeologist.

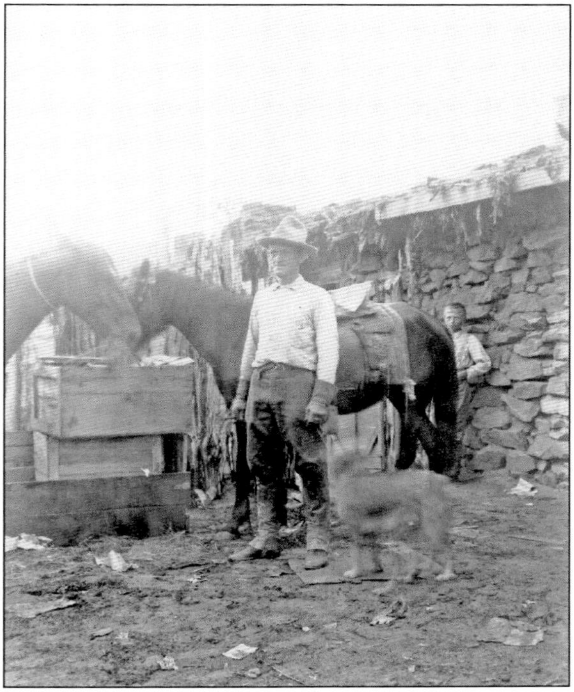

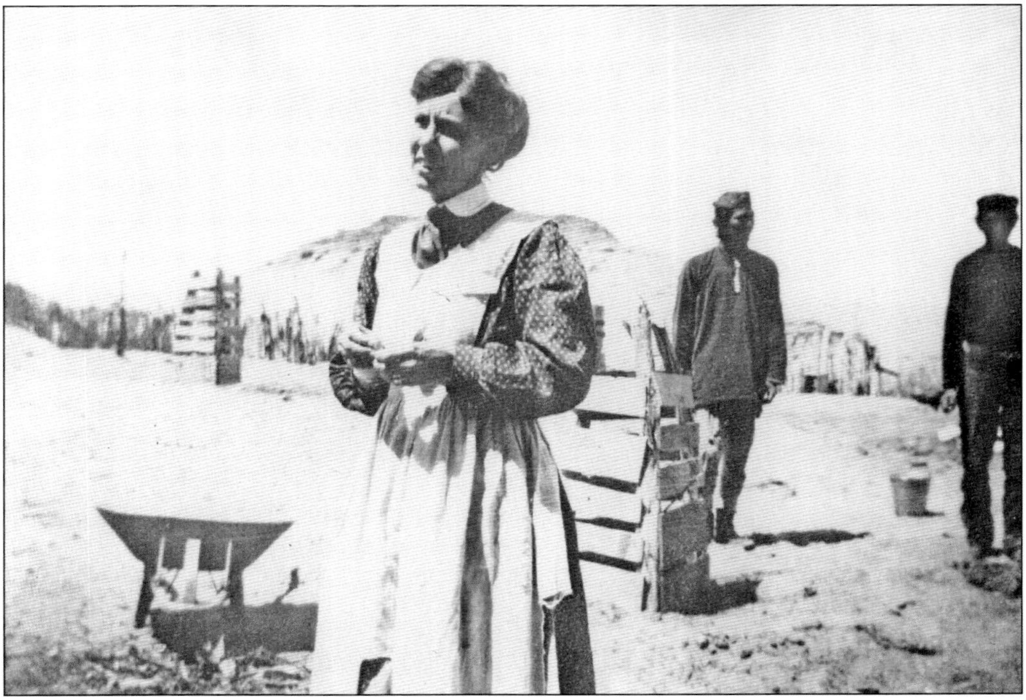

After their arrival at Oljato, the local Navajo headman Hoskininni claimed Louisa as a granddaughter. Much respected by the Navajos, Louisa spoke Navajo and learned their customs and traditions. The Navajos said that Louisa was one of them. In this 1909 photograph, the box structures protect young trees that Louisa planted to shade her Oljato home.

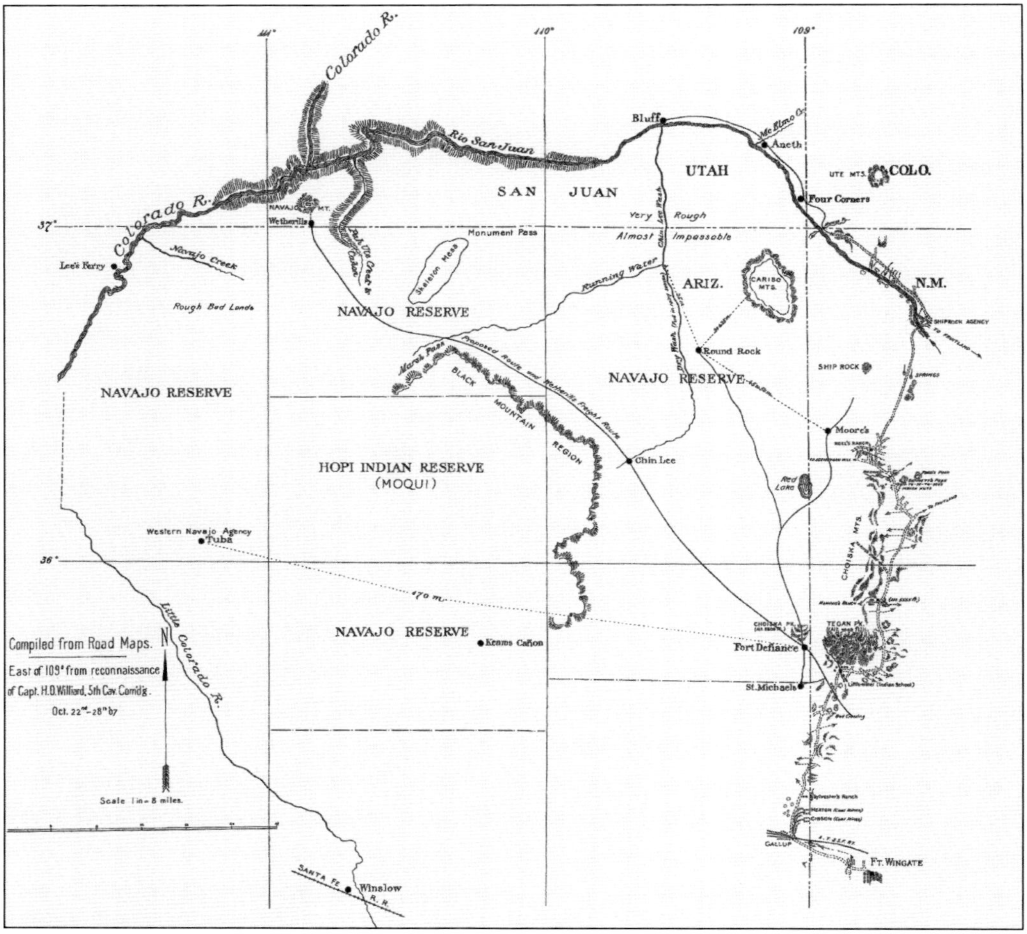

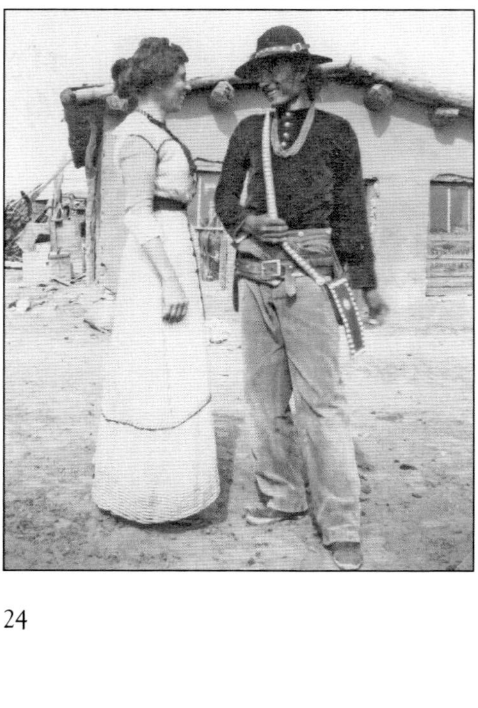

In 1908, six troops of cavalry, a machine gun platoon, a wagon train, and 50 pack mules were sent to Oljato in a show of strength when the local Navajos refused to send their children away to government boarding schools. The map above shows the route of the troops from Fort Wingate to Oljato. When the soldiers arrived at Oljato, in what became known as the Black Mountain Conference, they spread their tents across the flat land in front of the trading post. The Navajos hid the women and children in the remote canyons. John and Louisa intervened on behalf of their Navajo friends, and after peaceful talks between the Navajos and soldiers, agreements were peacefully reached. Louisa Wetherill, shown in this photograph with Sitsosie, acted as interpreter between the Navajos and the U.S. military. Sitsosie was a handsome and capable young man who often worked as a guide for the Wetherills.

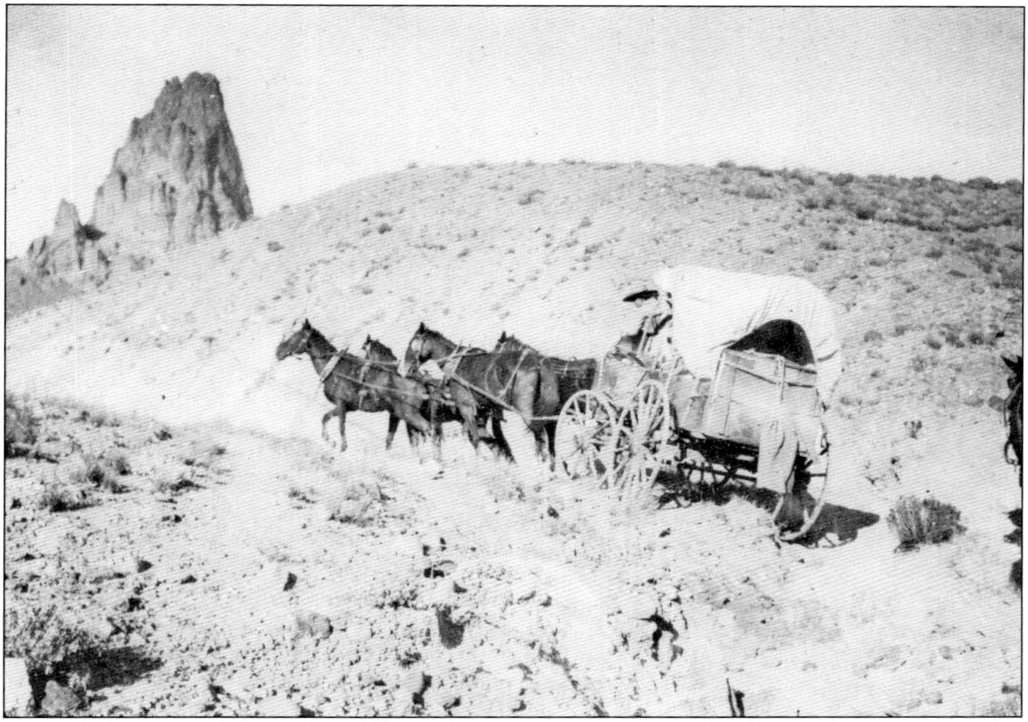
The wagon trail to Oljato went past Agathla Peak, also known as El Capitan.

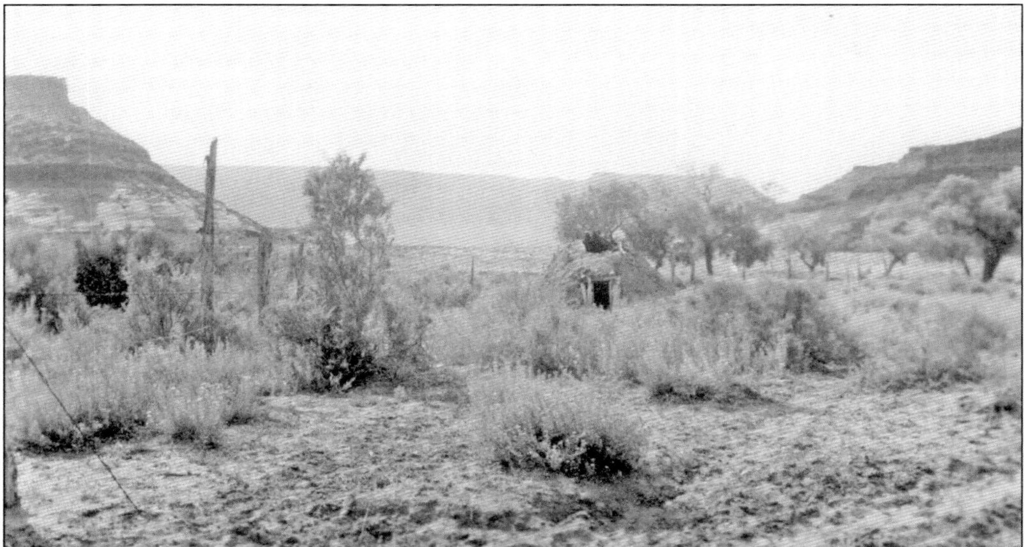
Remains of abandoned hogans can be seen in Navajo country. After a death, the hogan is abandoned. In order for the spirit of the deceased to leave this world, a hole is broken in the north side of the hogan wall, and the area is never visited, because it is considered unlucky or evil. A Navajo family will then typically move to a new place and build a hogan of logs and mud. Before it is used, a Blessing Way is held to bless the hogan, and sacred corn pollen is sprinkled around or on the walls.

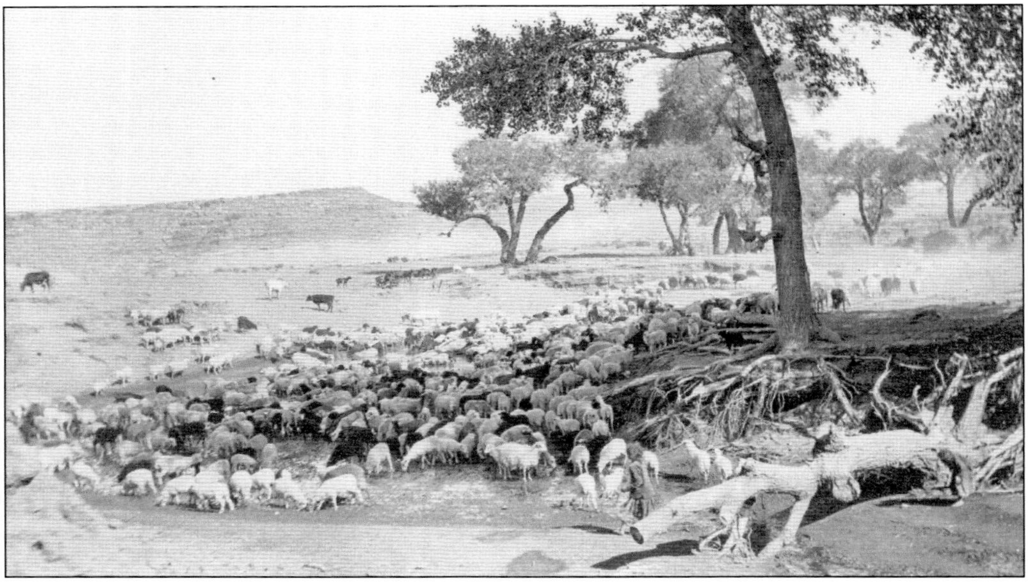

A young shepherdess at the lower right center of the photograph watches over a flock of sheep. Sheep provided food for the Navajos, and wool could be taken to the trading post to trade for goods. In older times, Navajo families were nomadic, traveling with their flocks to water and grass.

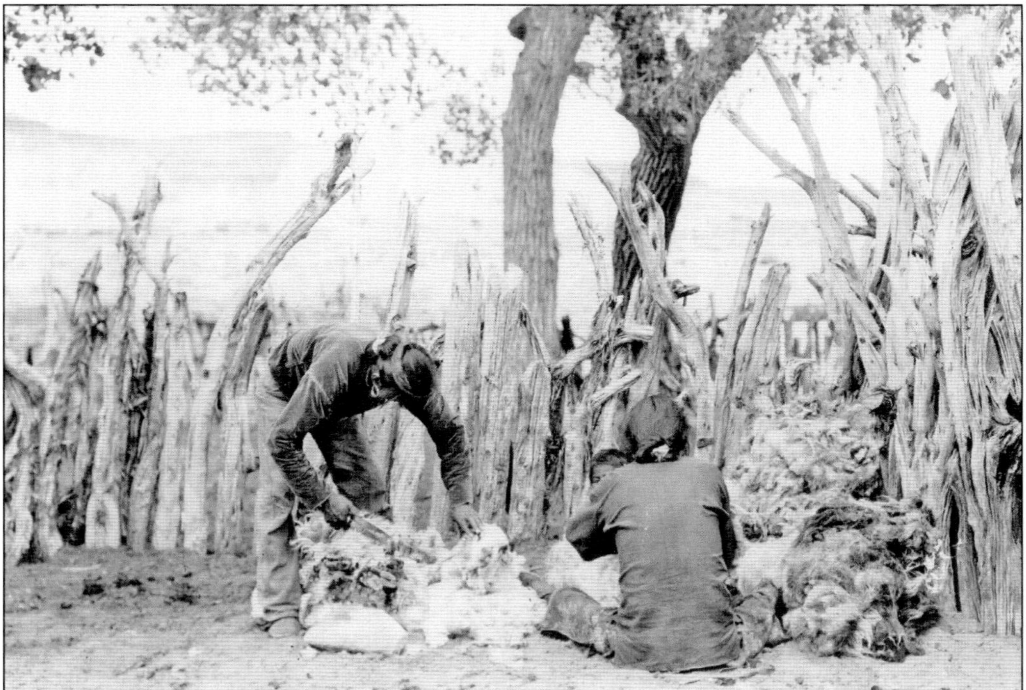

Two Navajo men at Oljato are shearing sheep with hand clippers. A good shearer could hold the sheep down with one hand and shear the wool off in one continuous clip so that all of the fleece was the same length. A large pile of wool is at the right, and a small boy can be seen peeking over the shoulder of the seated man.

Hoskininni Begay, the only son of the famous chief Hoskininni, stands in front of the Oljato Trading Post with 10-year-old Georgia Ida Wetherill. He was born on the mesa that bears his family name. In 1884, Hoskininni Begay and his cousin killed two white miners, Samuel Walcott and James McNally. Two previous prospectors, Mitchell and Merrick had been killed in Monument Valley four years earlier, and relations were hostile between Navajos and white miners coming into the country. Hoskininni Begay fled to Monument Valley, but his father was arrested. Eight months after the murders, a trial ended without an indictment, Hoskininni was released, and Hoskininni Begay was acquitted.

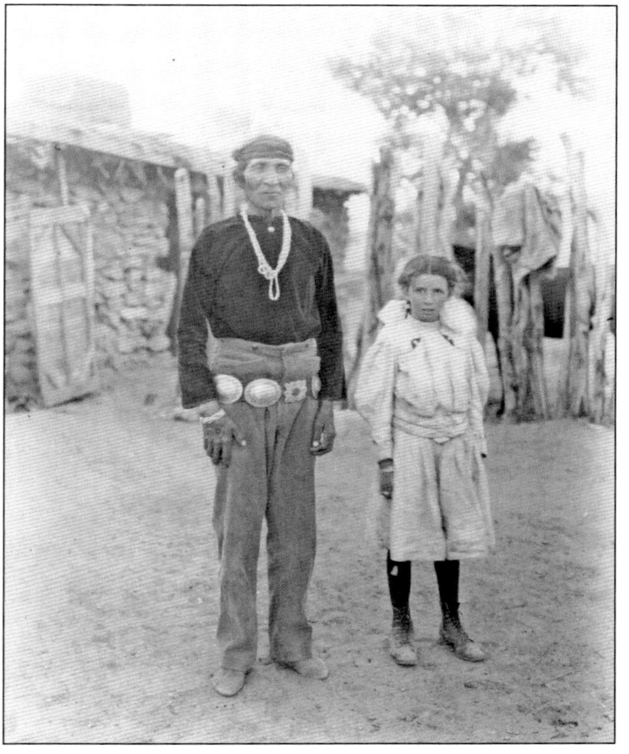

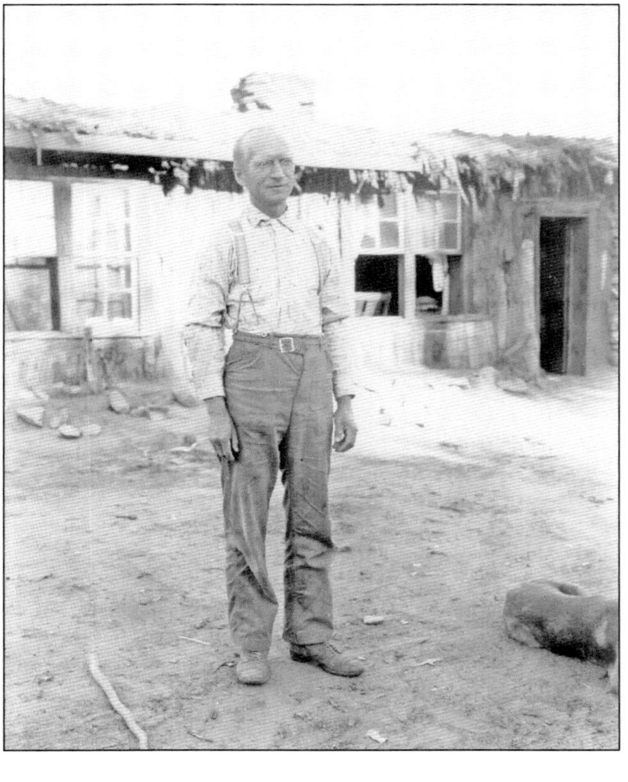

Byron Cummings, an archaeology professor from the University of Utah, based his 1908 field season at Oljato, hiring John Wetherill and his wranglers to guide him to cliff dwellings in Tsegi Canyon. The following year, Cummings was on the memorable trip with John Wetherill to locate Rainbow Bridge as well as other ruins in Tsegi Canyon. His young son Malcolm came with him on the 1909 summer expedition.

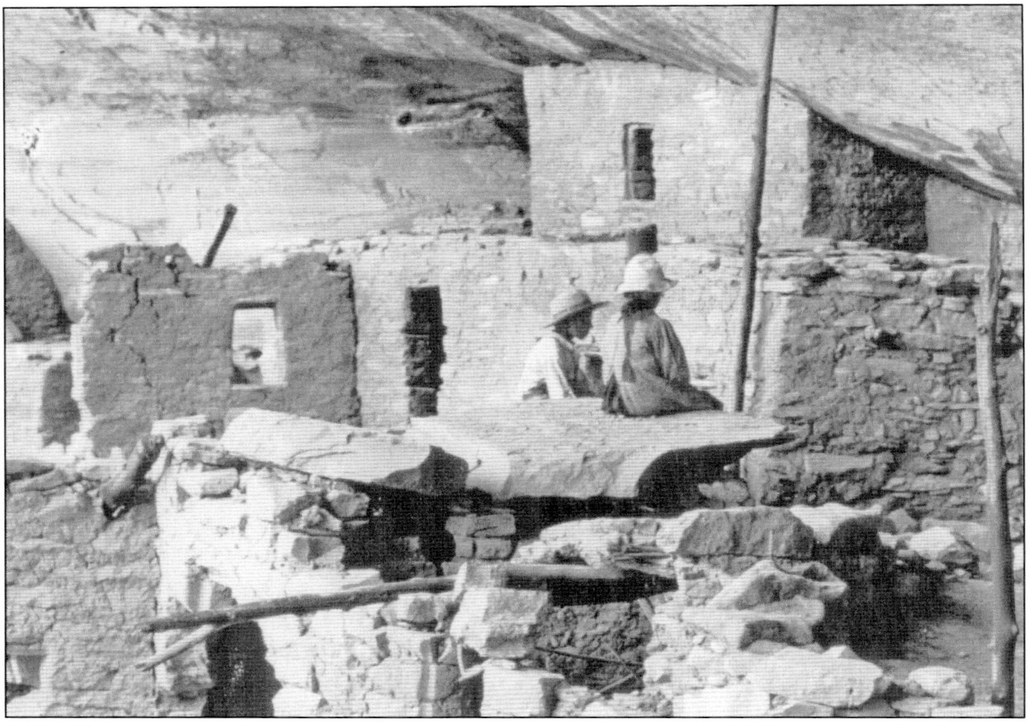

Malcolm Cummings and Georgia Ida Wetherill, along with Ben Wetherill (not pictured), visited a 74-room cliff dwelling with their parents in 1909. The children, all close to the age of 10 years, were the discoverers of the famous inscription on an interior wall of the dwelling that has been read as "1661 Anno Domino" and was thought to be Spanish. Although the date may have been later, the famous writing gave the site its name, Inscription House. The Navajo know it as Ts'ah Biis Kin, "House in the Sagebrush." This photograph was taken at Keet Seel.

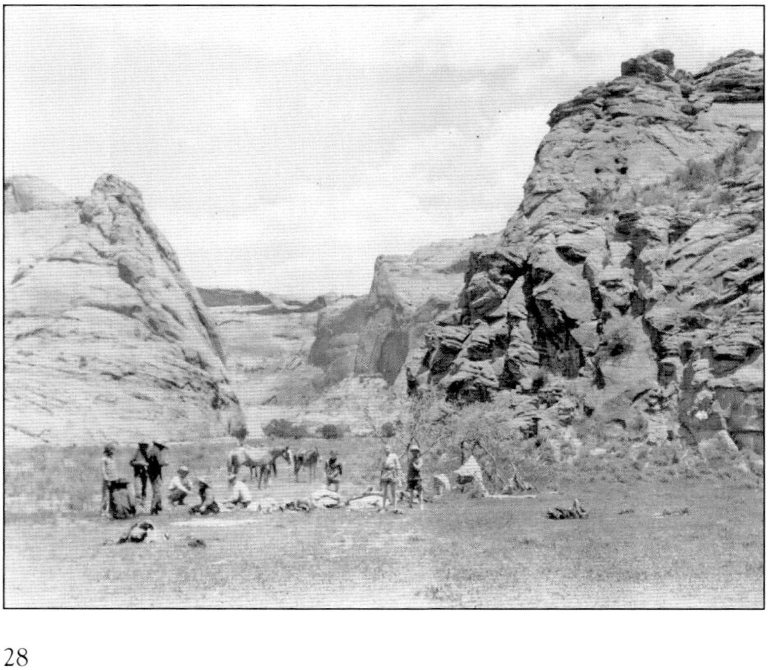

Members of the 1909 Byron Cummings expedition, led by John Wetherill, camp in a canyon at the base of the towering rock cliffs.

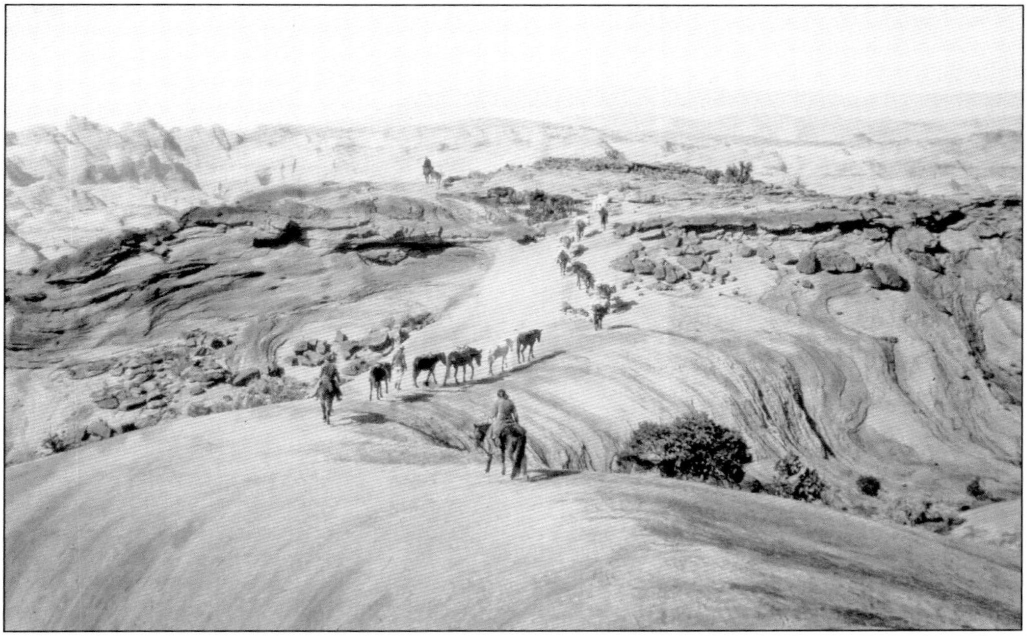

Glass Mountain was just one of the many dangerous spots on the trail to Rainbow Bridge where riders were forced to dismount and lead their horses and pack animals across the slick rock. Horses were reluctant to walk there, and a misstep would send an animal plunging to the bottom of a canyon.

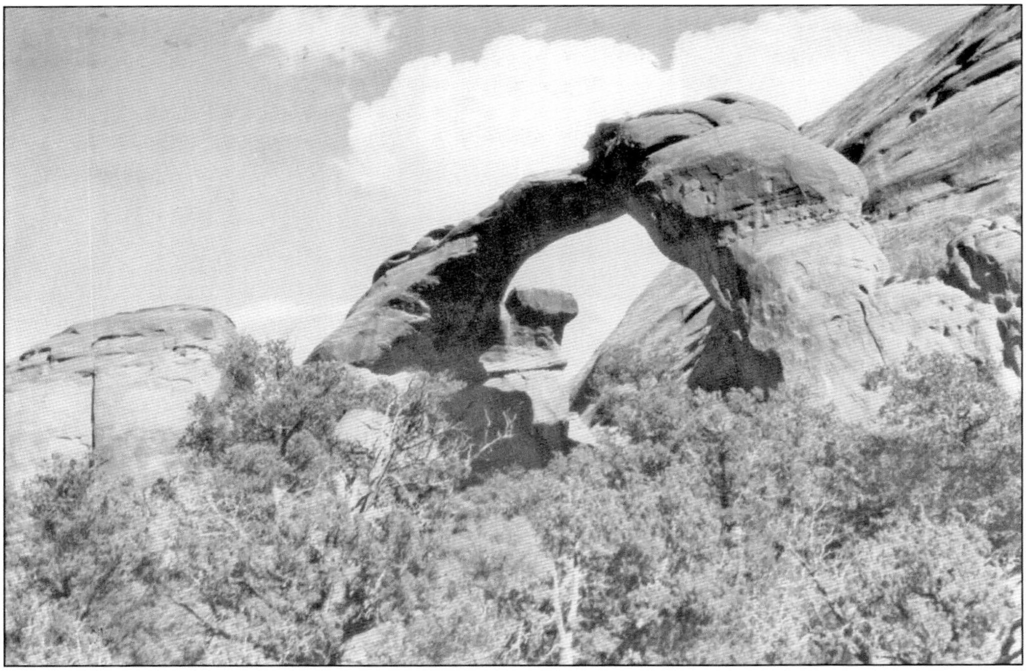

Owl Arch is in Surprise Valley on the Rainbow Bridge Trail. *Nasja* means "owl" in Navajo, and the arch was named for the Paiute man who knew of the bridge. His son Nasja Begay guided the 1909 discovery expedition on their final miles to Rainbow Bridge.

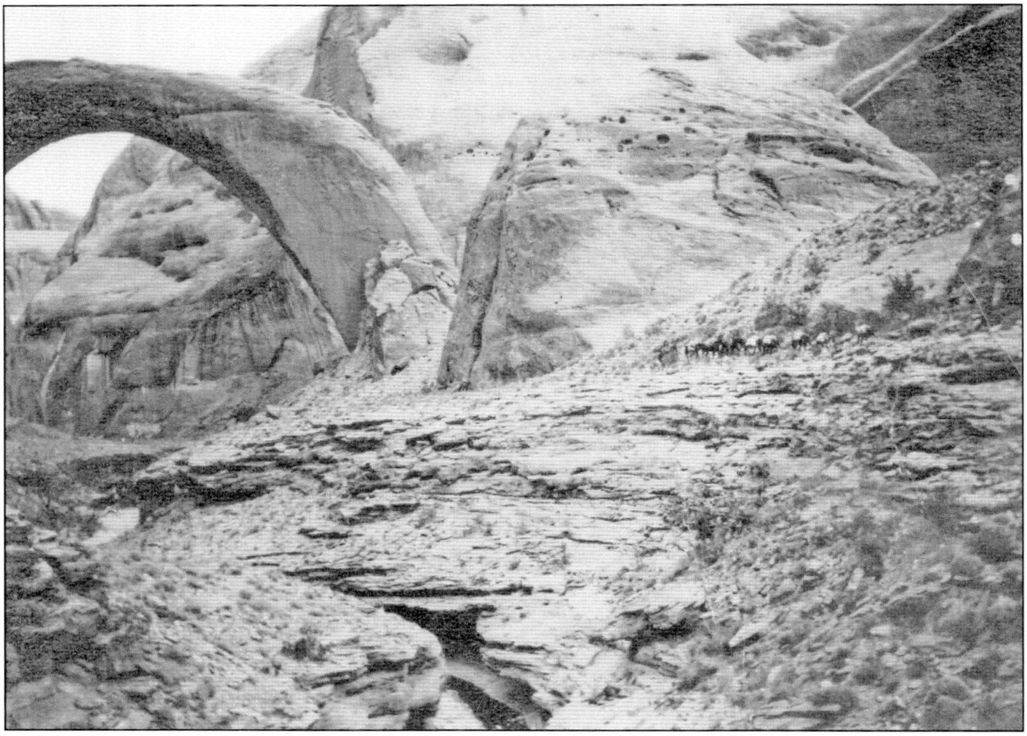

As the Cummings party, guided by John Wetherill in 1909, approached Rainbow Bridge, the riders dismounted and led horses and pack animals along a narrow ledge just below the stone arch. The pack train can be seen to the right of the bridge.

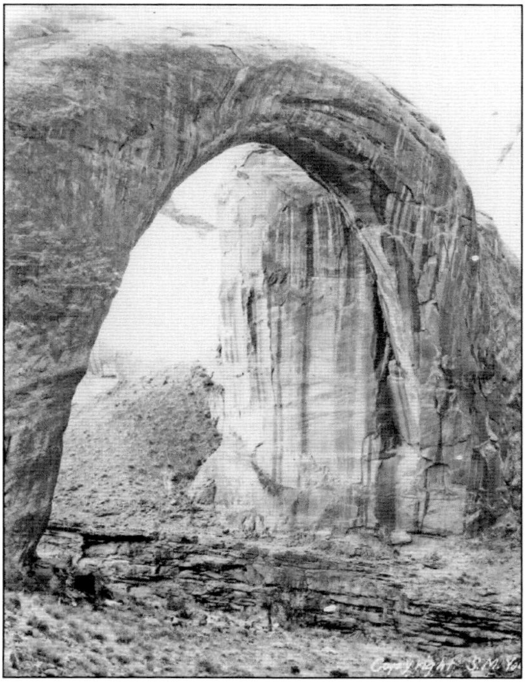

Rainbow Bridge rises to a height of 309 feet and has a span of 278 feet. The top of the arch is 40 feet thick. Louisa Wetherill heard stories from Navajos about a bridge of stone, and in August 1909, her husband led two rival groups on an expedition to locate the arch. Archaeologist Byron Cummings from the University of Utah, with Paiute guide Nasja Begay, organized one group, and William B. Douglass, a U.S. General Land Office surveyor, and his Ute guide Mike's Boy (as he was called) formed the second group. Late in the rugged journey, it became apparent that Douglass's guide was uncomfortable with continuing further, and Douglass and his party, believing that they would get fatally lost, wanted to turn back. As they trekked onward and entered Bridge Canyon, Douglass took risks to ride ahead of the group to stay in the front, but it was John Wetherill who was in the lead and was the first to ride under Rainbow Bridge on August 14, 1909.

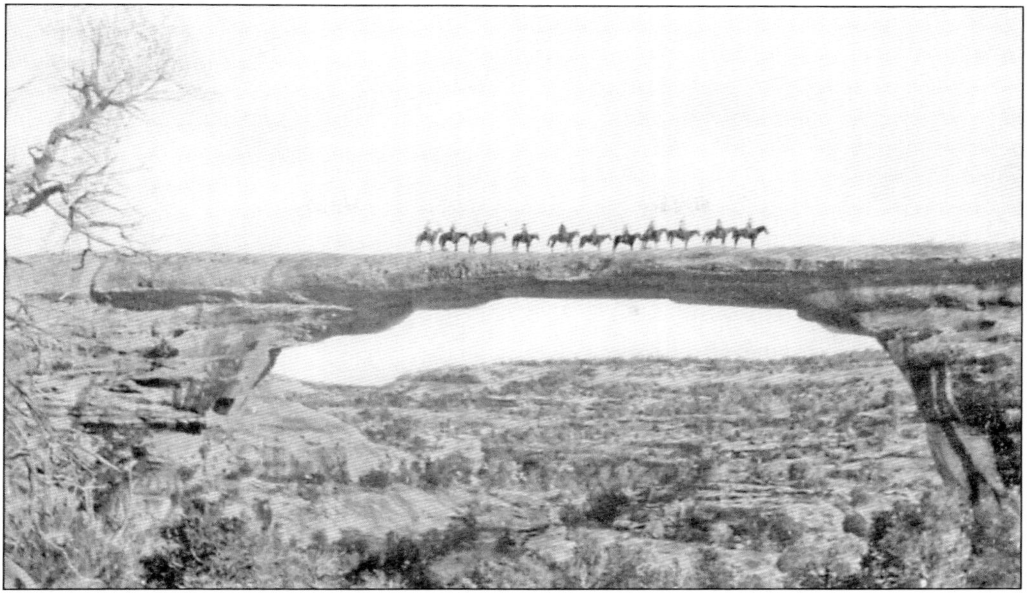

Owachomo means "rock mound," a feature at the eastern end of the bridge abutment. In 1908, Pres. Theodore Roosevelt signed the order creating Natural Bridges National Monument, which is located in Utah, north of the San Juan River. This early designation of a remarkable country with an extraordinary landscape created interest in the little-known area in northern Arizona and southeastern Utah.

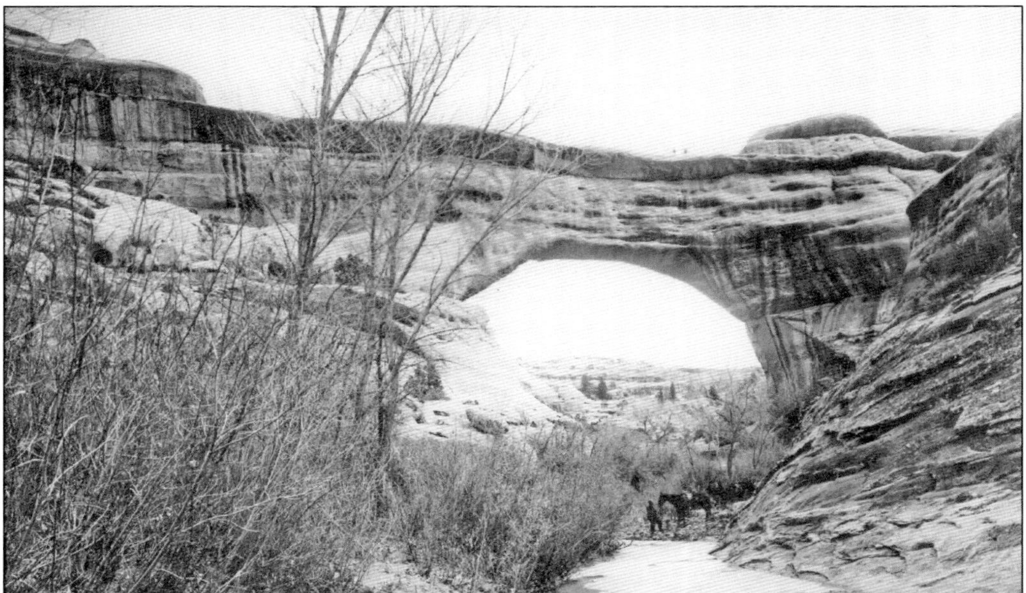

Utes and Navajos in the area knew of Sipapu Natural Bridge, but Cass Hite, a white prospector, was first taken to Sipapu in 1883 by the Navajo chief Hoskininni. In earlier times, the bridge was called Augusta, but after the national monument designation in 1908, the bridge was renamed Sipapu. Note the small figures of two people standing on top of the bridge. There are also several horses and a man holding the reins of a horse below the bridge at the edge of the water.

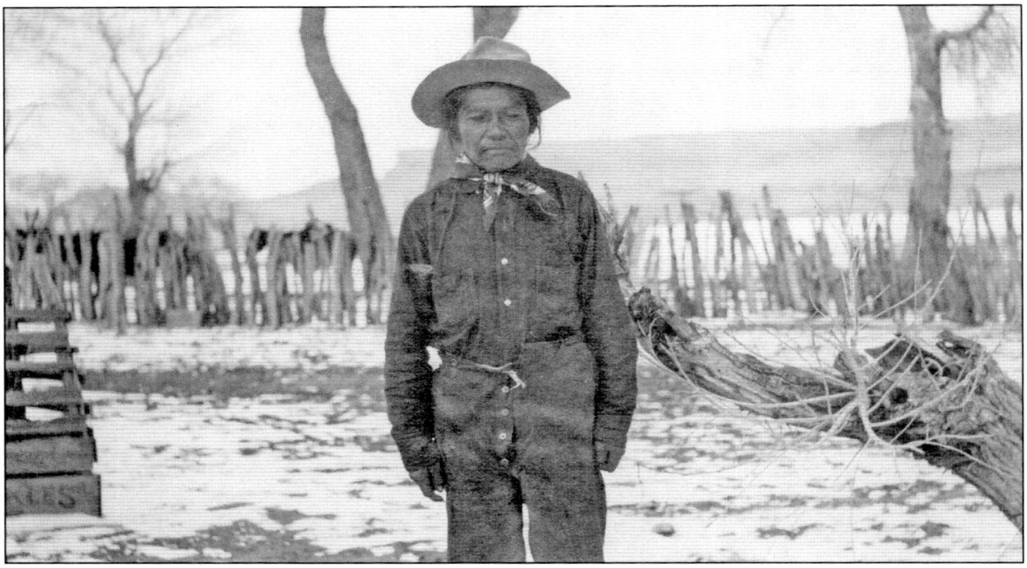

Glad Hand, posing for his photograph on a snowy day in the winter of 1909, was a young Navajo man who worked as a wrangler and guide at the Oljato Trading Post. He was known, however, to sometimes go off by himself. When he guided archaeologist Byron Cummings to ruins in Tsegi Canyon, he often disappeared for the entire day, leaving Cummings on his own. Cummings recalled a trip where they encountered some Navajos going to a "sing," a healing ceremony, at Red Lake. At lunch, Glad Hand was nowhere to be found; he had decided to follow the Navajos, and Cummings was left to find his way back to Kayenta, leading the pack animals in the dark. The guide was given the name "Glad Hand" because he was friendly and would always smile and shake hands when meeting people. Glad Hand died nine years after this photograph was taken in the influenza pandemic of 1918.

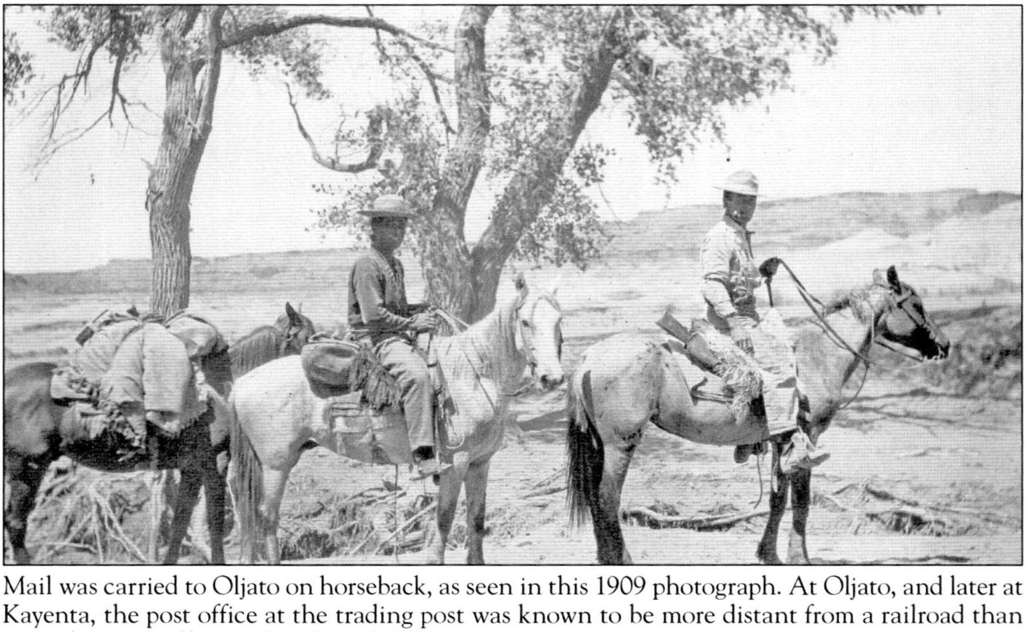

Mail was carried to Oljato on horseback, as seen in this 1909 photograph. At Oljato, and later at Kayenta, the post office at the trading post was known to be more distant from a railroad than any other post office in the United States.

Three

Diné Means "the People"

Kayenta has always been remote, and the Navajos who lived in the area were barely impacted by outside influences for many years into the 20th century. Oliver La Farge, a writer who visited Kayenta in 1930, wrote, "Around Kayenta we saw the last of the old times." The Navajos still wore velveteen shirts with buttons made from silver Mercury dimes and calico leggings, and on their feet were handmade leather moccasins. Bows and arrows were strapped to their saddles.

Navajos acquired sheep, goats, and horses from the Spanish; they also began farming, very likely learning dry-farming techniques from neighboring pueblo people. The introduction of domestic animals and agriculture had the consequence of creating a less nomadic life among the Navajo, but in earlier times their very survival required a more aggressive and competitive lifestyle. Their use of a sinew-backed bow, a powerful weapon, made them a group to be feared by the agricultural puebloans, as well as by the few Anglos who began to drift into the impregnable lands south and east of the Colorado River. Navajos also contended with their traditional enemies, the Utes, as well as Mexican slave traders who periodically raided Navajo camps. Additionally, the arrival of white settlers, prospectors, and soldiers would test the existence of the Navajo people in their rugged homeland.

The modern-day Navajo Nation covers 27,000 square miles in northeastern Arizona, northwestern New Mexico, and southeastern Utah. It is the largest Indian reservation in North America, and there are about 300,000 Navajos who live in the area, with some living outside the reservation in southwestern cities such as Phoenix and Flagstaff, Arizona. The center of modern Navajo government is in Window Rock, Arizona.

The word *Navajo* is Spanish; the Navajos call themselves Diné, which means "the People." Navajos have lived in the Four Corners area for over 500 years. According to the old stories, the Diné have passed through three worlds before coming into the present world—the Fourth World or Glittering World.

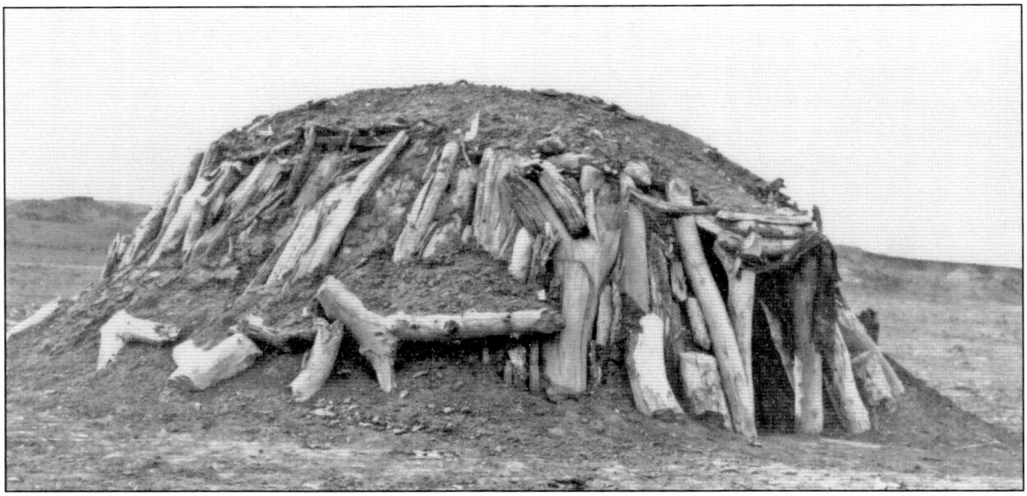

The traditional Navajo home, a hogan, is round and is built with sides of logs if wood is available. Spaces are filled in with dirt and mud. To the Navajo, hogans are not just homes, they are also sacred places. The Holy People, Navajo spiritual beings, built the first hogans of turquoise, white shell, or abalone. The positioning of people and objects inside of the hogan is prescribed according to Navajo tradition.

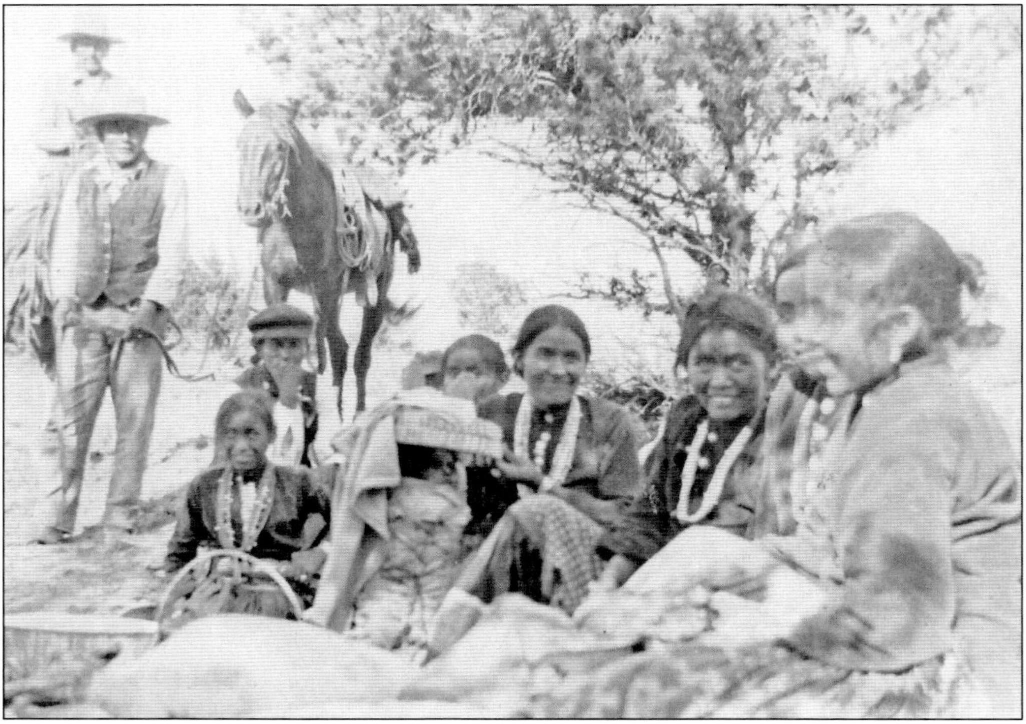

A Navajo family and friends have gathered under the meager shade of a cedar tree to visit. Most likely it was a special occasion, because the ladies are beautifully dressed in velveteen shirts with silver-coin buttons and strings of necklaces around their necks. The baby in the cradleboard has a "rainbow" over him—the round piece that is attached to the top of the cradleboard—which signifies happiness and good health.

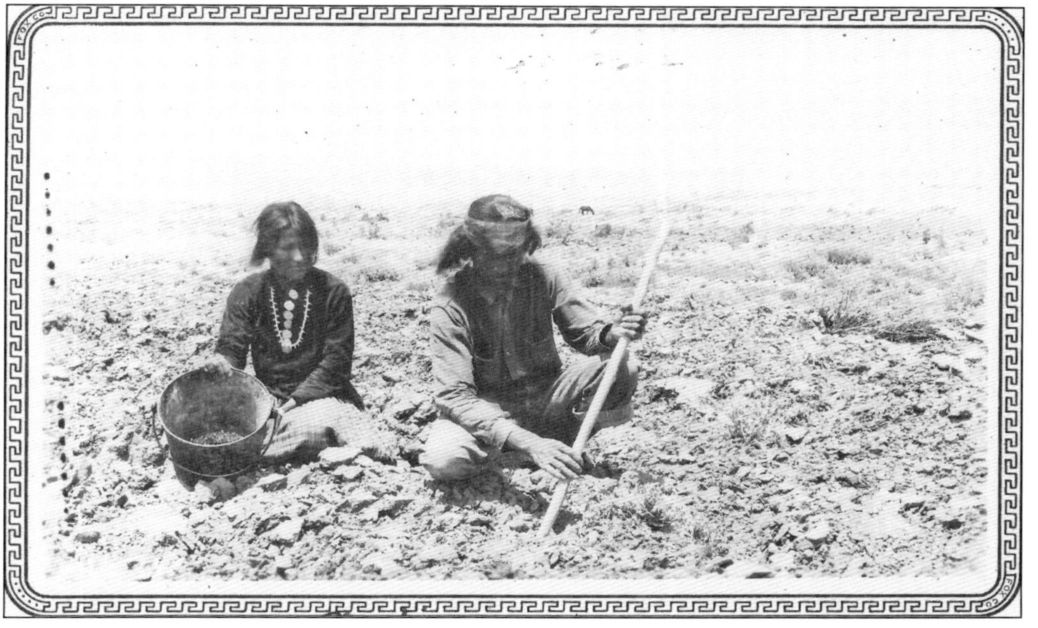

Small fields of corn provided food that could be dried and stored. The couple above is using a digging stick to make a hole to plant two or three kernels of corn. Plots of corn are generally small because of a lack of good soil and a water source. Ground near washes provides moisture, but even today, dry farming is commonly practiced.

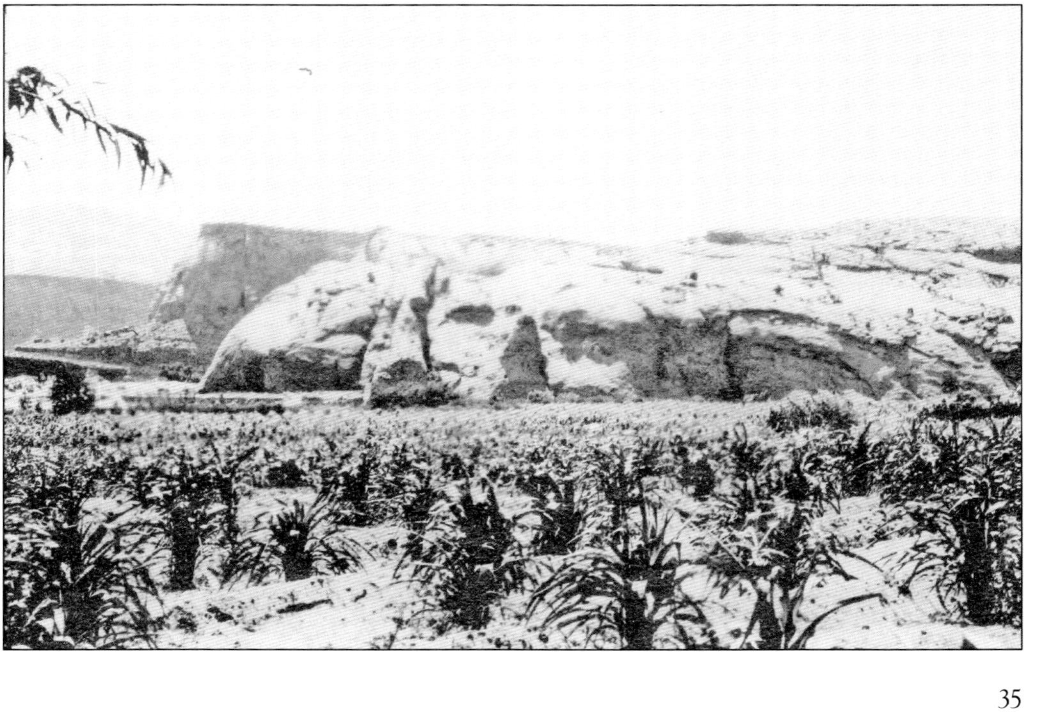

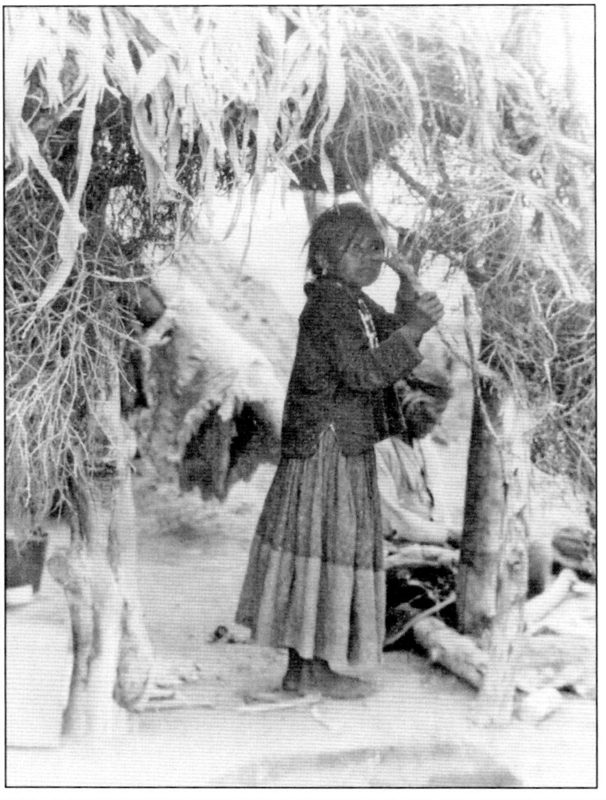

A Navajo girl stands under a ramada built with support poles and covered with brush for shade. Ramadas were used as living spaces in the summer. The girl is wearing typical Navajo dress—a full, gathered skirt and a loose shirt. Shirts were made of cotton and velvet and often were adorned with silver buttons made from coins.

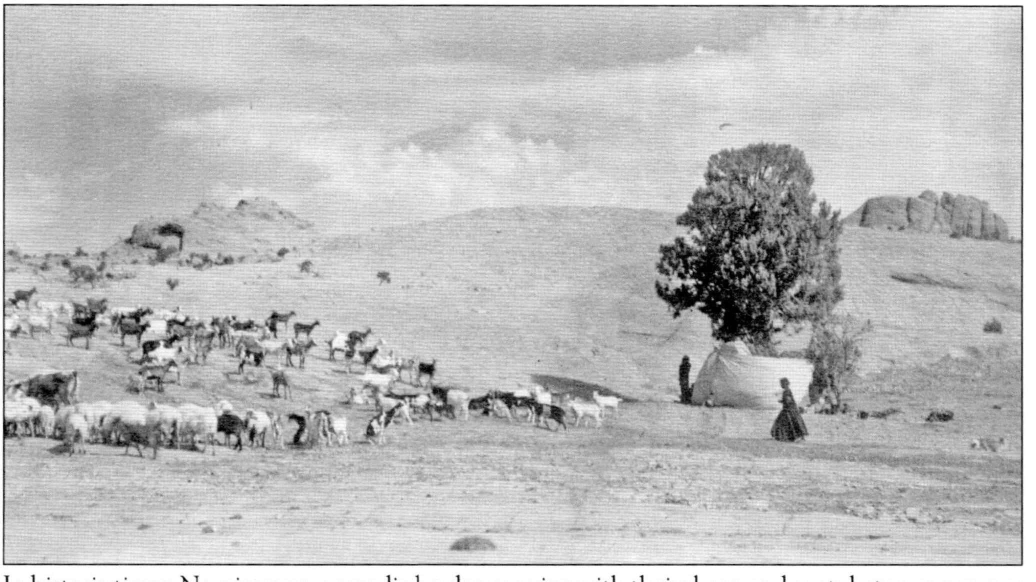

In historic times, Navajos were nomadic herders moving with their sheep and goats between summer and winter ranges. A brush shelter next to a single tree in the stark landscape provides shade while a shepherdess watches her herd. Sheep were historically a measure of wealth; they provided food, pelts, wool for weaving, and objects for trade with other Navajos as well as at the trading post. According to Navajo tradition, women own the sheep, the goats, and their homes.

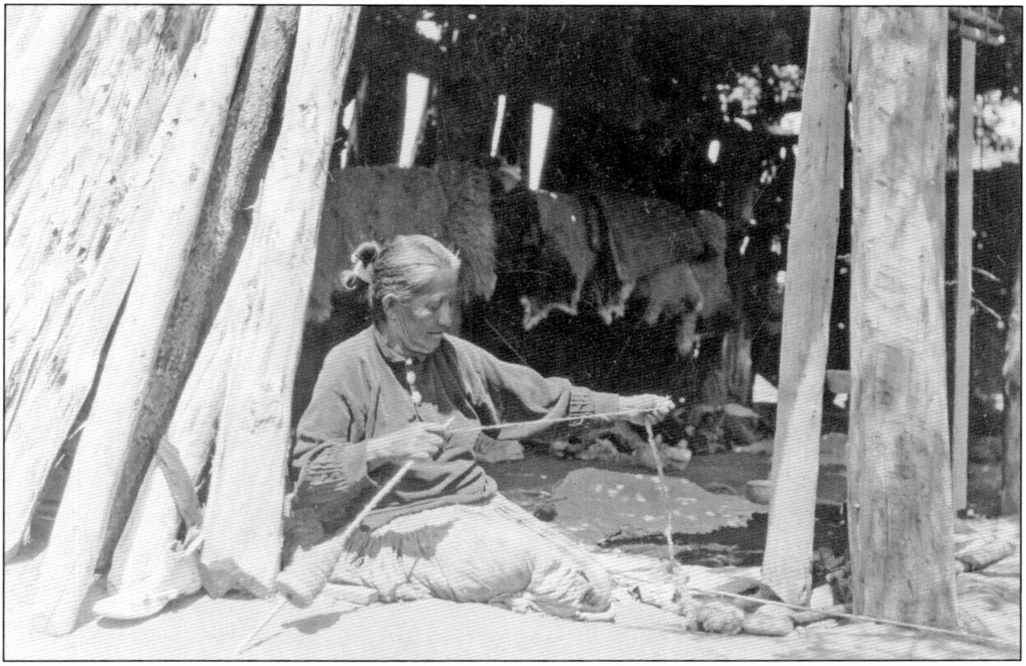

A Navajo woman is shown here spinning wool into yarn to be used in a rug. She is seated at the entrance to a log-and-brush ramada. The open design of the structure would allow summer breezes but would also provide shade and keep out sand and wind. After the wool is spun, it is dyed in pots and hung on tree branches and bushes to dry.

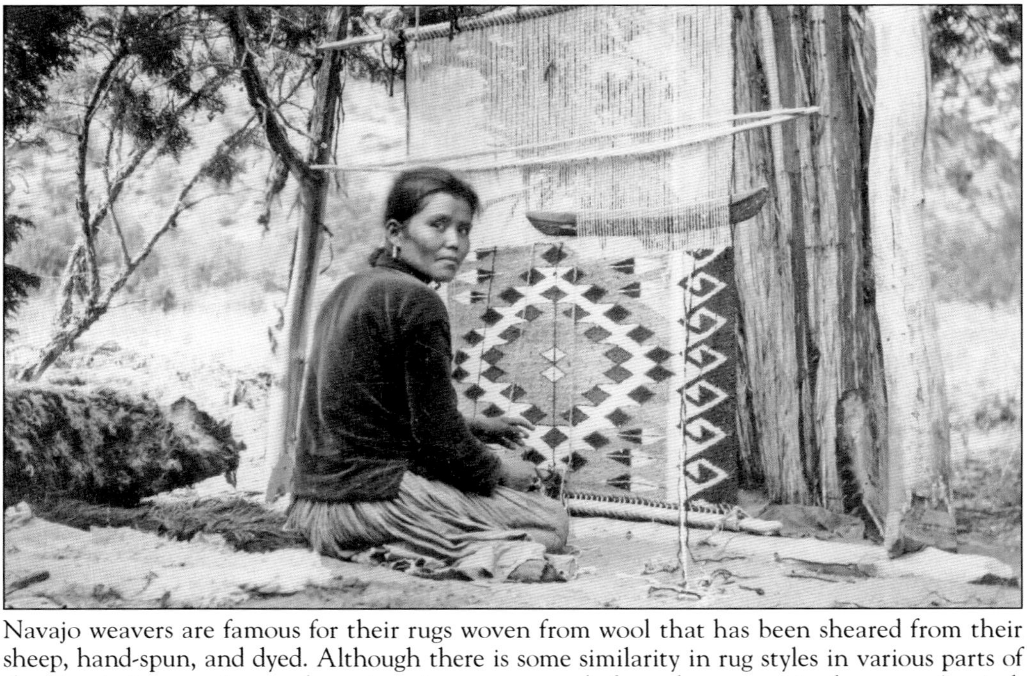

Navajo weavers are famous for their rugs woven from wool that has been sheared from their sheep, hand-spun, and dyed. Although there is some similarity in rug styles in various parts of the Navajo Reservation, each rug is unique, woven only from the pattern in the weaver's mind. This lady's loom is set up in the open air, next to a tree that provides shade.

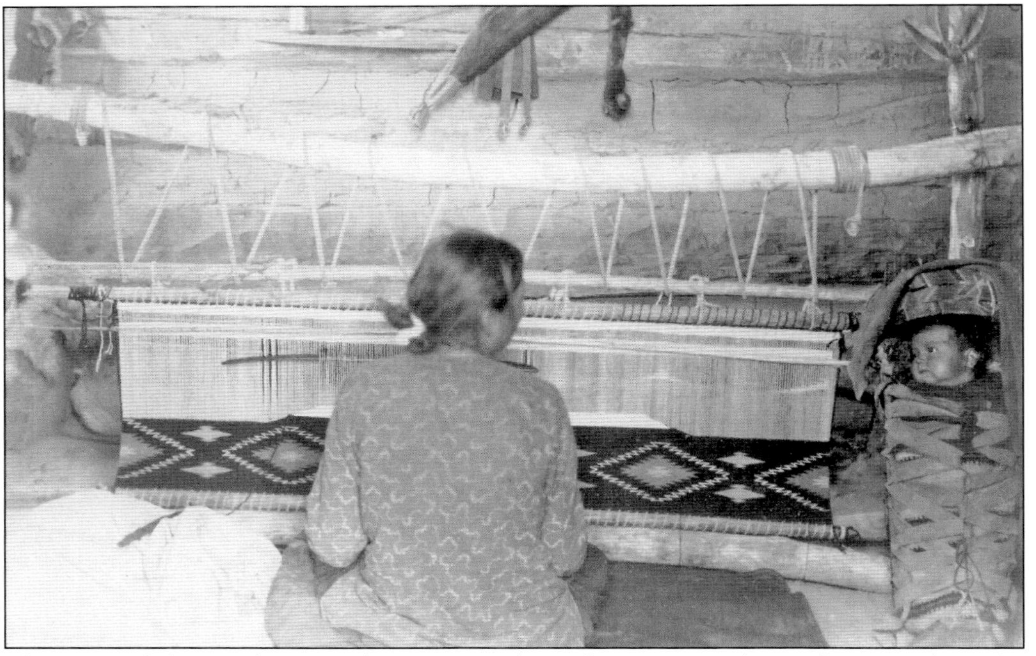

This Navajo lady is working on a large rug on a loom that appears to be inside a room (note the horizontal logs with plaster between them). Her baby is happily secured in a cradleboard nearby, watching intently as she weaves.

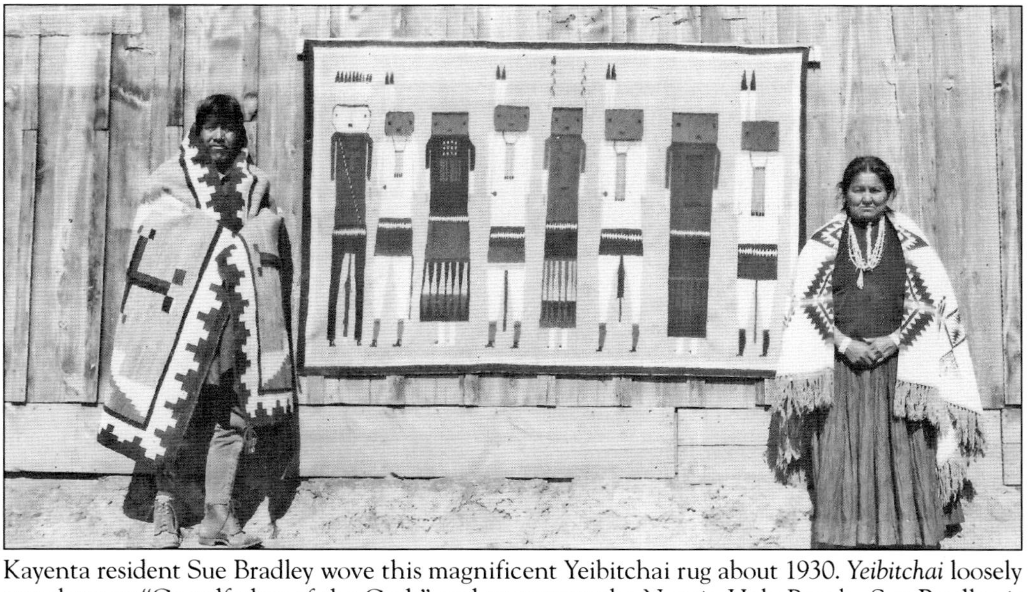

Kayenta resident Sue Bradley wove this magnificent Yeibitchai rug about 1930. *Yeibitchai* loosely translates as "Grandfather of the Gods" and represents the Navajo Holy People. Sue Bradley is posing here in front of Warren's Trading Post with her husband, John.

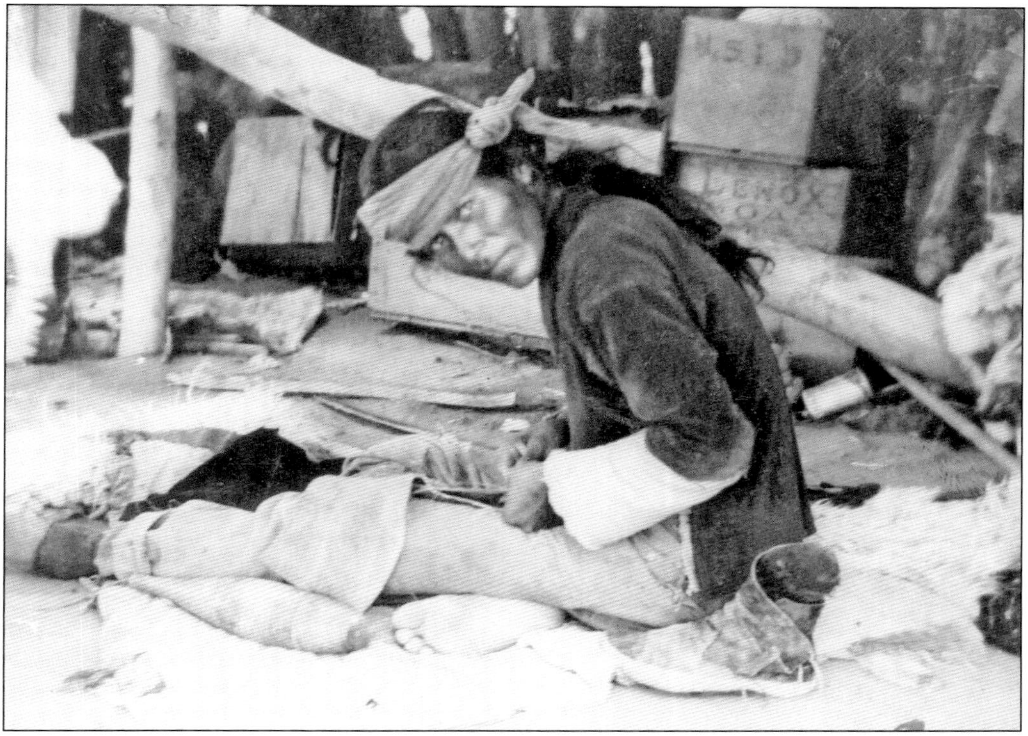

This man is making moccasins. If a person desired a pair of shoes, he would take a sheepskin to a moccasin maker, who would take an impression of the person's feet and then make a pair of customized moccasins from the soft, tanned leather.

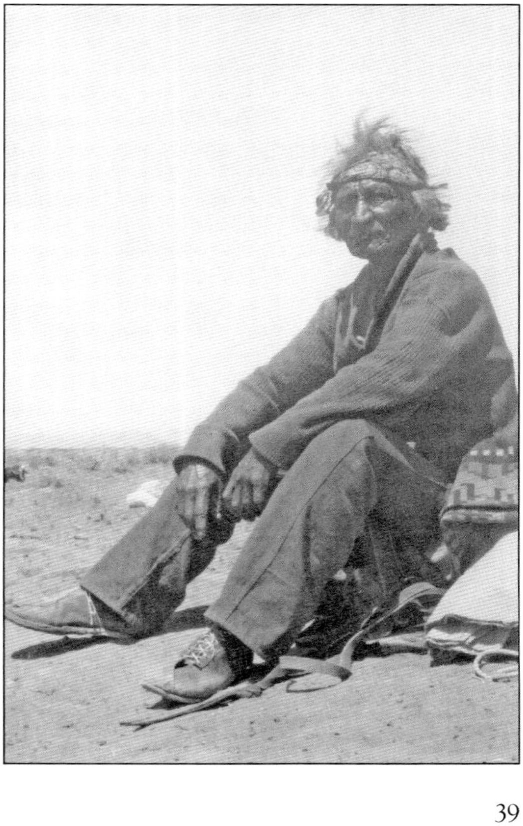

An elderly Navajo man rests on a pile of blankets. He is wearing handmade leather shoes with hard leather soles and white string laces.

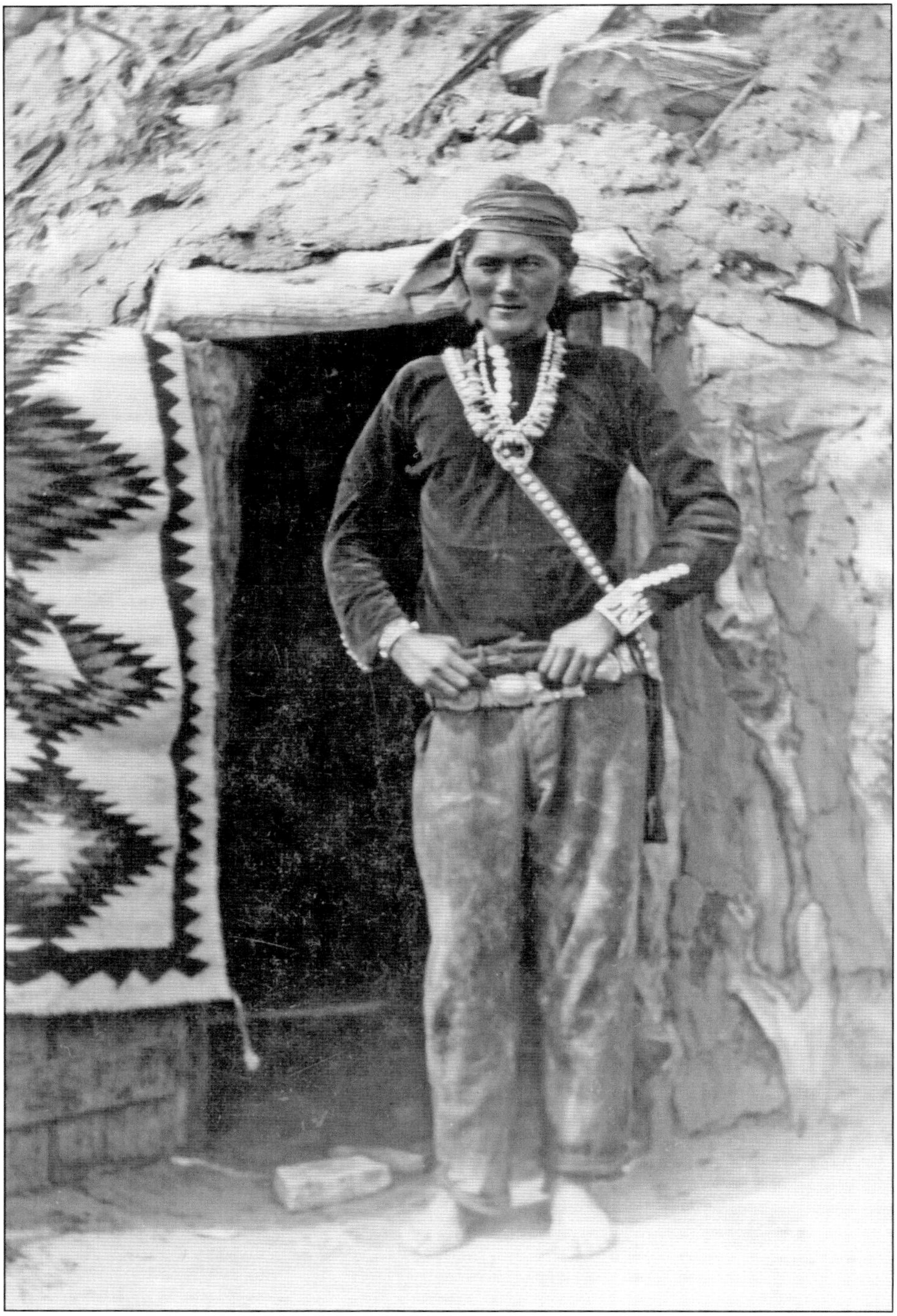

This handsome Navajo man, Frank Parrish, is wearing many examples of fine silver: a concho belt, bracelets, and a silver necklace. He lived near Agathla Peak and appeared in many of the John Ford movies filmed in nearby Monument Valley, including *She Wore a Yellow Ribbon* and *Cheyenne Autumn*. Parrish is also wearing a leather bag slung across his shoulder and adorned with Mercury head dimes. In a bit of contrast to all of his finery, he is barefoot.

Navajo artists are renowned for their beautiful silver jewelry. A Navajo blacksmith, Atsidi Sani, is credited with being the first Navajo to become a silversmith about 1850. Sani knew how to work with iron, but by learning to work with silver, he could make the highly prized pieces used on horse bridles. Using American coins and Mexican pesos, Navajo artists soon began developing their skills, creating silverwork to adorn saddles and bridles, buttons for velvet shirts and leather bags, concho belts, and striking bracelets and necklaces.

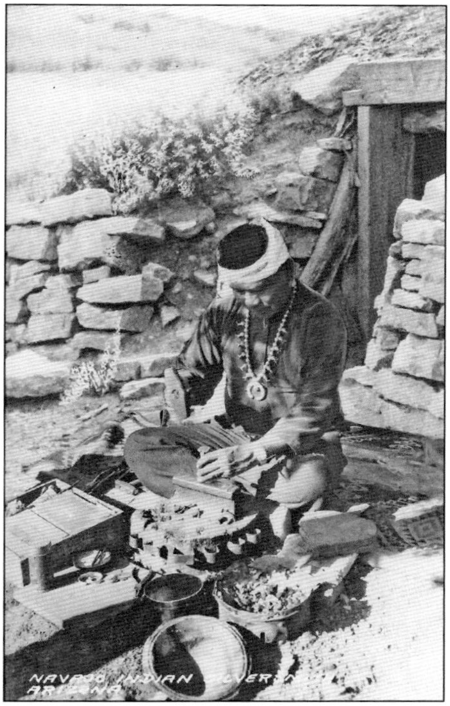

The young men on the horses are wearing their finest clothes. The man at the left has a silver necklace and silver buttons on his shirt. The man in the center also has silver buttons on his shirt and a leather bag decorated with silver buttons. The skin of an angora goat is slung across the back of his saddle.

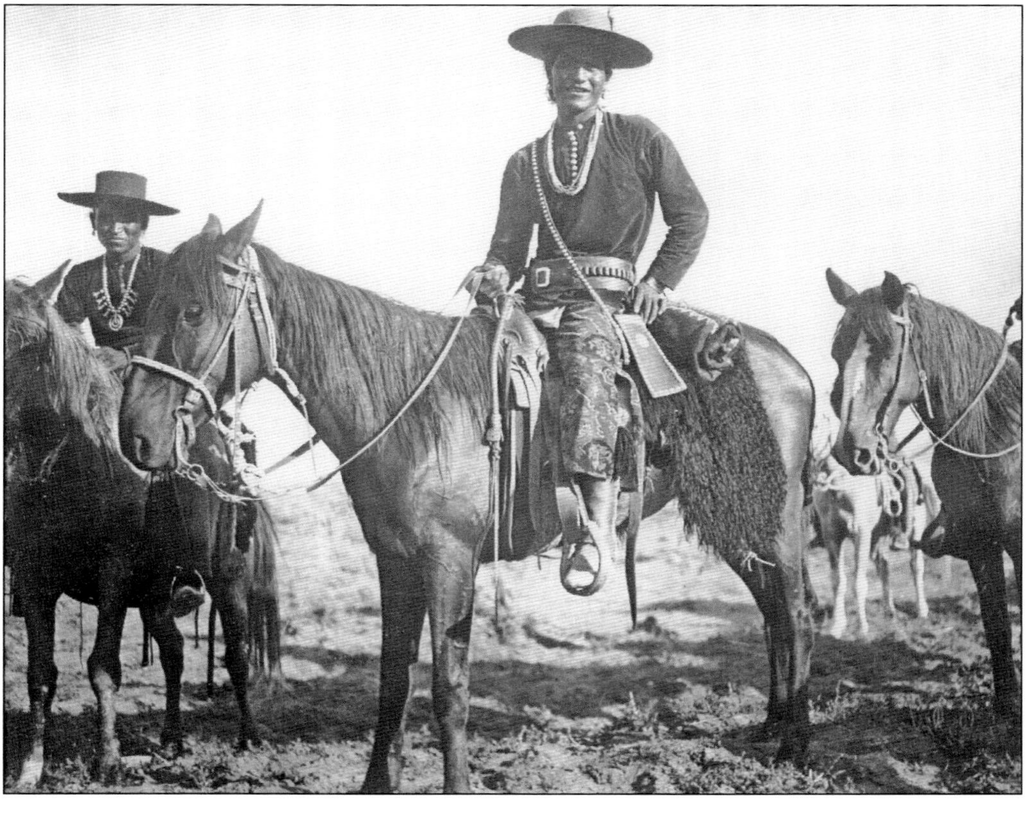

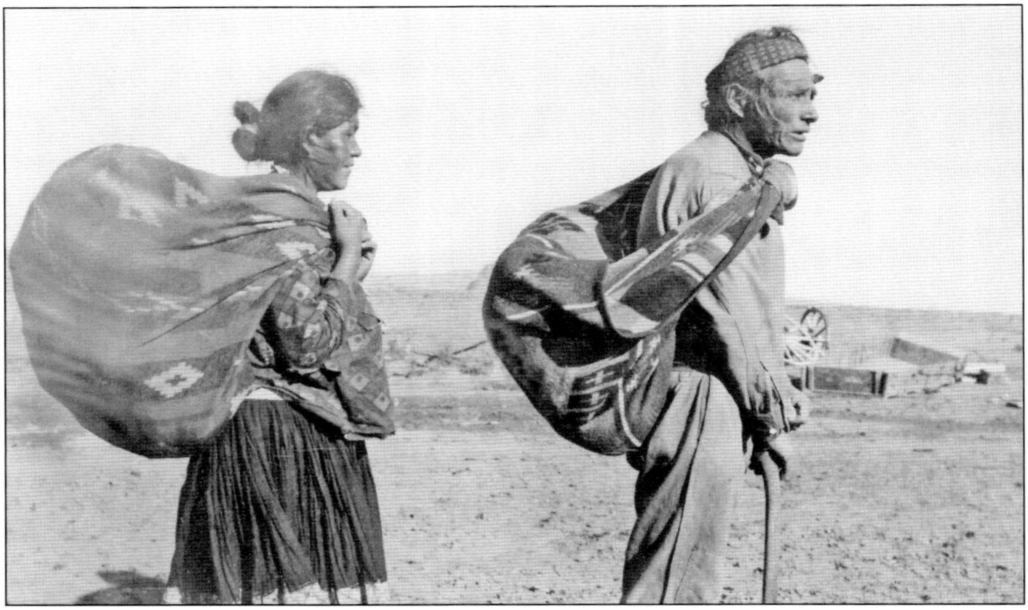

People lacking a horse, mule, or wagon in early times had to carry their belongings in bags slung across their backs, like this couple walking in the Kayenta area, probably in the 1930s. One elderly Navajo, when shown this photograph, remarked, "This is how people used to travel." But another viewer noted that there is a broken wagon in the background.

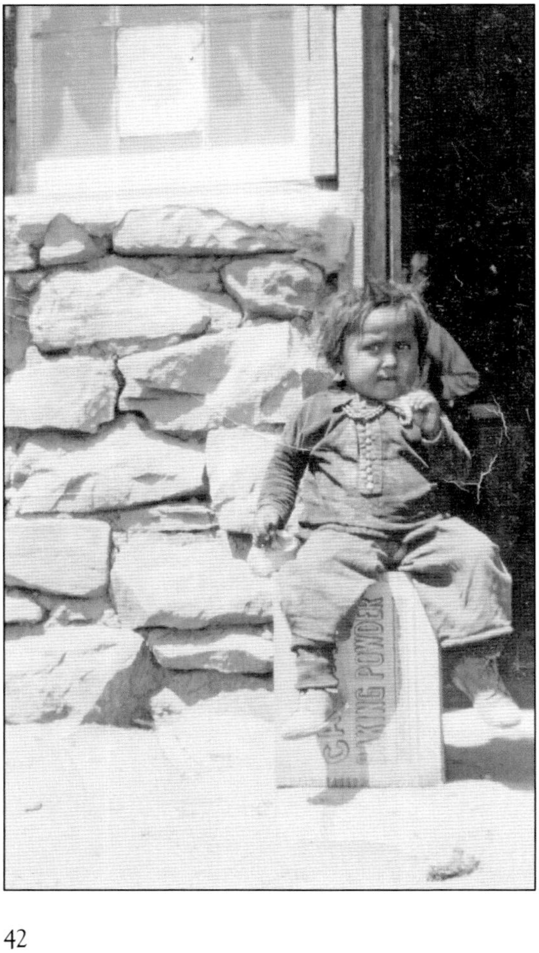

While seated on a Calumet Baking Powder box outside the trading post doorway, a young Navajo boy enjoys a rare piece of stick candy, likely purchased by his parents at the Wetherills' store.

Tsé dix is an old stick game played mainly by Navajo women. Three sticks are held up over the rock in the center of the circle, and according to how they fall, the player gets points and moves around the circle of smaller rocks. The first person to get all the way around the circle wins the game.

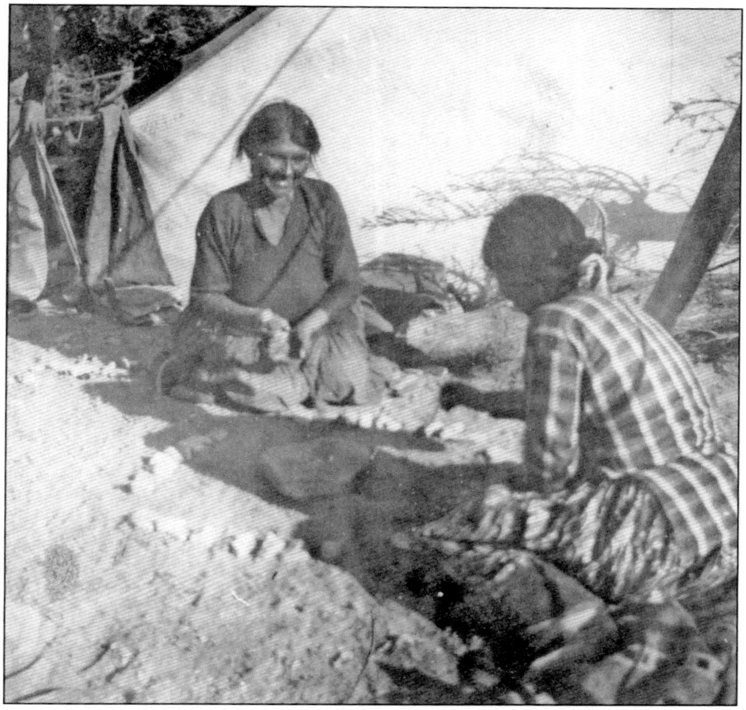

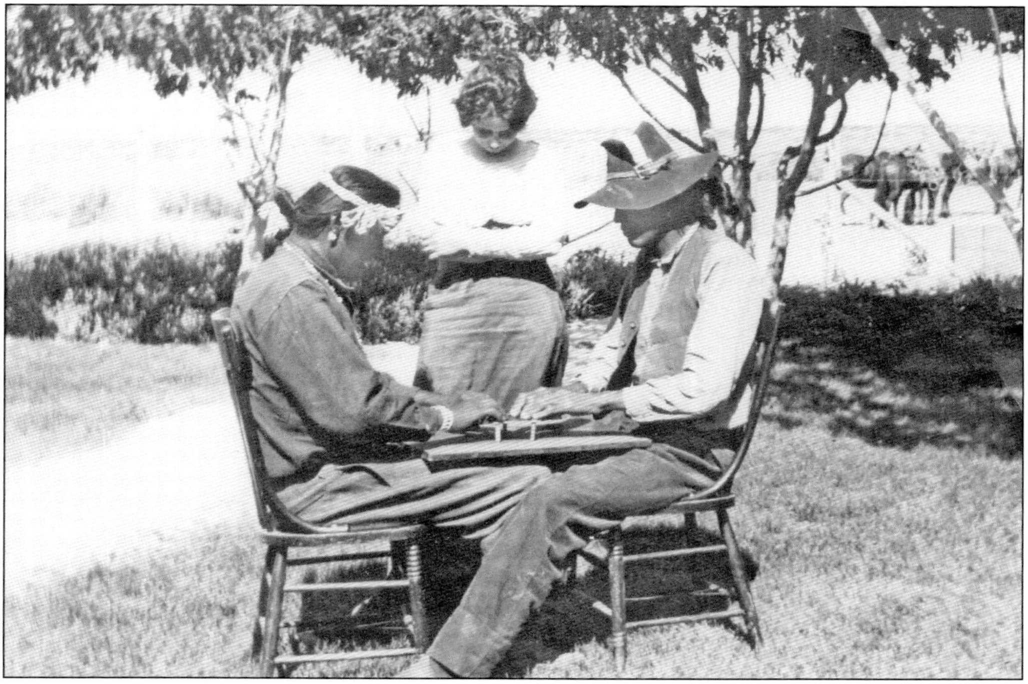

In a very untraditional game, two Navajo men are playing with a Ouija board and pointer while Georgia Ida Wetherill looks on. It is tempting to guess what they may have wanted to learn from the mysterious powers of the Ouija. This photograph was taken on the lawn of the Wetherill's home sometime in the 1930s.

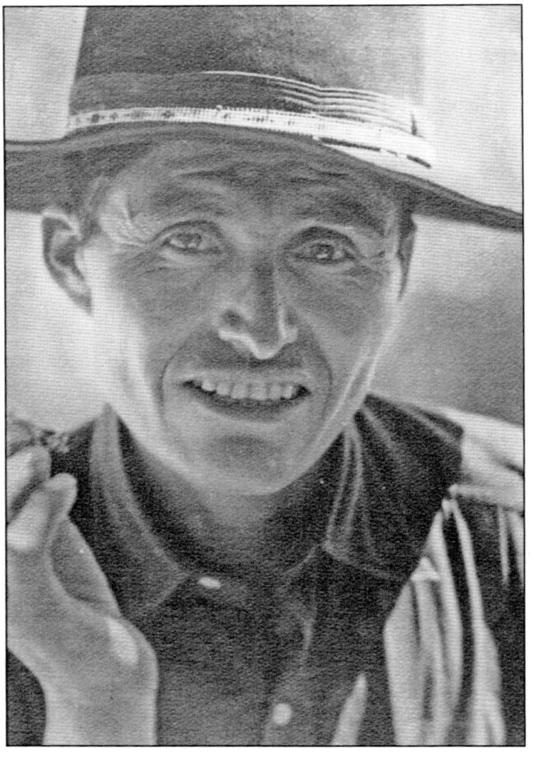

Billy Nash (left) was one of the first Navajo people in the Kayenta area to get an education. He strongly believed in the advantages of schooling and also made certain that his children were educated as well. Other Navajos who looked at this photograph remarked on his short hair, which was unusual in a time when most Navajo men still wore their hair pulled back in the traditional knot. The young man in the photograph below is wearing his hair down, rather than tied in the hourglass-shaped knot. One Navajo woman commented that perhaps he was going to a ceremony, and another person said that perhaps he had just washed his hair with soap made of the root of the soapweed yucca.

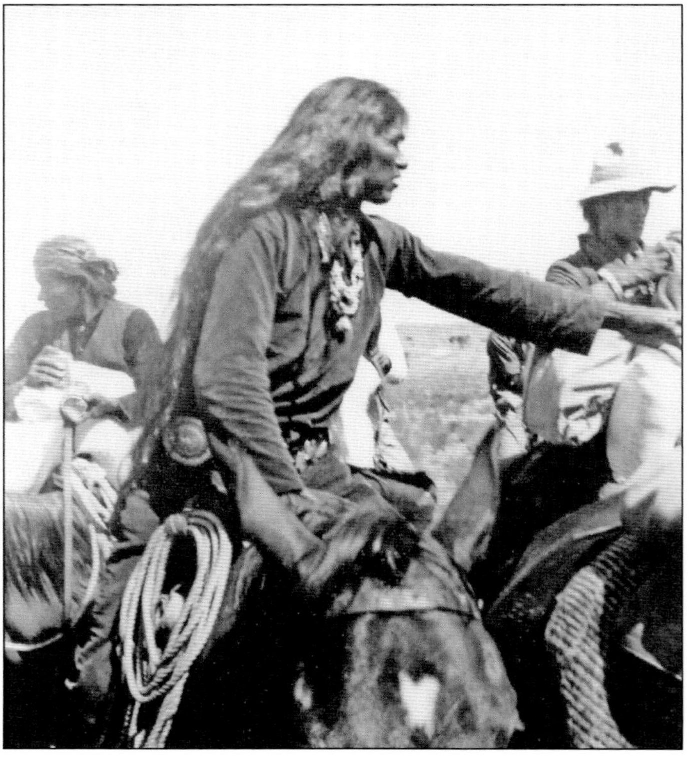

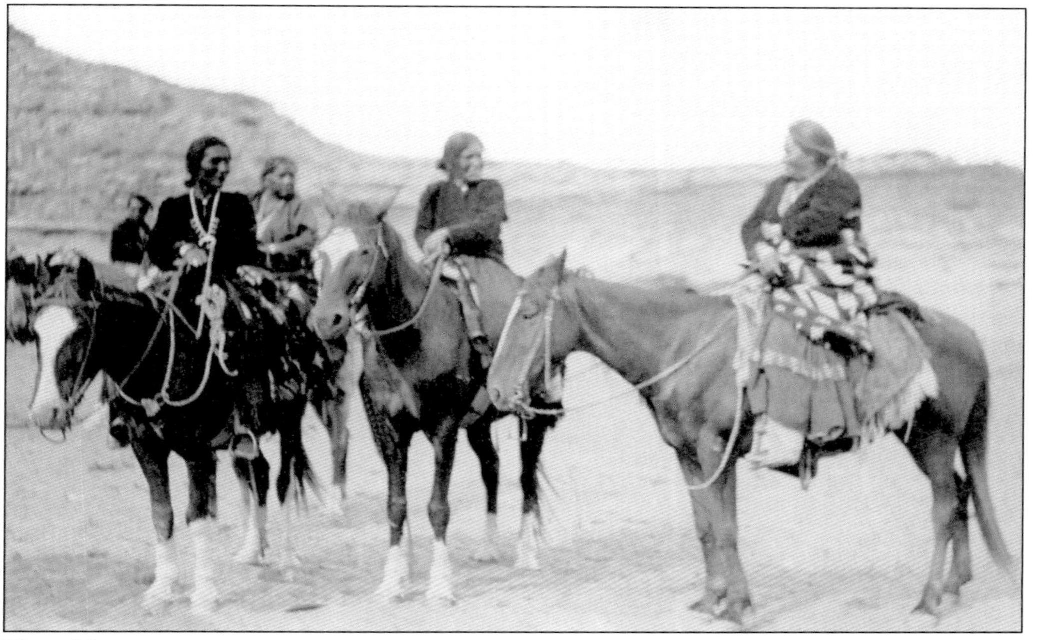

These Navajo women are dressed in their traditional full skirts and velveteen shirts and wear an abundance of jewelry as they enjoy a chat while mounted on their horses in front of the trading post.

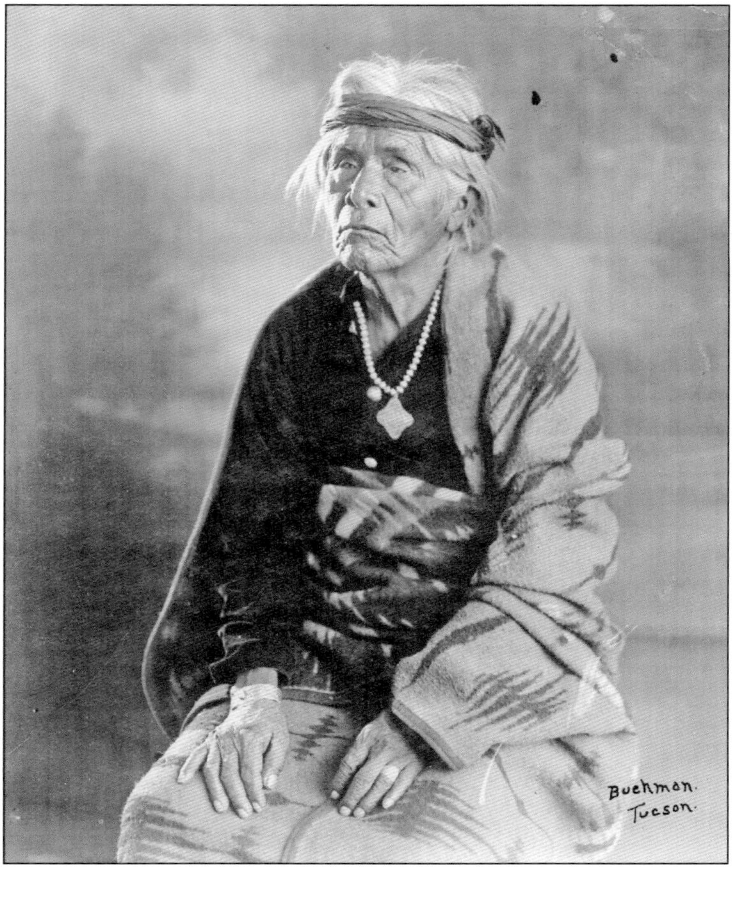

Hosteen Luca was a chanter and a medicine man. He is wrapped in a fine blanket for this formal photographic portrait. Like many Navajo men, he generally wore his hair in a traditional hair bundle at the back of his head, with a red bandana tied around his head.

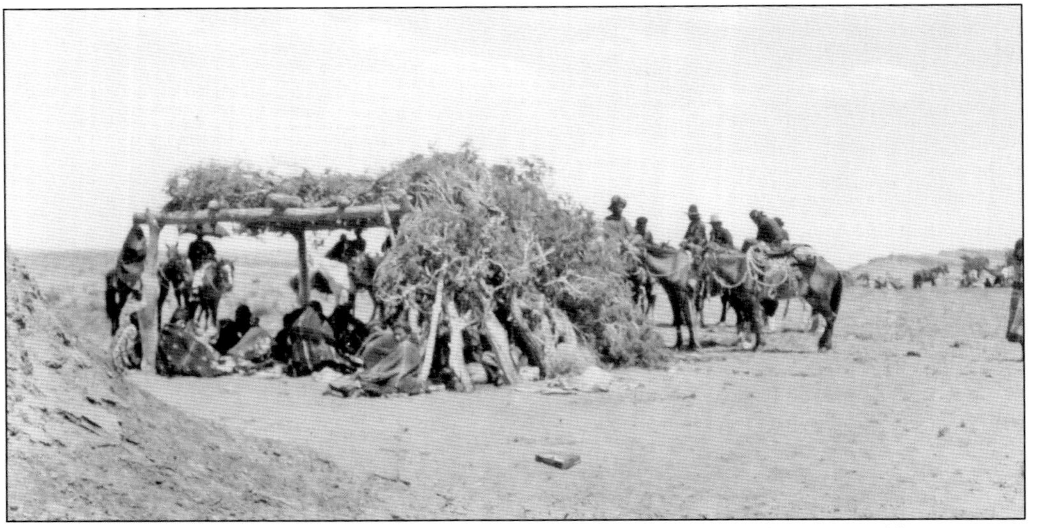

At the Girl's Dance, also known as the Squaw Dance, young women of marriageable age invite single men to dance with them. Traditionally, it was a time when matches were made. Everyone dressed in their finest clothes and jewelry, and mothers urged their daughters to approach a boy, particularly if he came from a family with many sheep and horses. The ceremony went on for several nights, and the dancing lasted until morning.

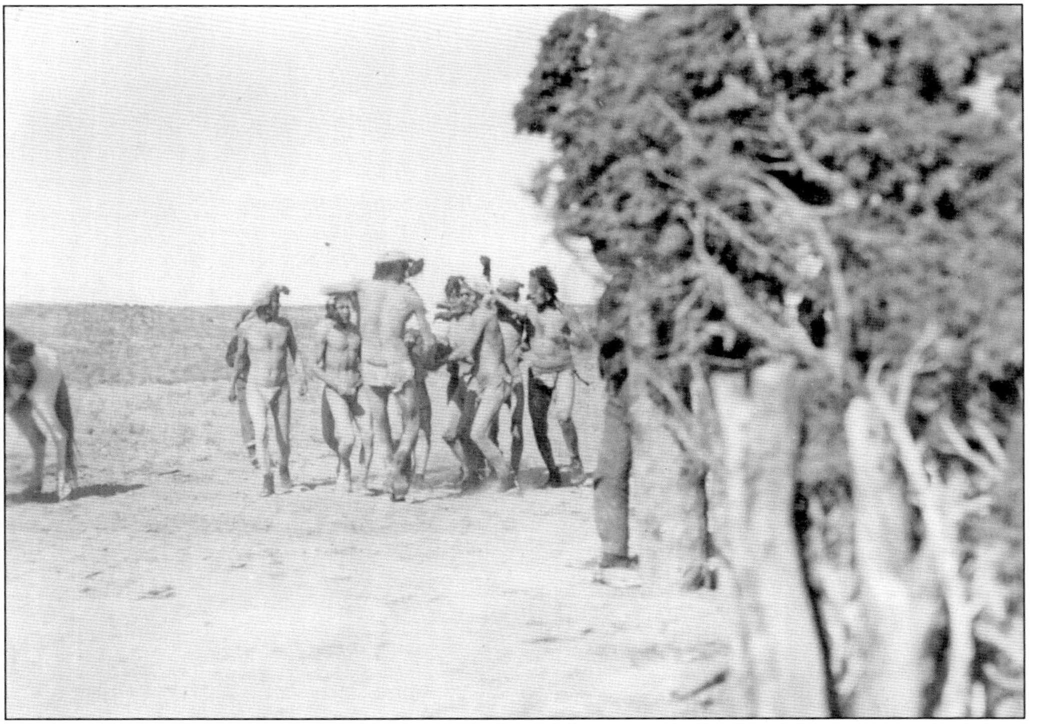

In this 1923 ceremony, the mud men appear during the Squaw Dance. The mud dancers have to enter and exit the hogan through the smoke hole at the top; they cannot use the door. After the solemn part of this healing ceremony, the dancers grab spectators and try to throw them in the mud hole.

These Navajo Yeibitchai Dancers appeared at Kayenta in this winter ceremony, the Night Way. The Yeibitchai figures beg for food or money that will be used during the nine-day ritual. The lead dancer wears a feathered mask with a cedar ruff around the neck and a deerskin-hide cape. Other dancers cover their bodies in thick white clay, which also helps give protection from the cold. The distinctive Kayenta landmark, the Toes, can be seen on the horizon in this 1930s photograph.

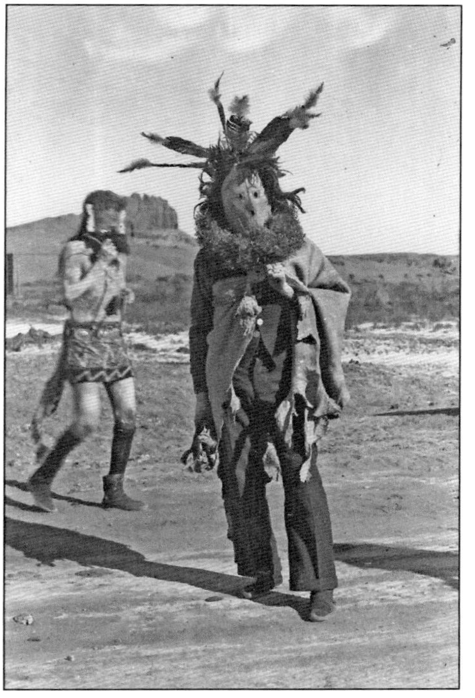

The row of wooden hoops in this 1930s photograph is part of a sacred Navajo healing ceremony. Each part of the hoop is constructed with certain plants, usually gathered by a person with special knowledge of the traditional use of plants available in the area.

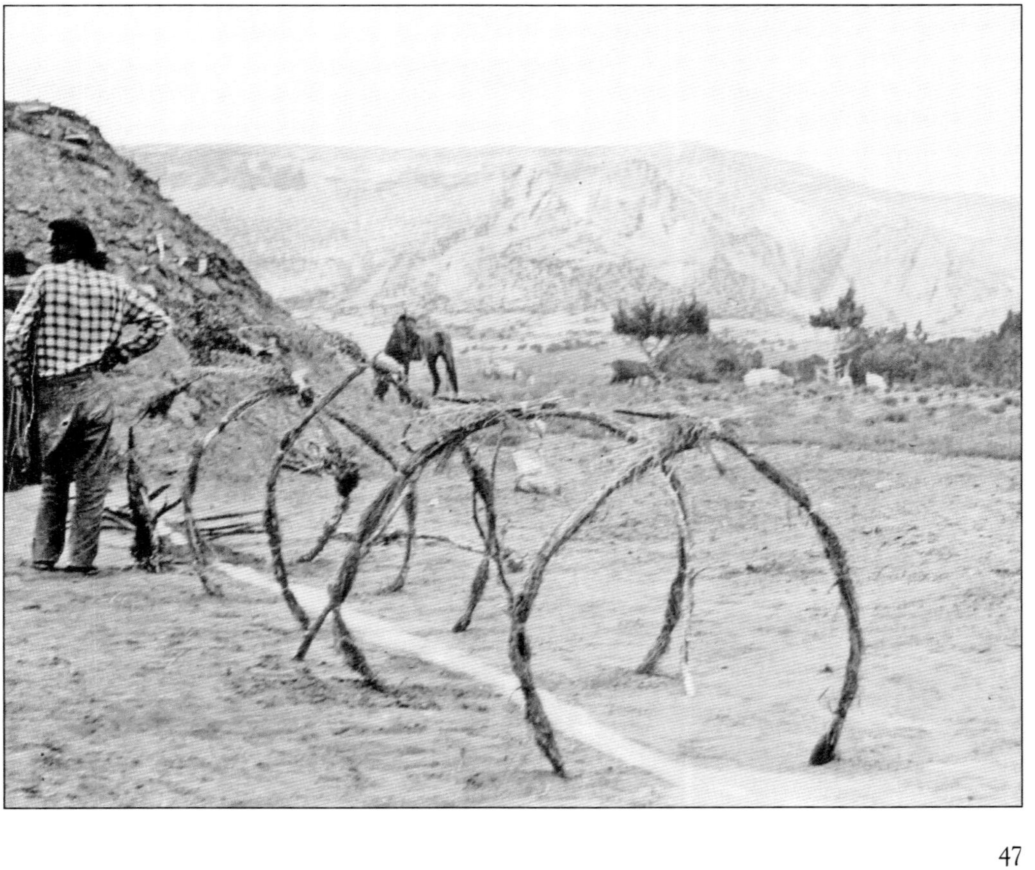

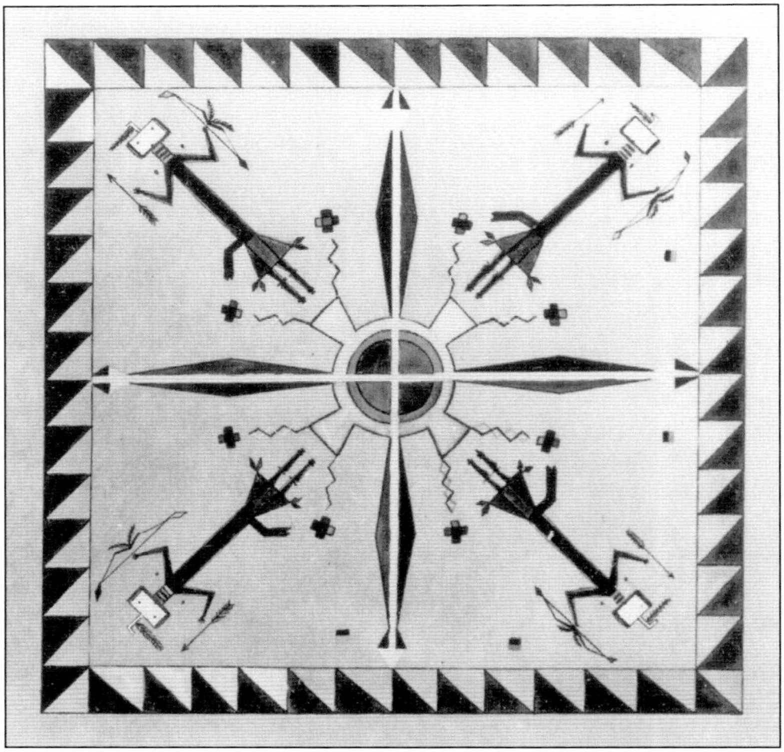

Special religious leaders, called singers, create sacred pictures of stylized images using colored sand and other crushed minerals. These paintings are usually created for healing rituals, begun as the sun rises. When the ceremony is finished—always by late afternoon, before the sun goes down—the painting is destroyed and the sand is gathered up and taken away to be deposited in designated places.

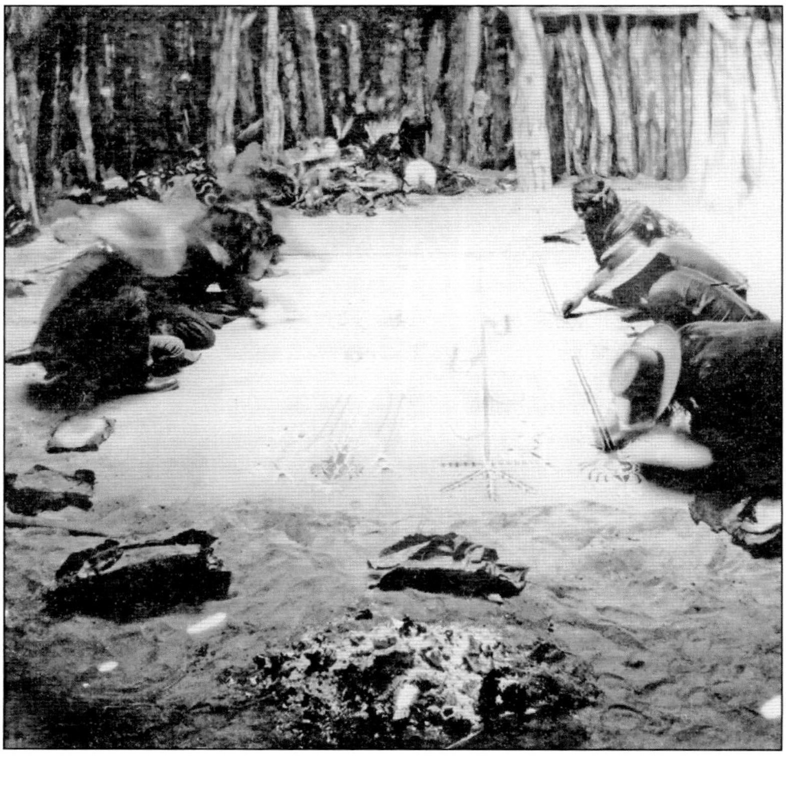

Four

Kayenta, Where Water Comes Like Fingers out of a Hill

In December 1910, John and Louisa Wetherill and their partner, Clyde Colville, moved their trading post to a new site that would put them on the south side of Laguna Creek—a temperamental creek that had dangerous crossings and often experienced torrential floods. At Oljato, supplies had to be freighted from Gallup, New Mexico, across 190 miles of sand and mud and over a dirt track cut with deep arroyos. A move to Kayenta put the Wetherills 30 miles closer to Gallup and eliminated the necessity of crossing Laguna Creek, even though it was still 150 miles to a railroad. Another advantage of the move to Kayenta was that it was less isolated, especially in the winter, when deep snows cut off any possibility of travel to and from Oljato. Additionally, the bridge across the San Juan River near Mexican Hat in southern Utah washed out soon after it was completed in 1909, further isolating the inhabitants at Oljato.

To the southwest of Kayenta is Marsh Pass, a narrow pass flanked by Laguna Creek. John Wetherill and Clyde Colville hired workers to oversee work on the road that would open up travel from Tuba City to Flagstaff, Arizona, 150 miles to the southwest, a five-day trip in a wagon.

Located in northern Arizona, Kayenta is on the western edge of the Navajo Reservation, just south of the Utah border and a few miles south of Monument Valley. Traditional Navajos called it Tó Dínéeshzhee, or "Fingers of Water," although the town is actually named after the bog hole Téé'ndééh, which means "Animals Fall into Deep Water." The site of the bog hole is about 3 miles west of town, and Kayenta itself is located at the spring downriver on Laguna Creek.

Soon after the Wetherills moved to Kayenta, a day school was built nearby, followed by a tuberculosis sanitarium. A dam on Laguna Creek often washed out but did provide water for local agriculture.

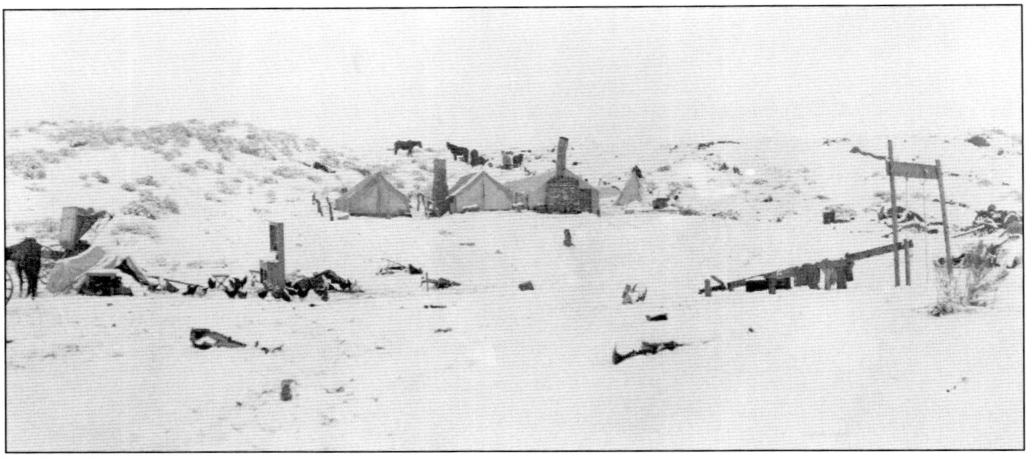

In December 1910, John and Louisa Wetherill and Clyde Colville moved to Kayenta, about 30 miles south from their previous trading post at Oljato. Leaving behind their Oljato home, they pitched tents in the snow, one for living quarters and the other to hold trade goods. A wooden plank across two barrels became the counter, and the Wetherill and Colville Trading Post was opened for business.

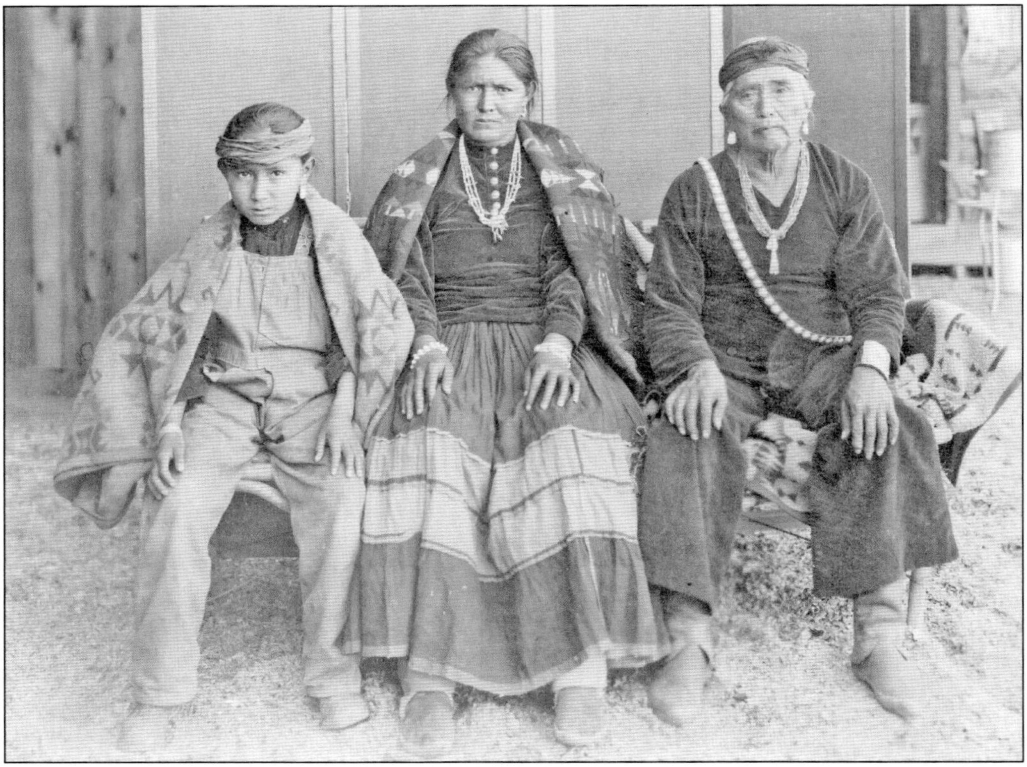

In 1906, when the Wetherills traveled to Oljato to build a trading post, they had camped at the future site of Kayenta. At that time, Sam Chief, a respected medicine man among the western Navajos, had asked them to build their trading post there. Sam Chief, shown here with his wife and son, was also known as Yellowsinger. He knew the chants for healing ceremonies, including the Yeibitchai, and had a talent for sand paintings used in the ceremonies.

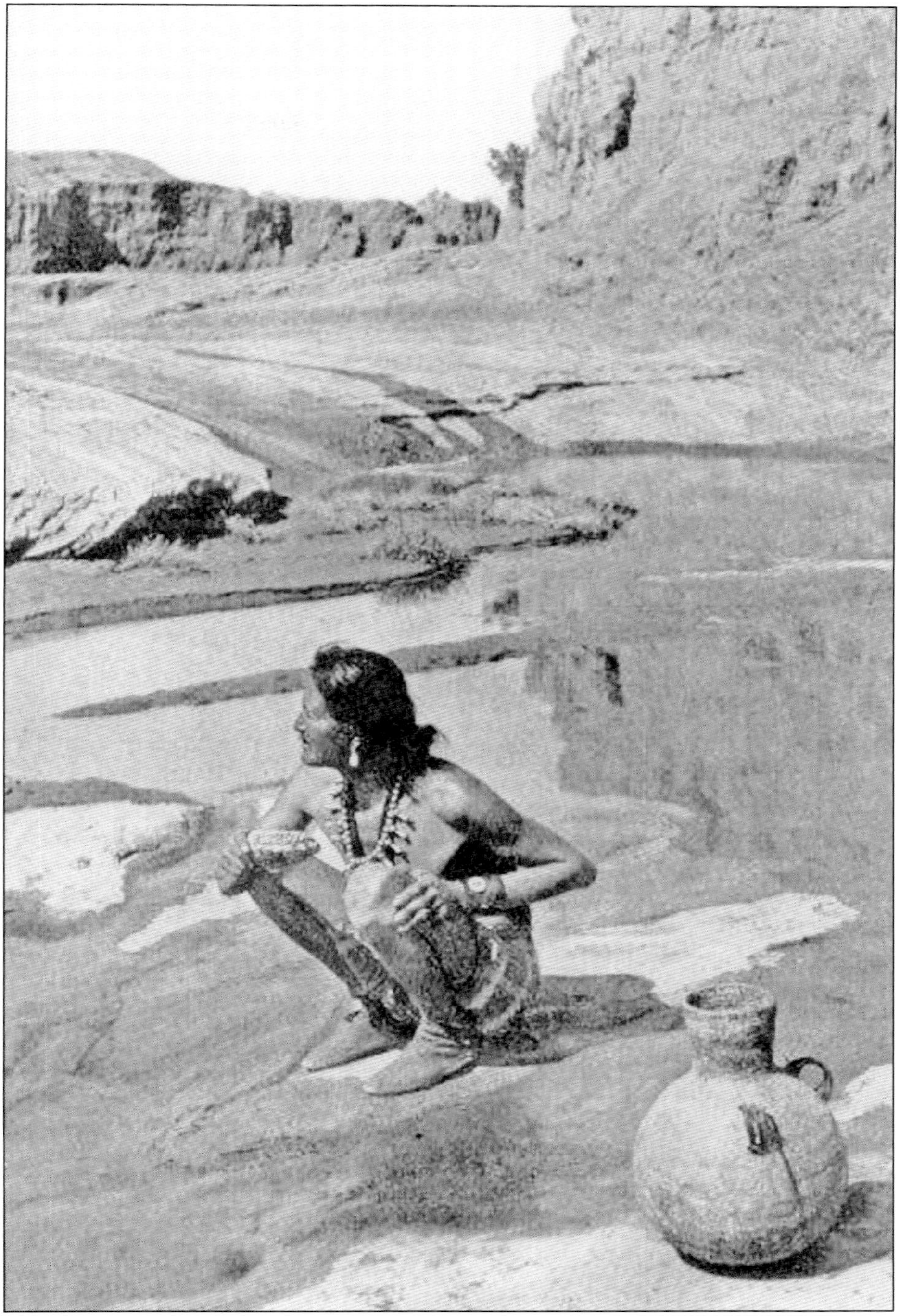

Kayenta is named for this natural tank or bog in Laguna Creek about 3 miles west of the town. At the town site is another spring named Tó Dínéeshzhee'. Navajos and other early travelers used both water sources for many years. When a post office was established, the government chose the name of Kayenta because it was easier for Anglos to read and pronounce. Unlike the poetic Tó Dínéeshzhee, "fingers of water coming from the hillside," Kayenta is named for a bog hole.

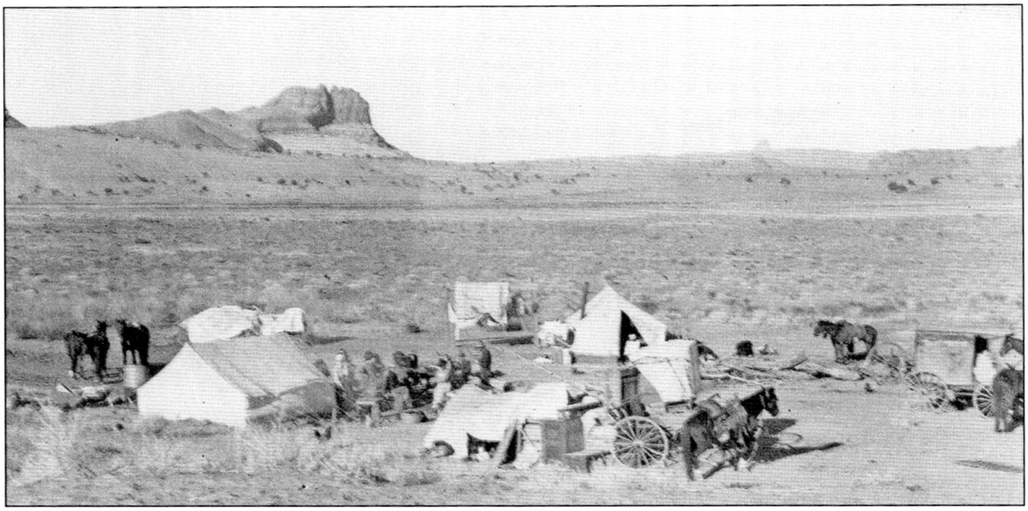

As winter passed, John Wetherill and Clyde Colville began building a home and trading post while still living and trading in the tents. In this 1911 photograph, the Toes can be seen on the skyline.

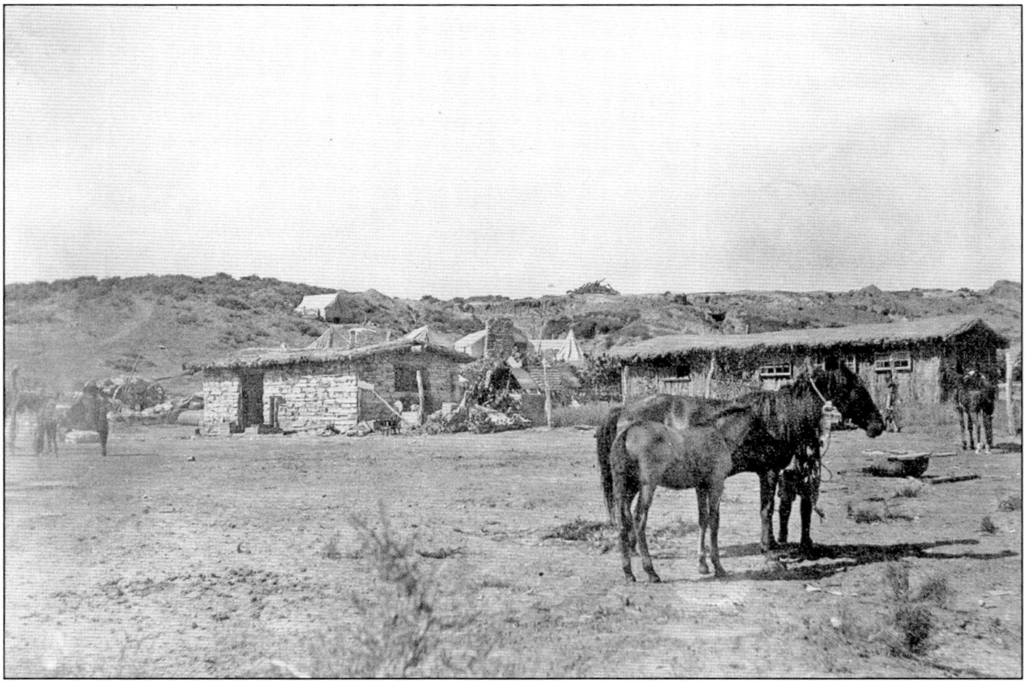

In this 1911 view of the Wetherill and Colville Trading Post, the store, constructed of stone, is at left, and the house is to the right. The house was built of logs set vertically with a roof of poles and brush. Tents behind the buildings provided lodging for guests.

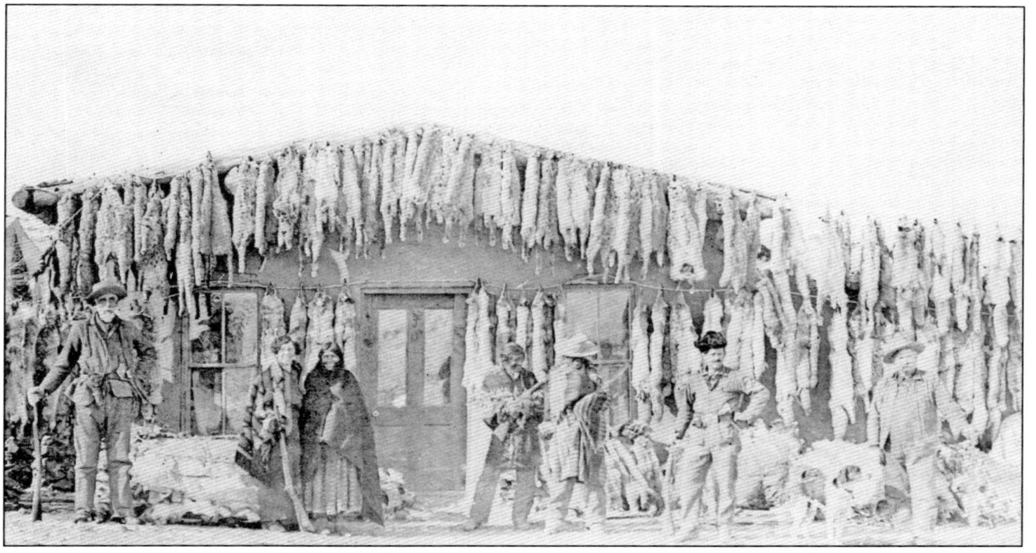

By Christmas 1911, the Wetherills had built a home and trading post, and family and friends gathered to celebrate the holiday. The men hunted bobcats and coyotes, whose pelts could be sold and traded. From left to right are Justus Tompkins (John Wetherill's uncle), Louisa Wetherill (holding the rifle), Mrs. Joe (formerly one of Hoskininni's Ute slaves), two unidentified Navajo men, John Wetherill, and Mr. Douglas.

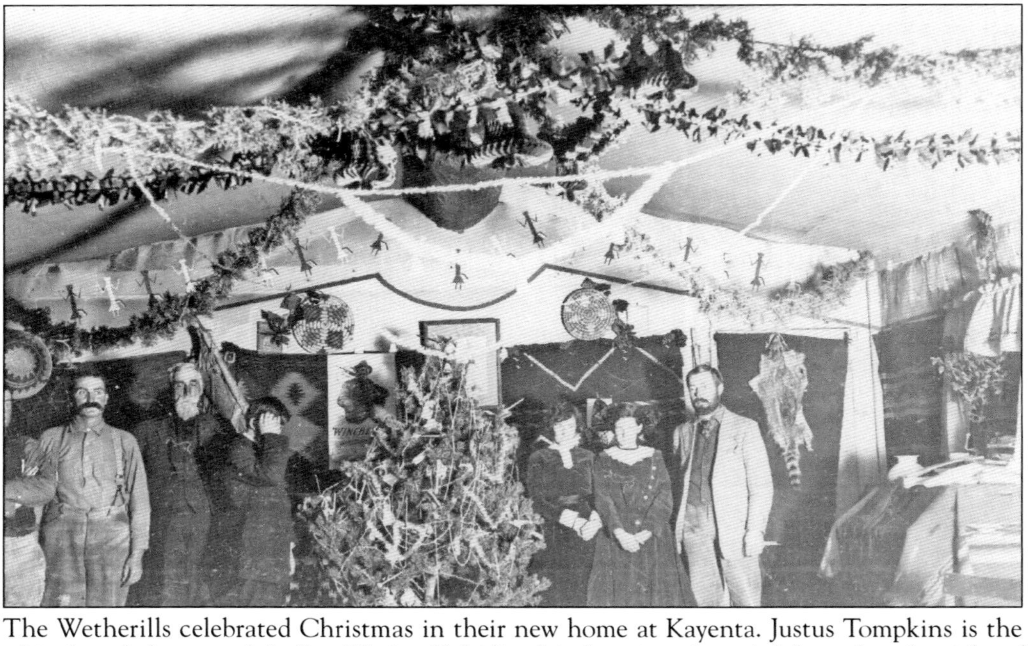

The Wetherills celebrated Christmas in their new home at Kayenta. Justus Tompkins is the white-bearded man at left; Ben Wetherill, hiding his face, is to Justus's left, and to the right of the Christmas tree are Louisa Wetherill and her daughter, Georgia Ida. The identities of the other men are unidentified.

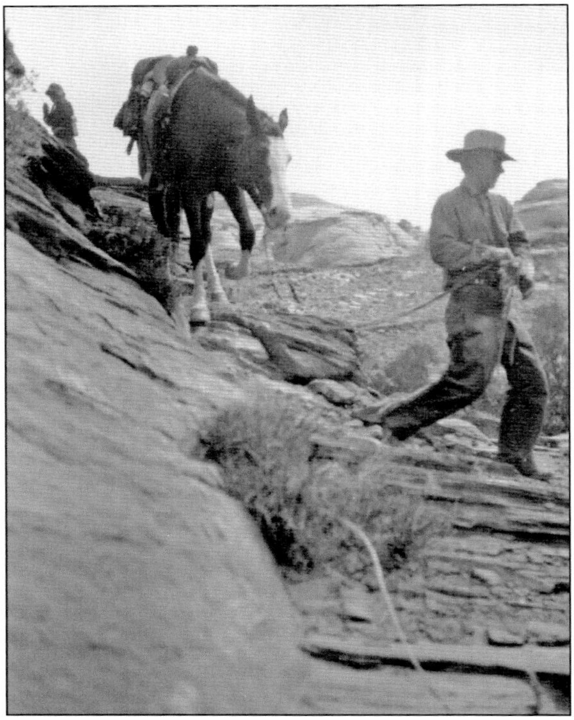

Famed novelist Zane Grey made the first of his many visits to Kayenta in 1913, when he made the long pack trip to Rainbow Bridge with John Wetherill serving as guide. In 1912, Grey's popular novel *Riders of the Purple Sage* was published, and as a result of the trip in 1913 with Wetherill, Grey later wrote *The Rainbow Trail*. Grey was captivated by the country and returned many times. In this 1922 photograph, Grey leads his horse down a steep sandstone incline.

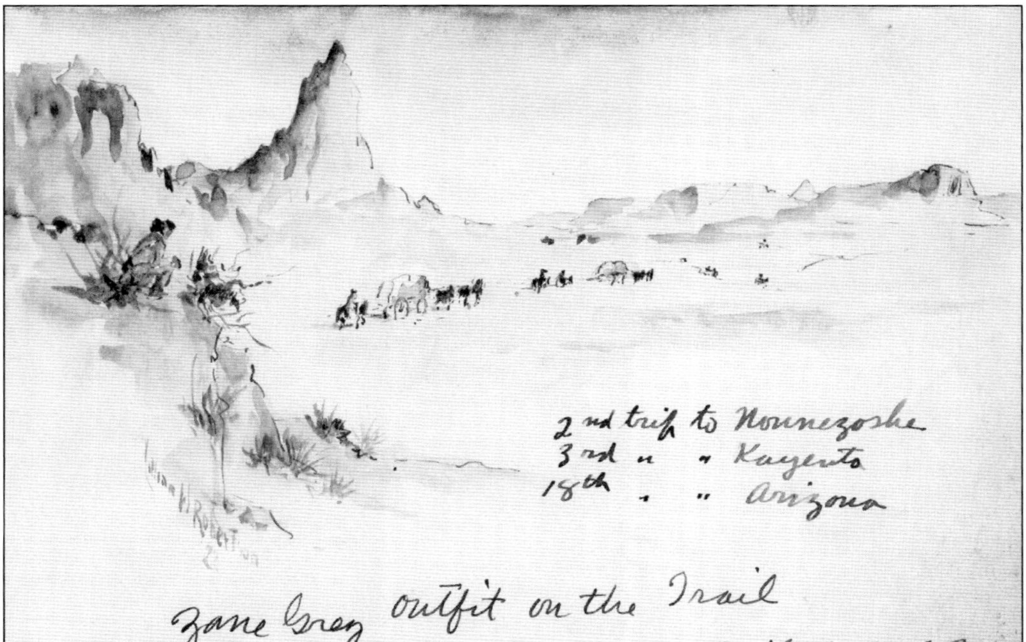

In a 1922 trip to Rainbow Bridge, Zane Grey's son Romer accompanied his father. In the Wetherill guest book, Grey noted that it was his second trip to the famed bridge, his third visit to Kayenta, and his 18th trip to Arizona. Artist Lillian Wilhelm Smith sketched the image of the pack train.

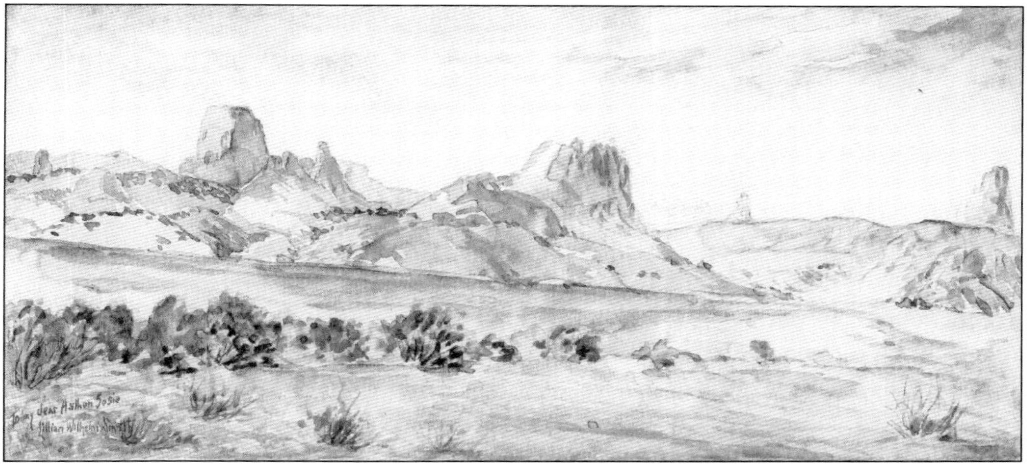

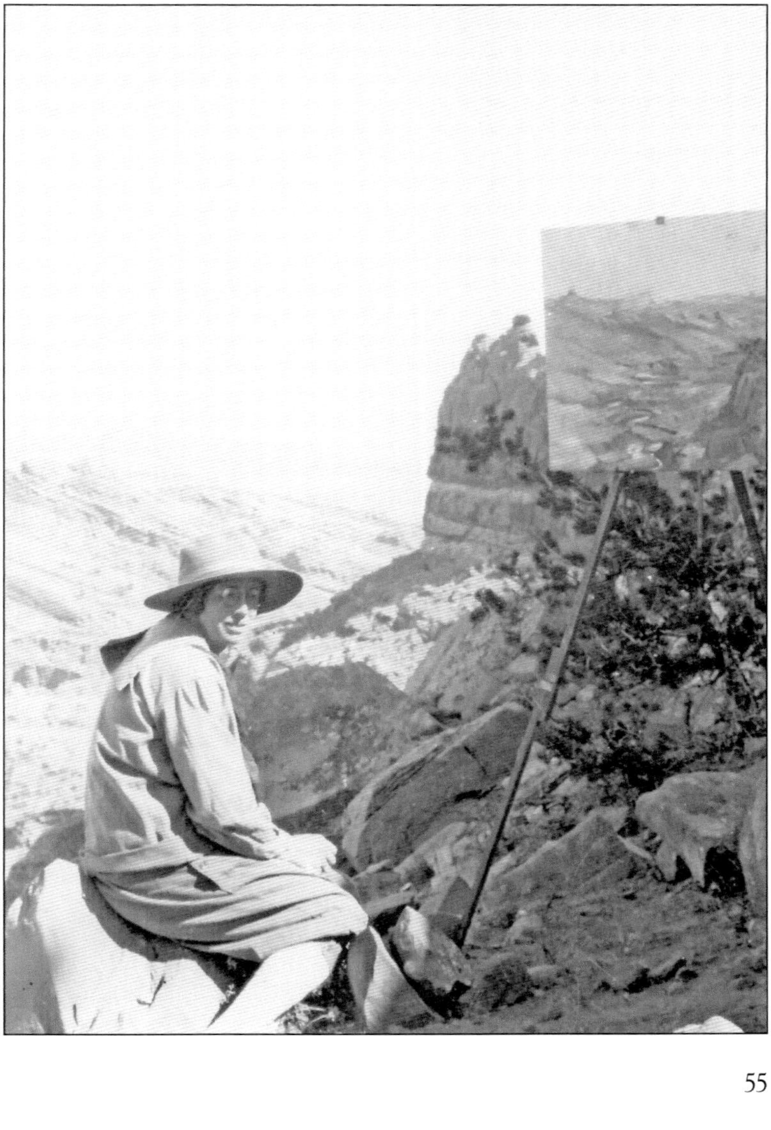

Lillian Wilhelm Smith (1882–1971) was born in Germany but lived most of her life in Arizona. Her cousin was the wife of writer Zane Grey, and Smith came west to paint illustrations for his books. She married Jesse Smith, a cowboy and guide, and she rode with her husband across miles of remote stretches in northern Arizona. Smith was the first artist to paint Rainbow Bridge, having seen the amazing sight on one of the arduous pack trips in 1913 with Zane Grey's party. Her painting of the Toes captures the unique rock formation at Kayenta. Smith dedicated her watercolor to "my dear Asthon Sosie," her friend Louisa Wetherill.

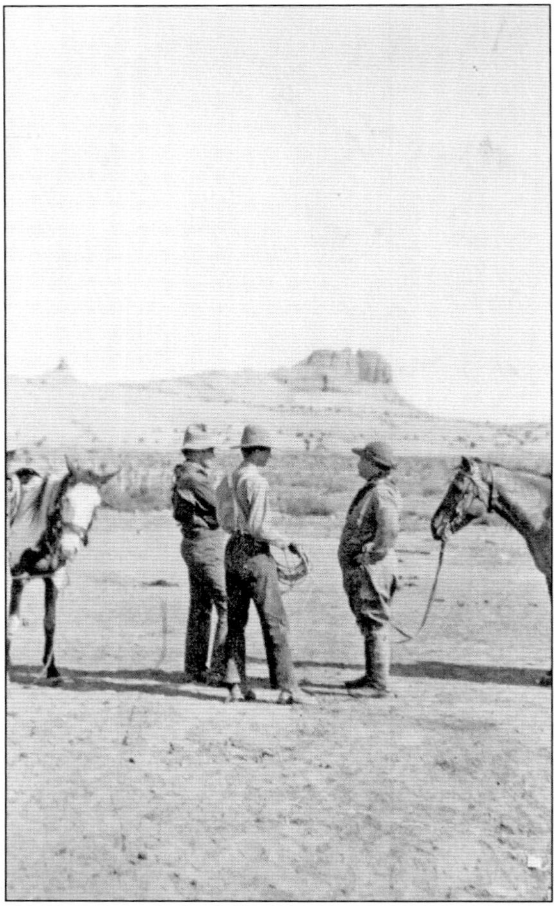

In 1913, four years after he left office as the 26th president of the United States, Theodore Roosevelt made the long trip to Kayenta, where he stayed with the Wetherills. At left, John Wetherill led the former president (right) and his sons Quentin (left) and Archie (center) on a pack trip to Rainbow Bridge. Roosevelt's subsequent article in *Outlook* magazine and his book *A Book-Lover's Holidays in the Open* shone a spotlight of national attention on the scenic wonders of the area around Kayenta, bringing an ever-growing flow of people with each year. In the photograph below, Roosevelt can be seen leading his horse across a treacherous spot on the Rainbow Bridge trail at Glass Mountain.

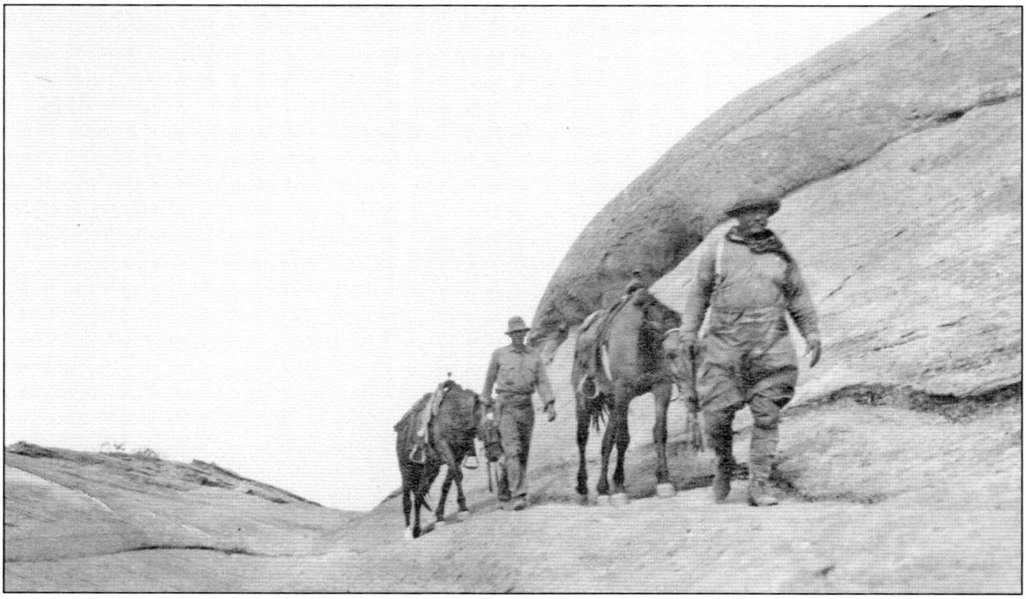

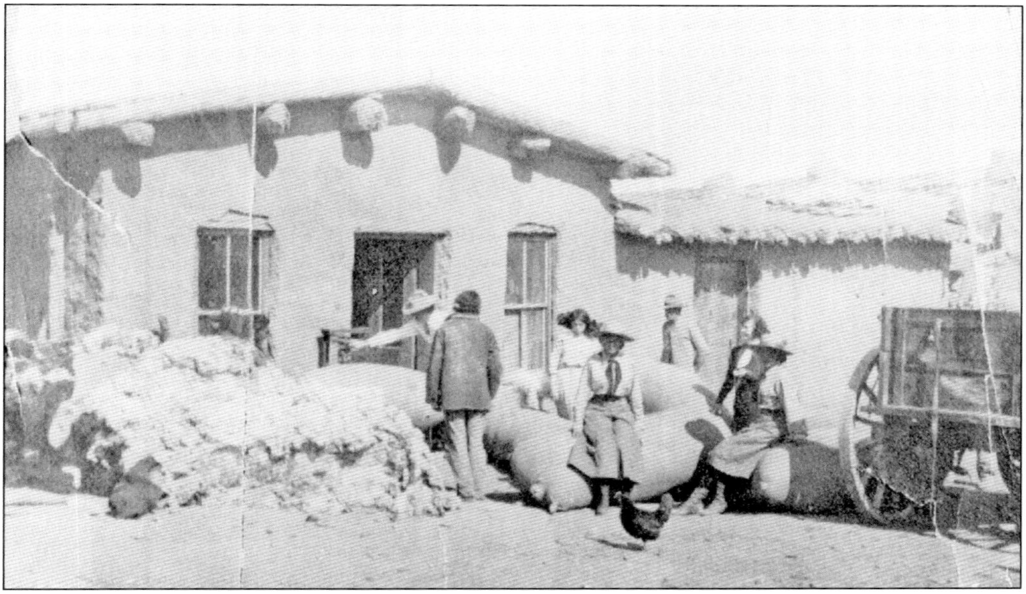

Shortly after it was built, the trading post was covered with mud stucco, although it all eventually fell off. In this 1922 photograph, John Wetherill is weighing bags of wool brought in by the Navajos. An unidentified Navajo man is in front of John, and to the right are Georgia Ida, the artist Lillian Wilhelm Smith, an unidentified man, and Louisa Wetherill, who is standing just behind Mildred Smith, who is sitting on a wool bag.

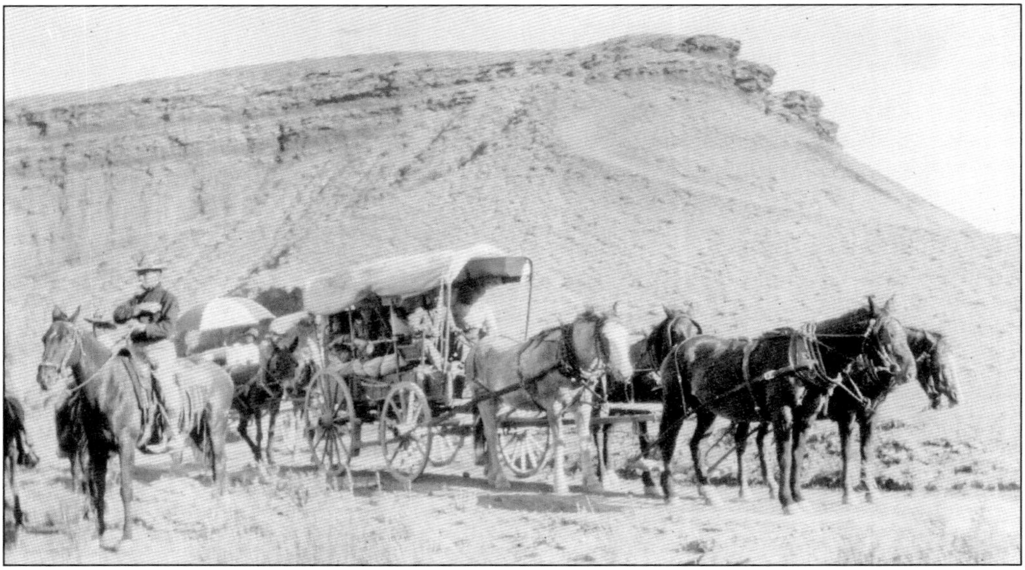

Samuel J. Guernsey, at left on the horse, and Alfred Vincent Kidder excavated rock shelters and pit house ruins in the summer of 1914 in an expedition funded by Harvard's Peabody Museum. The objective of their trip was to investigate the existence of prehistoric inhabitants of the Marsh Pass area, then called "Basket People." John Wetherill's younger brother Clayton, driving the wagon, guided the Harvard archaeologists.

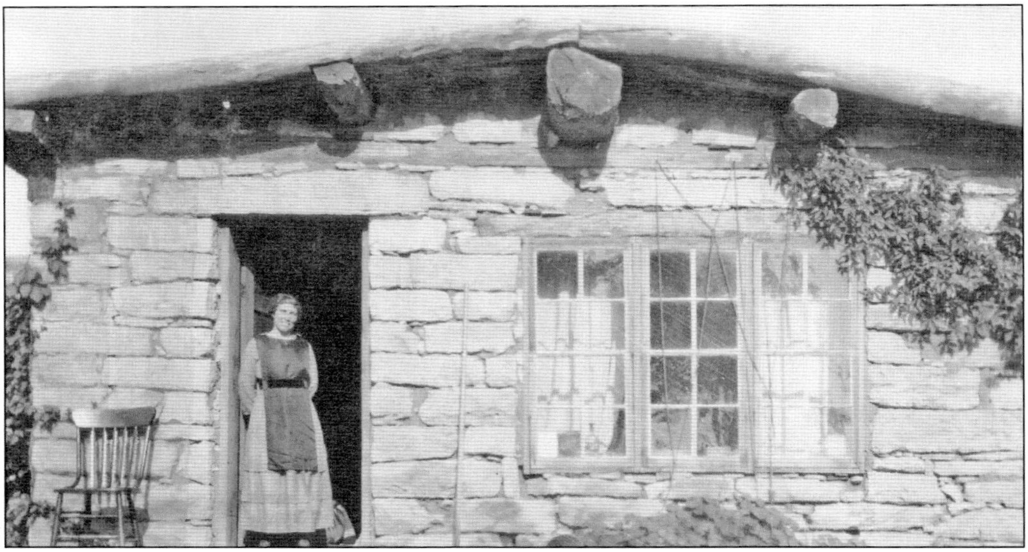

Louisa Wetherill is pictured in the doorway of her house in 1914. She impressed guests with her refinement and education. Even though she was the only white woman in the area, she created a comfortable and inviting home, welcoming guests, Anglo tourists, and Navajo friends alike. She could converse with famous people such as Theodore Roosevelt and Zane Grey as easily as she could pack a horse and ride out to a remote hogan to nurse flu victims. She was the liaison to the Navajos and hostess to the outside world. Her inviting home was decorated with Navajo rugs and baskets. Clyde Colville painted the corn and Yeibitchai pattern on the walls.

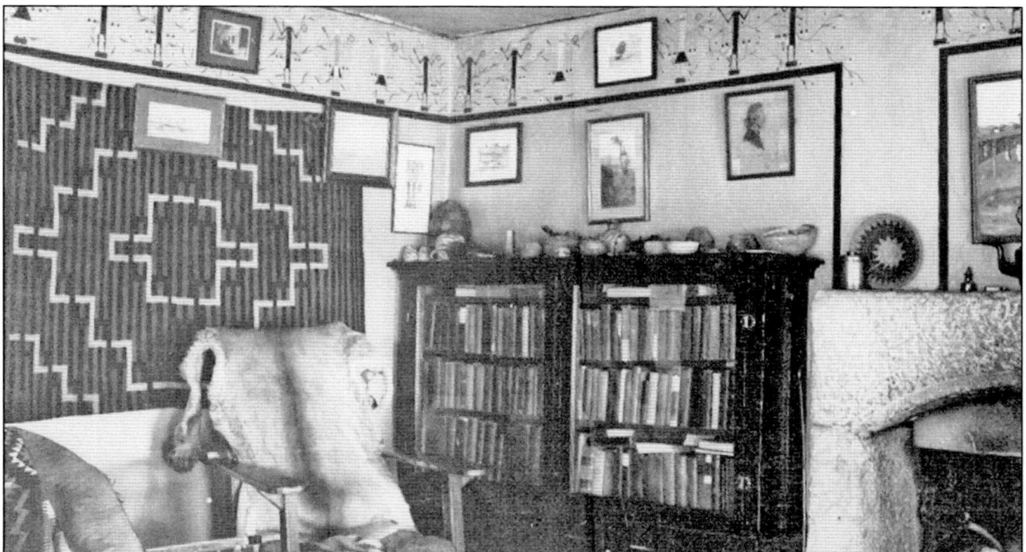

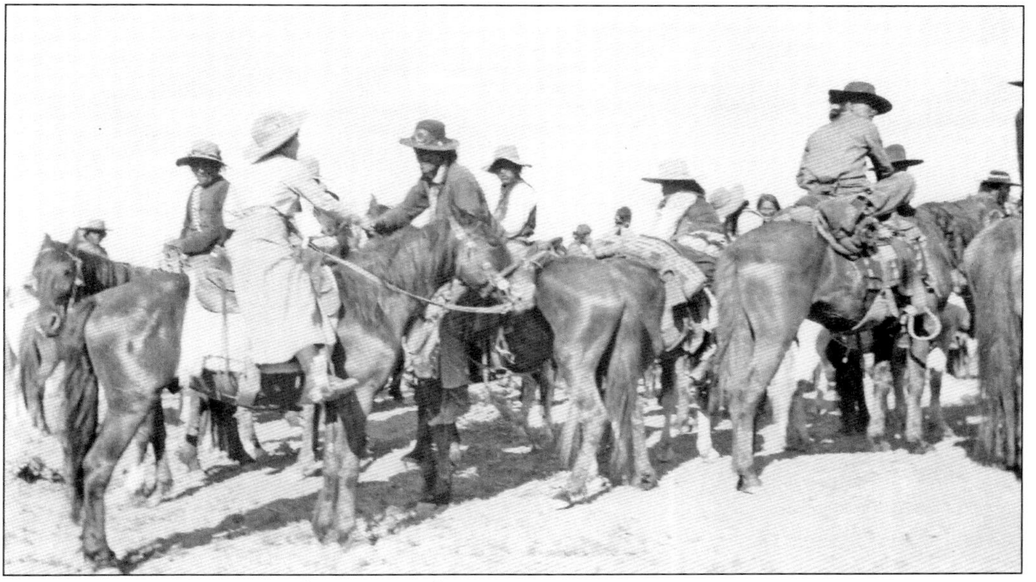

A visitor to Kayenta wrote that in regard to the Navajos, Louisa Wetherill "speaks their tongue like a native, and has their confidence as they seldom give it to any of the white race. They have entrusted to her secrets of their tribe, and because she keeps their secrets, they reveal others to her." Above, Louisa is on horseback chatting with a group of Navajos. In the photograph at right, taken in the early 1920s, she is with Hoskininni Begay, her friend of many years. Like his father, Hoskininni Begay had many wives. At the time of his death in 1941, he had eight wives and 28 children.

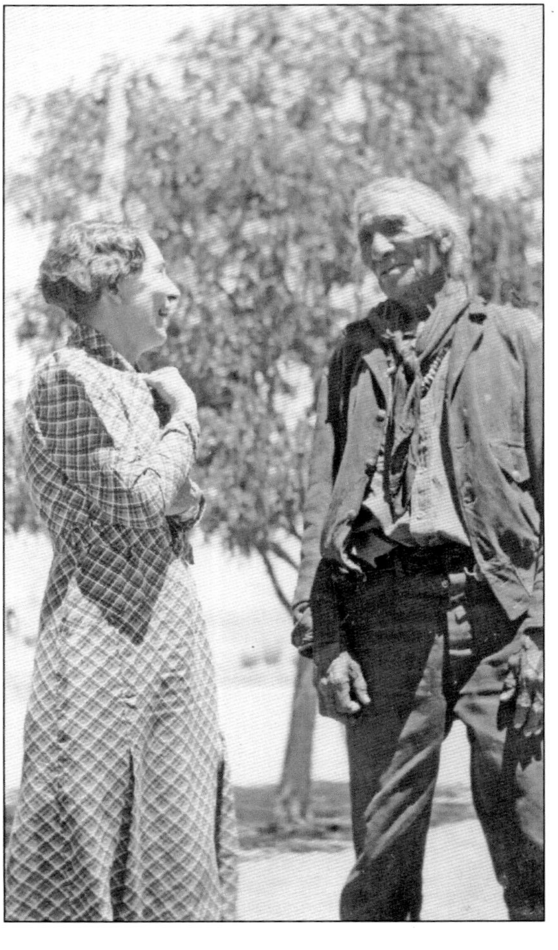

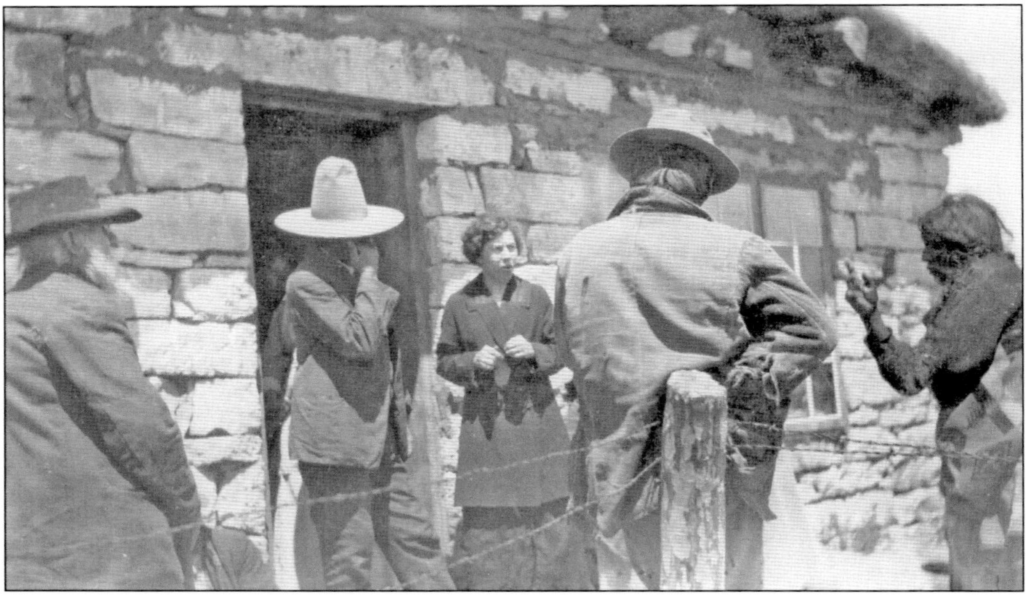

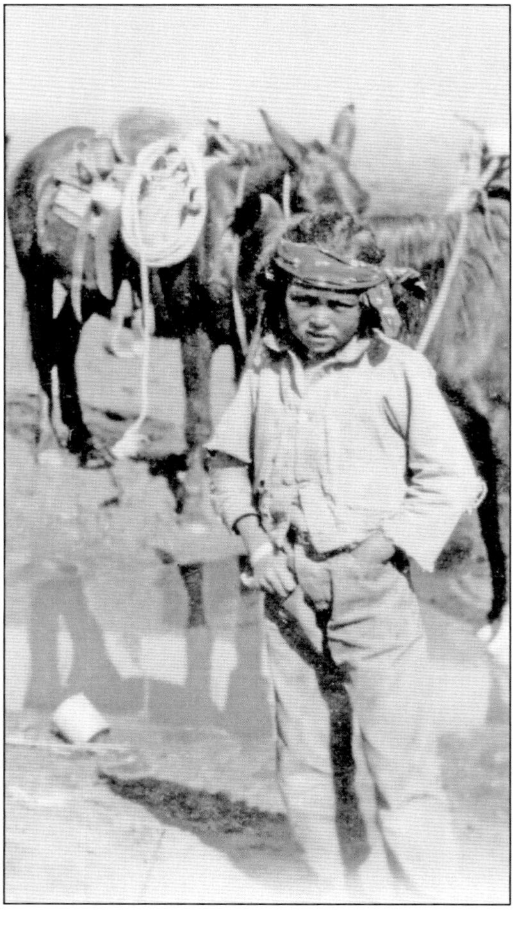

As the result of some raids and the killing of a Mexican shepherd in 1914, a posse was organized to arrest a group of Utes led by Old Polk and Posey. After a two-hour gun battle, several of the Utes escaped and hid out in the country between Kayenta and the San Juan River. Louisa Wetherill was able to talk to the Utes and convinced them to turn themselves in to Gen. Hugh Scott and avert more bloodshed. After a trial in Salt Lake City, Utah, the accused Ute man was acquitted and returned to the Navajo Springs Reservation. The Ute leader Old Polk stands next to Louisa Wetherill in the doorway of the trading post, where she was negotiating with the Ute leader. Louisa's grandfather James Rush is at the left, and at the right is a Navajo, Happy Bill. The man with his back to the post is an unidentified Ute man.

A Navajo boy visiting the trading post is wearing a bandana tied around his head.

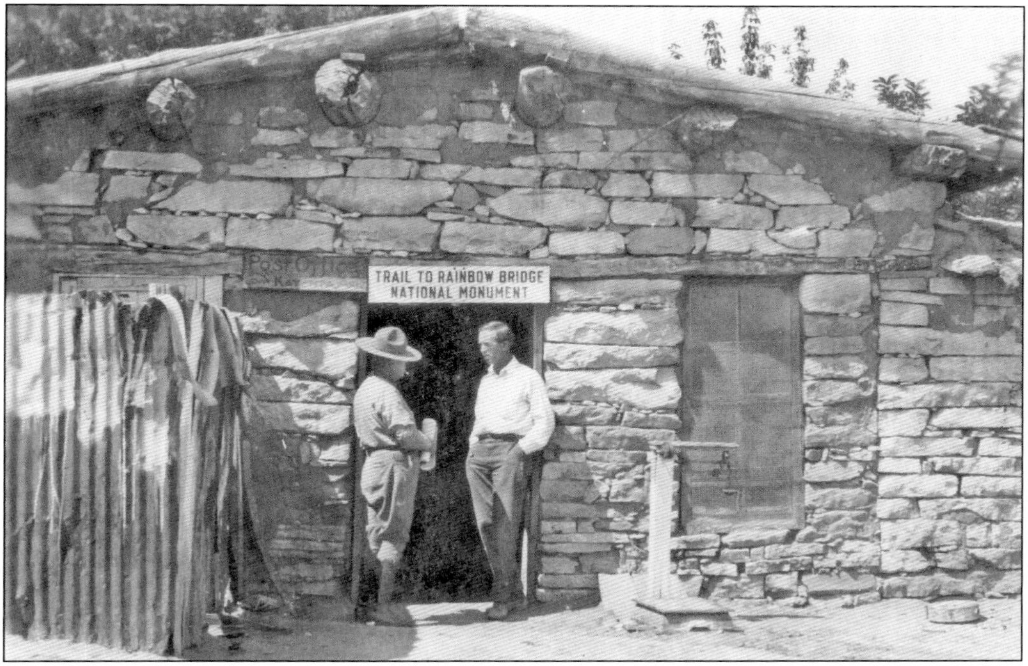

Jimmy Swinnerton, a California artist, made several visits to Kayenta. This photograph was taken about 1920. Swinnerton, wearing the hat, is visiting with Clyde Colville, the Wetherills' partner. Colville, known to the Navajos as Pelicana Naez, "the tall American," did most of the trading post management, ordering goods and selling to customers.

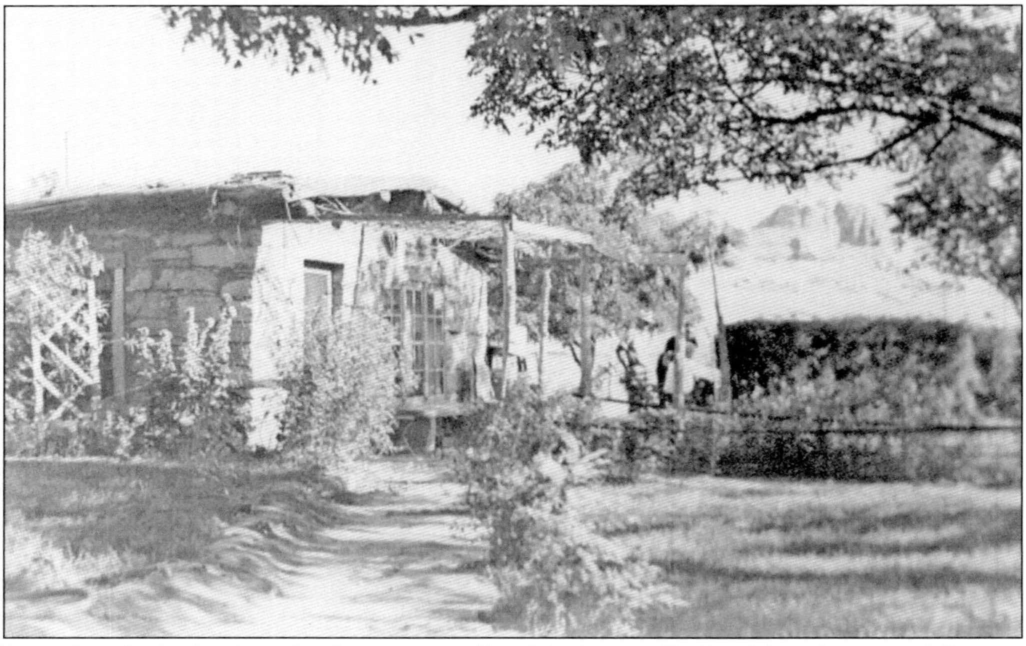

Even though she lived in the desert most of her life, Louisa Wetherill loved trees and flowers, and at Kayenta she created a lush, green oasis in the arid, sandstone country. The Toes can be seen through the trees at the right of the house.

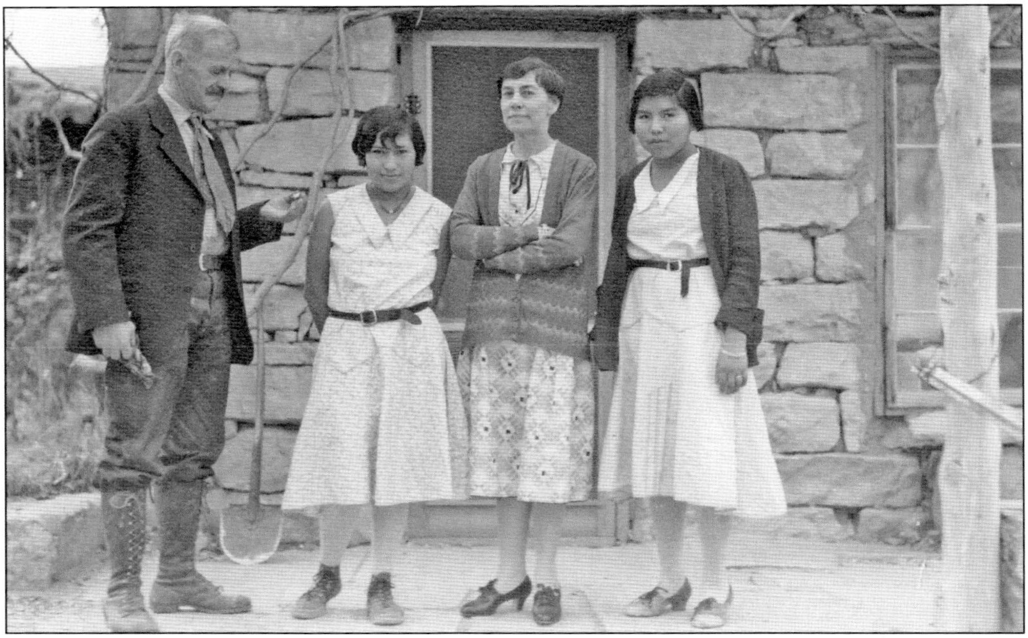

The Wetherills adopted Esther and her sister Fanny (at right), the daughters of a Ute slave woman, about 1920. Unfortunately, Esther died of tuberculosis. A few years later, the Wetherills adopted Betty, shown here about 1930 standing between John and Louisa, and both girls lived at the trading post until they were grown and married.

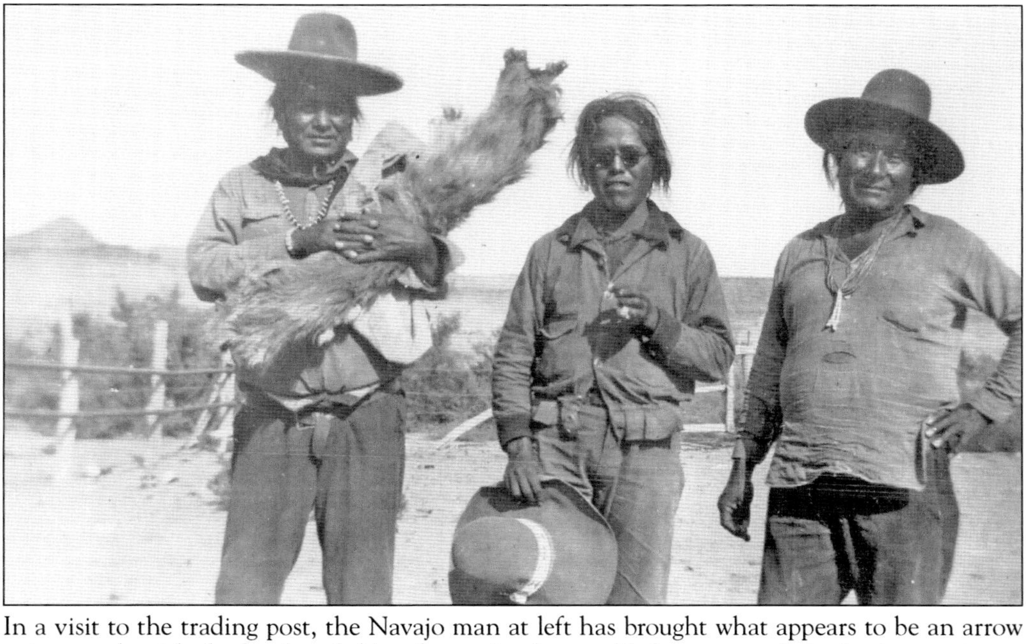

In a visit to the trading post, the Navajo man at left has brought what appears to be an arrow quiver made with the hardened skin of an animal, most likely a coyote. It is also interesting to note that the unidentified man in the center is wearing sunglasses. It is rare to see sunglasses in vintage photographs, and especially in Kayenta, a place so far from a town.

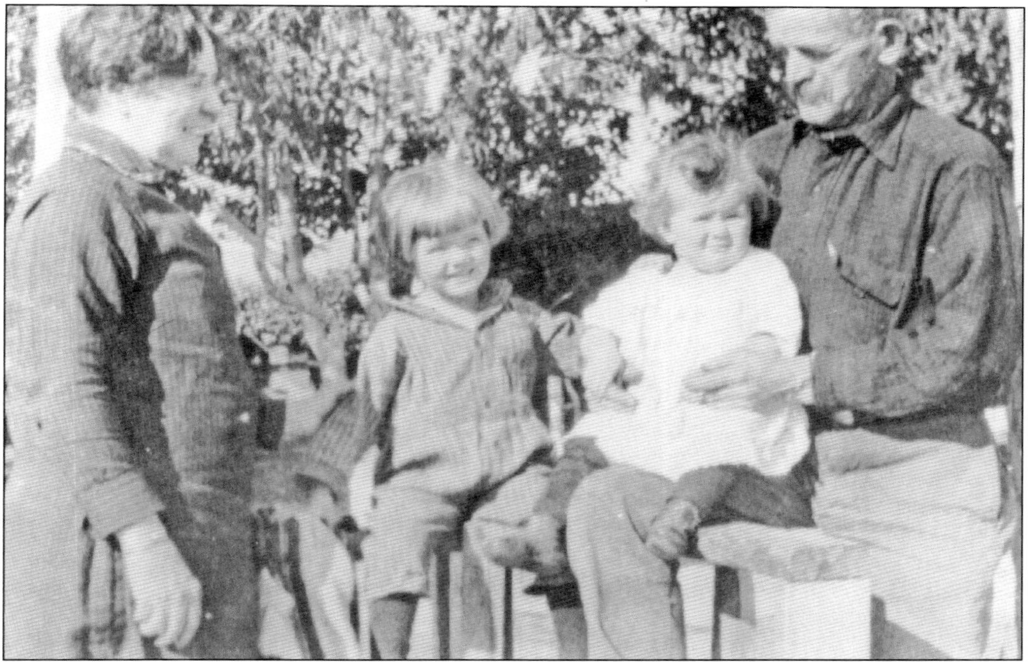

Louisa and John Wetherill pose with their granddaughters Johni Lou (left) and Dorothy (right) in 1926. When the girls were 11 and 13, they ran away from their home in southern Arizona to spend the summer with their grandparents at Kayenta. They rode the bus and then hitched rides, and when they finally got to Kayenta, they were allowed to stay.

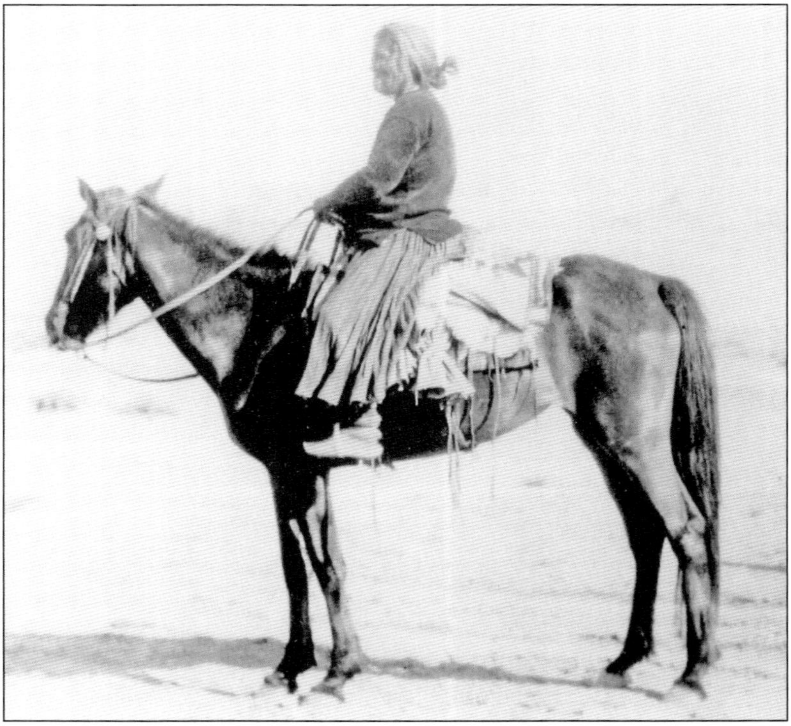

A dignified Navajo grandmother sits astride her horse on a visit to the trading post. She is wearing a velvet shirt, a full skirt, and moccasins. Her bags and blankets are tied on behind the saddle.

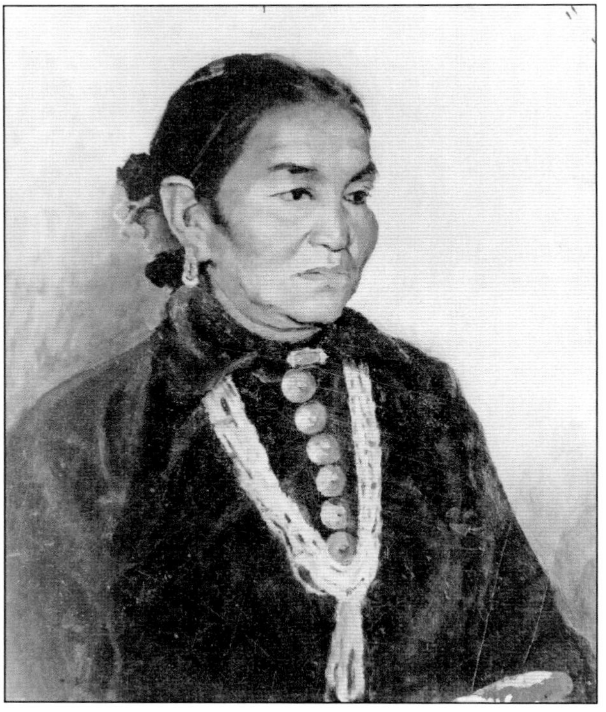

Over the years, many artists visited Kayenta. Boston artist Marion Boyd Allen traveled to the area in 1922 and painted Sue Bradley, a local Navajo woman and weaver (creator of the exquisite Yeibitchai rug). Sue Bradley wore those turquoise and shell earrings every day.

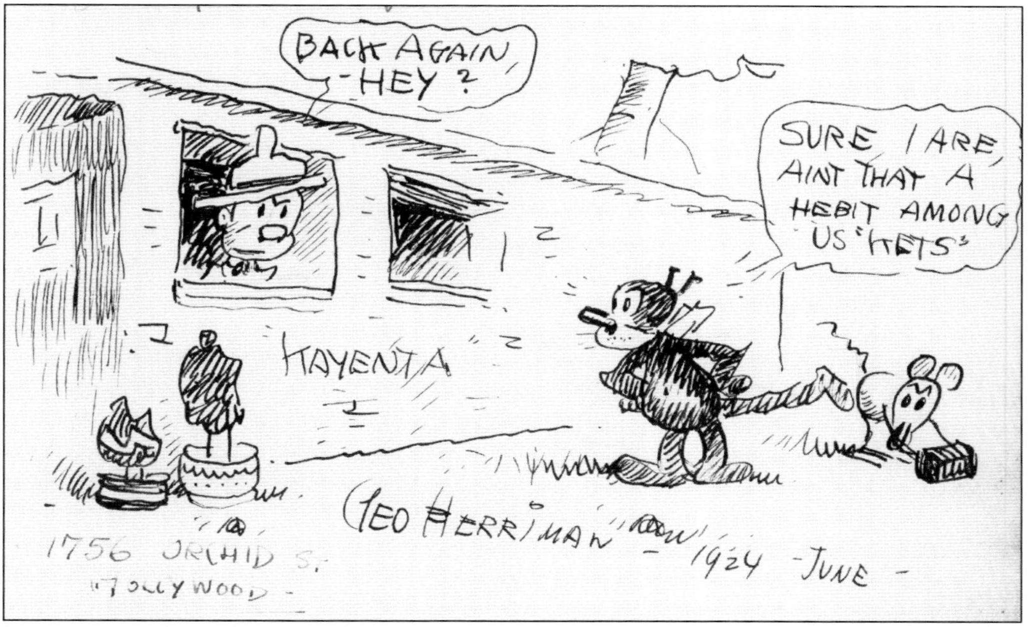

Beginning in the early 1920s, George Joseph Herriman made nearly annual visits to Kayenta, staying with the Wetherills and painting cartoon sketches in their guest book. Herriman was the creator of the popular cartoon character Krazy Kat, which appeared in newspapers across the country. Although Herriman lived most of his adult life in Los Angeles, California, so deep was his love for the Kayenta country that at his request, after his death in 1944, his ashes were scattered in Monument Valley.

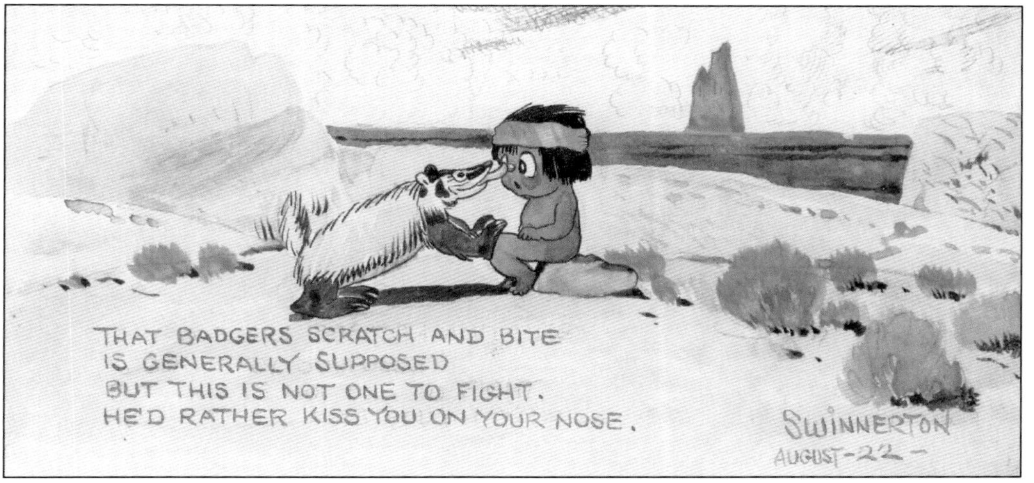

James G. Swinnerton made many trips to Kayenta to visit John and Louisa Wetherill. In the 1928 photograph at right, Swinnerton is on the left, Louisa is in the middle, and Irvin S. Cobb is at right. Cobb was a novelist who also wrote for the *Saturday Evening Post*. Swinnerton began his career as a cartoonist for the *San Francisco Examiner*. For nearly two decades, he produced a cartoon series titled *Canyon Kiddies* for *Good Housekeeping* magazine. Swinnerton later became known for his paintings of the Southwest landscape.

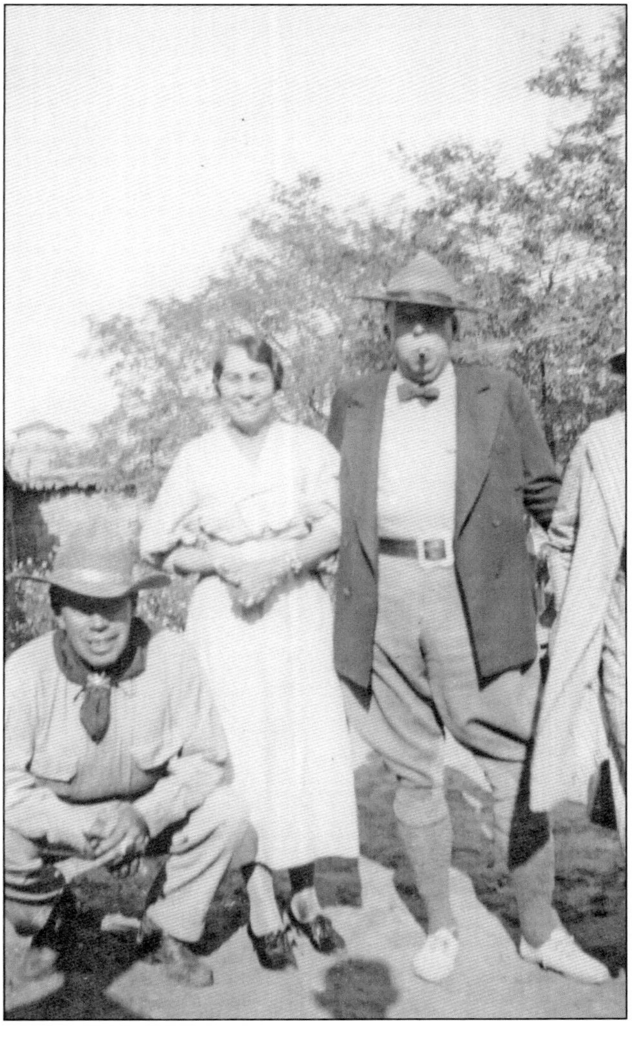

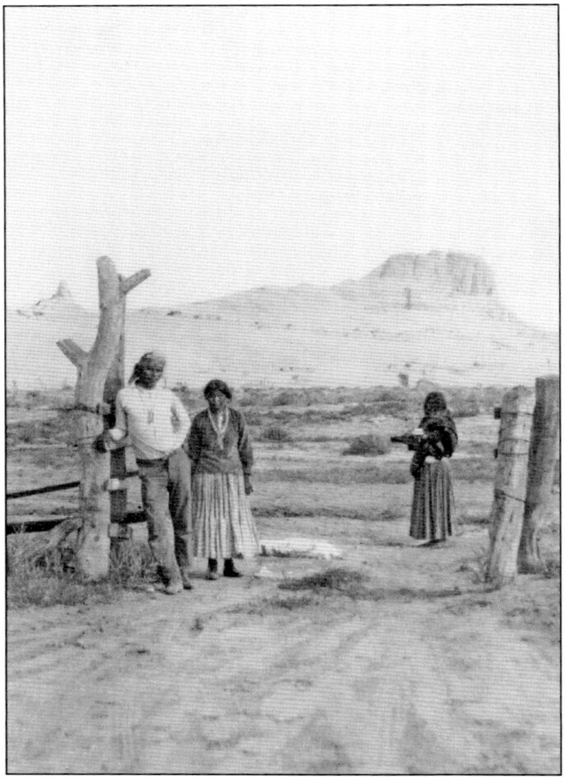

Navajos were daily visitors to the Kayenta trading post. Here a group of three pauses at the front gate to have their photograph taken; the Toes can be seen on the distant skyline.

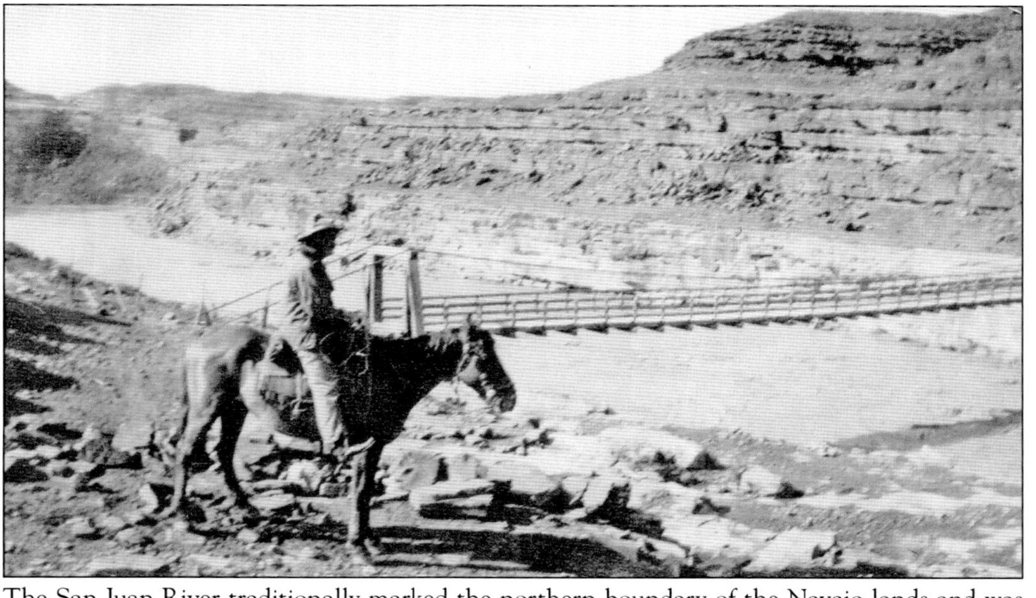

The San Juan River traditionally marked the northern boundary of the Navajo lands and was a barrier to most travel north and south. Fording the river was often dangerous, and travelers camped on the banks, sometimes for days, waiting for the water level to drop. The first bridge washed out; the second was a swinging bridge. On the back of this photograph of John Wetherill he wrote: "Kayenta—45 (?) mi, Bluff—27 mi.; Hell—1 mi."

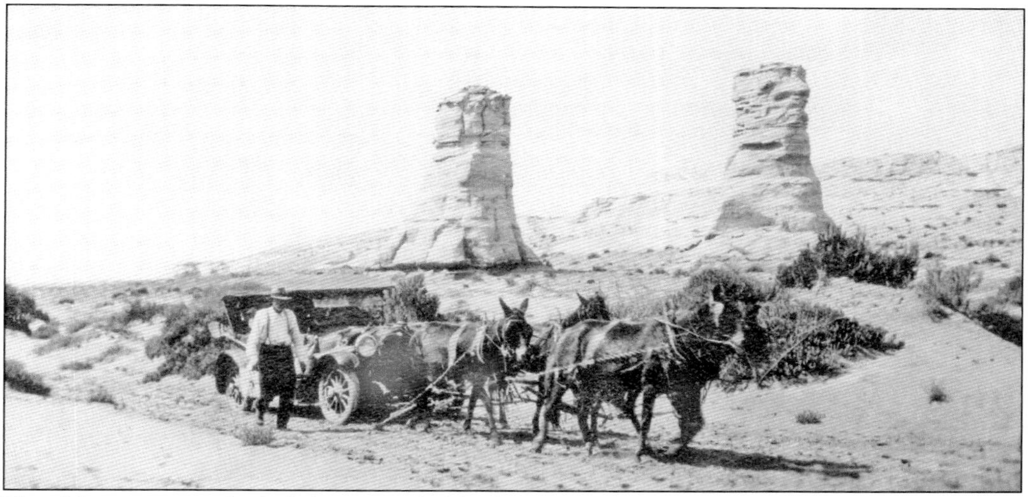

Travel by car was only slightly more reliable than wagon or horseback in the early years of the 20th century. A team of mules was called in to pull a car through the sand near a local landmark known as the Elephant's Feet in the early 1920s.

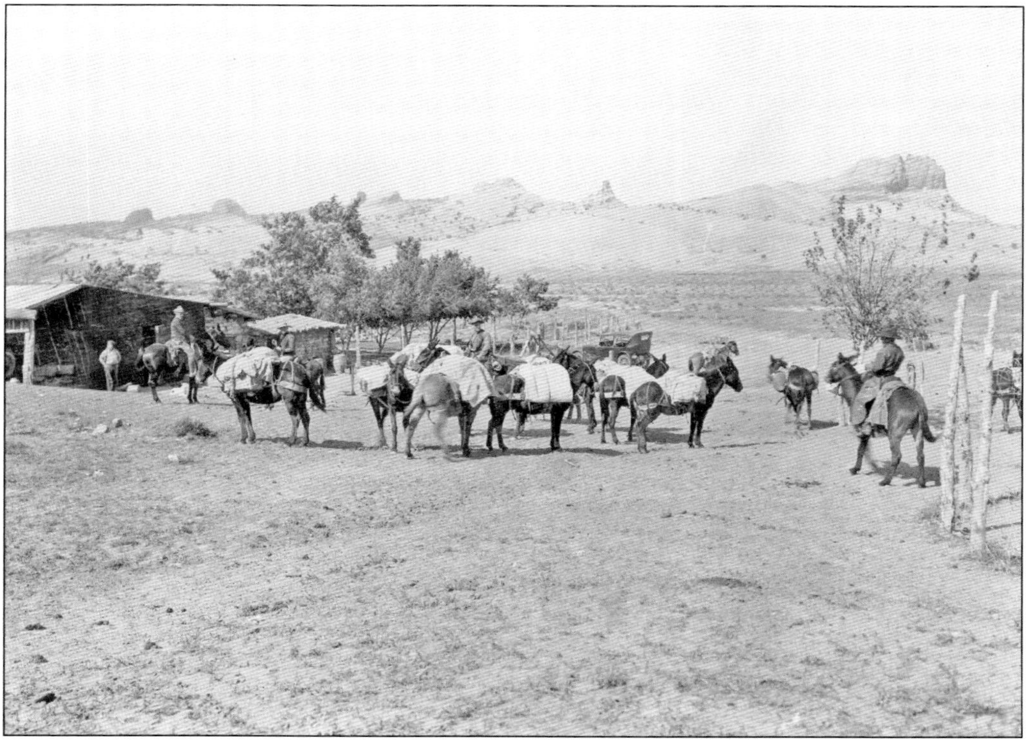

In the 1920s, the wonders of Monument Valley and Rainbow Bridge became more known to the outside world, and John Wetherill led many expeditions and pleasure trips into the remote country. Most trips required 10 to 14 days spent riding and camping on the ground. This group is setting off in 1923 from the Wetherill and Colville Trading Post with a long pack string. The Toes are visible in the distance.

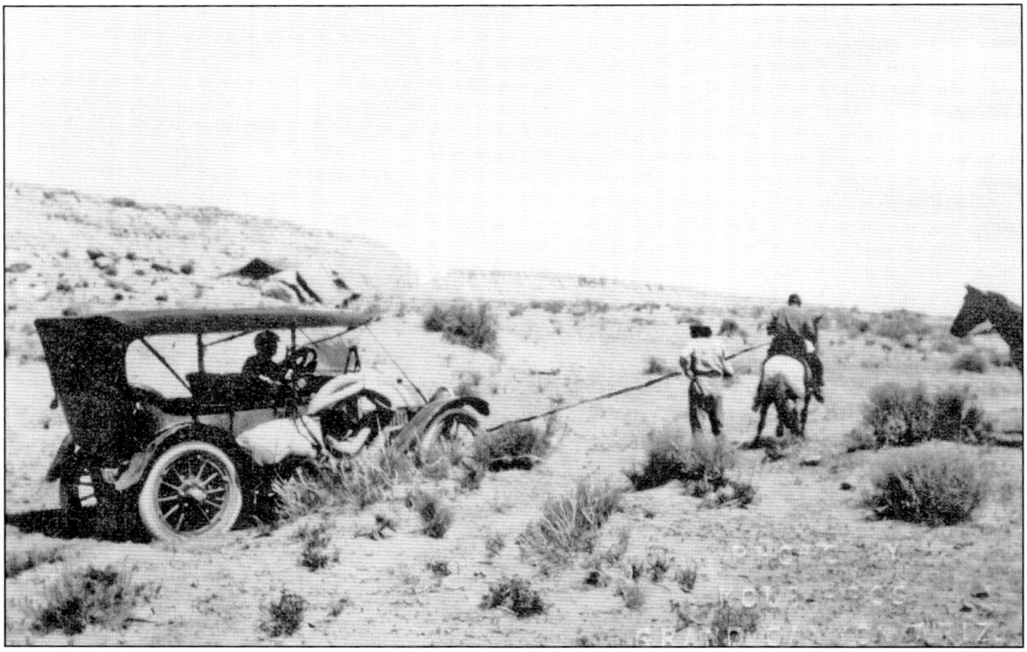

The first automobile to arrive at Kayenta was a four-cylinder Franklin (with a top speed of 28 miles per hour) driven by the five Zahn brothers in 1915. Most of their trip was cross-country; they carried shovels, winches, and sticks of dynamite to clear stubborn obstacles. But even with all that preparation, the Zahns, like the driver shown in this photograph, still had to resort to a team of Navajo horses at times. At Kayenta, the residents gathered to see their first automobile, and one Navajo commented that the car was a "horse with smoke coming out if its rear."

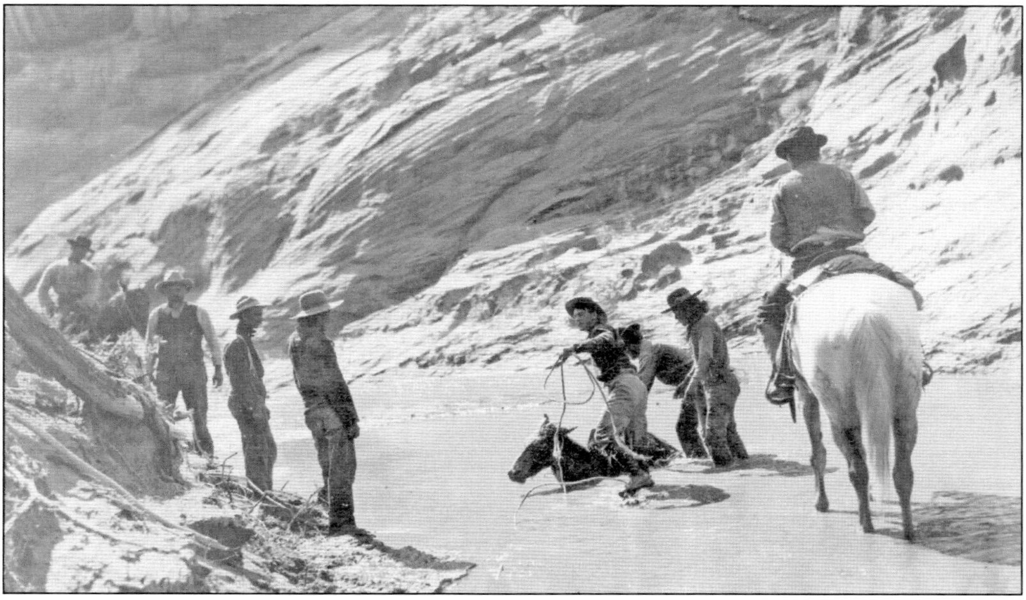

In the west, crossings at rivers and arroyos are often dangerous. Flash floods can roar down normally dry creek beds, and sandy bottoms become quicksand when wet. This group of men is attempting to extricate a horse mired in quicksand.

Keet Seel cliff dwelling is at the bottom of the deep and twisting Tsegi Canyon west of Kayenta.

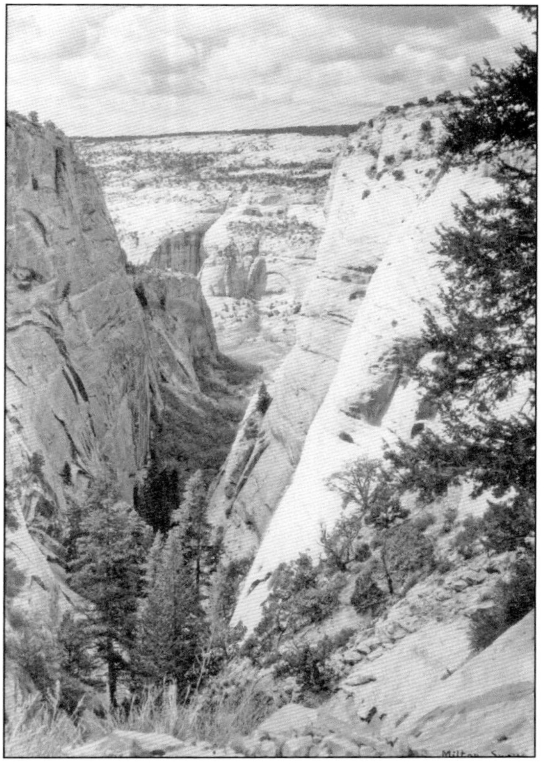

George Wharton James went to Kayenta in 1914 and hired John Wetherill as a guide with the following "reasonable" rates: "Each pack or saddle horse in the party, $1.50 per day; guide and his horse, $8.00 per day; if the party is large enough to require it a helper must be engaged at an extra $3.50 per day. In addition, the traveler pays for all provisions for himself and guides and all feed needed for the animals." Wetherill guided many groups to see the cliff dwellings and geological formations around Kayenta. This group, with John Wetherill in the lead, is crossing a shallow wash in the late 1920s.

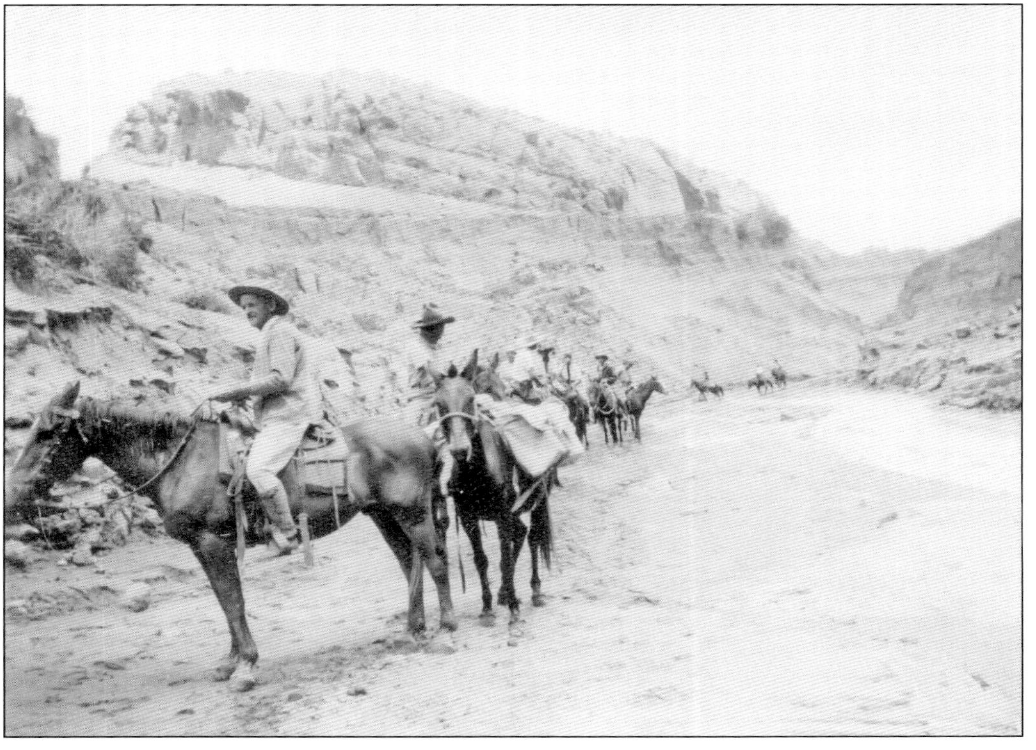

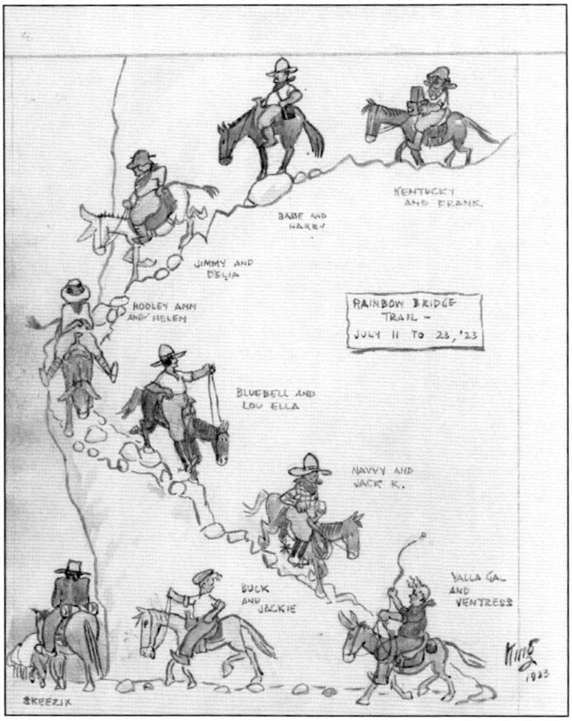

Frank King was a guest at the Wetherills' trading post in July 1923. King, creator of the popular *Gasoline Alley* comics, sketched this rendition of the group of tourists that made the adventurous 12-day horseback trip to Rainbow Bridge led by John Wetherill.

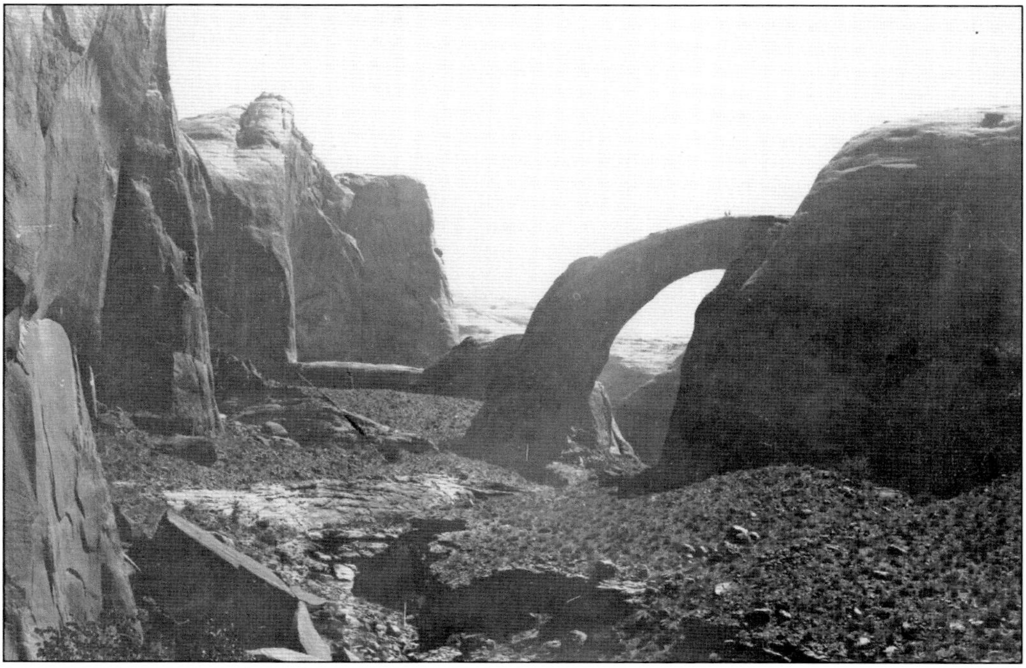

Surprisingly, New Yorker Eleanor Townsend, the first woman tourist to see Rainbow Bridge, journeyed there with her brother Arthur Townsend in September 1909, just a few weeks after it was first visited by John Wetherill. In this photograph taken from the downstream side, two figures can be seen standing on top of the stone arch. Perhaps they are Eleanor and Arthur.

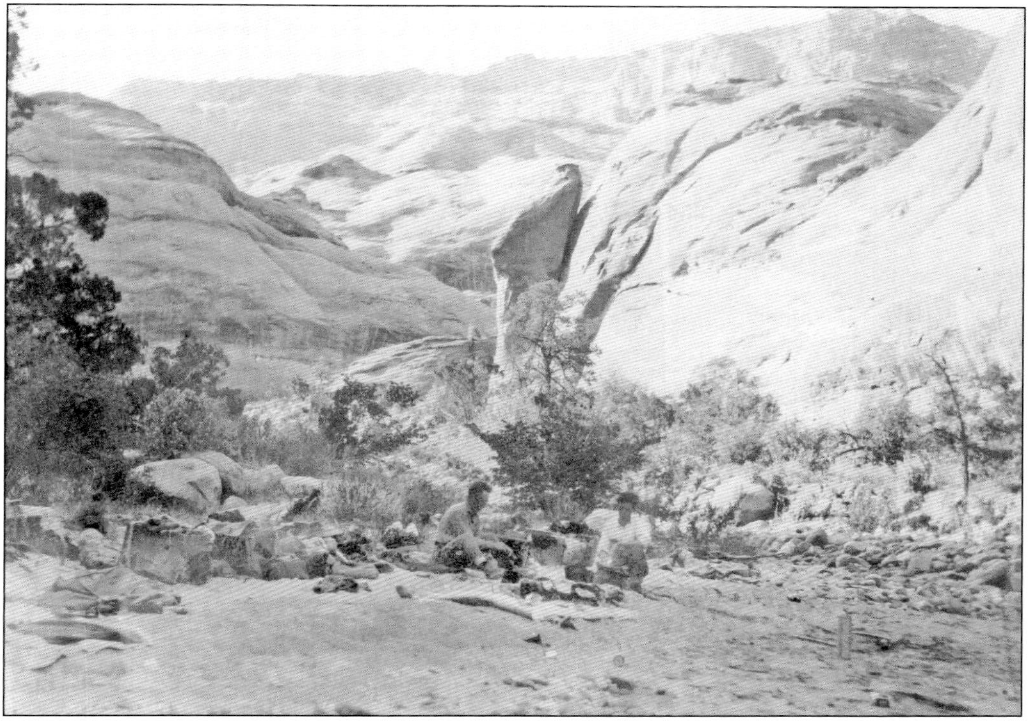

After Theodore Roosevelt and Zane Grey wrote about Rainbow Bridge, John Wetherill guided more people to see the stone rainbow each year. This is one of the camps on the Rainbow Bridge trail.

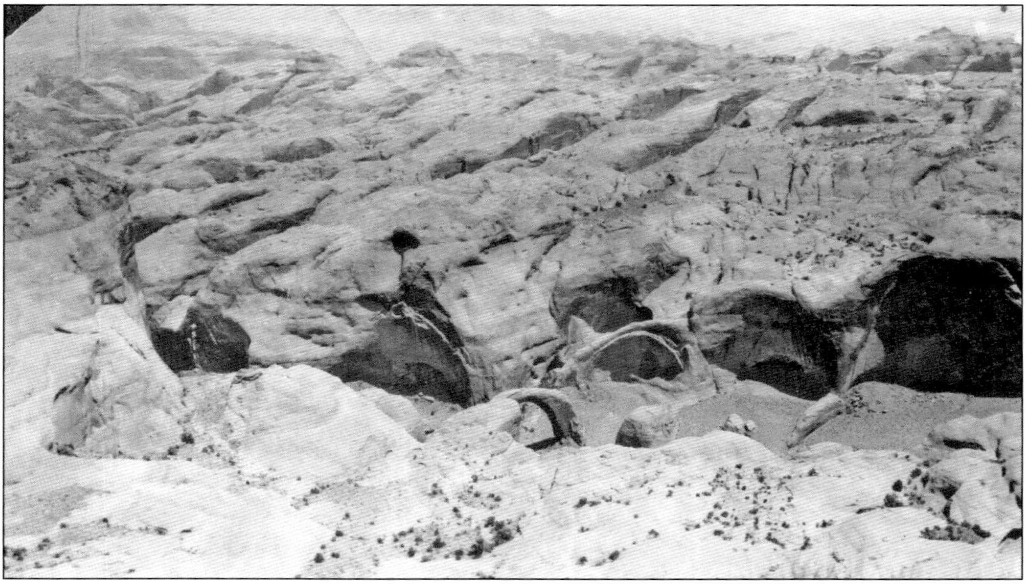

Rainbow Bridge (Nonnezoshe, "Where the Rock Goes across the Water") was known to local Navajos and Paiutes, but it was not until 1909 that the natural wonder was officially brought to the attention of the world by an exploring party. Seen from above, it is apparent that the terrain is nearly an impenetrable maze of slickrock and sheer drops.

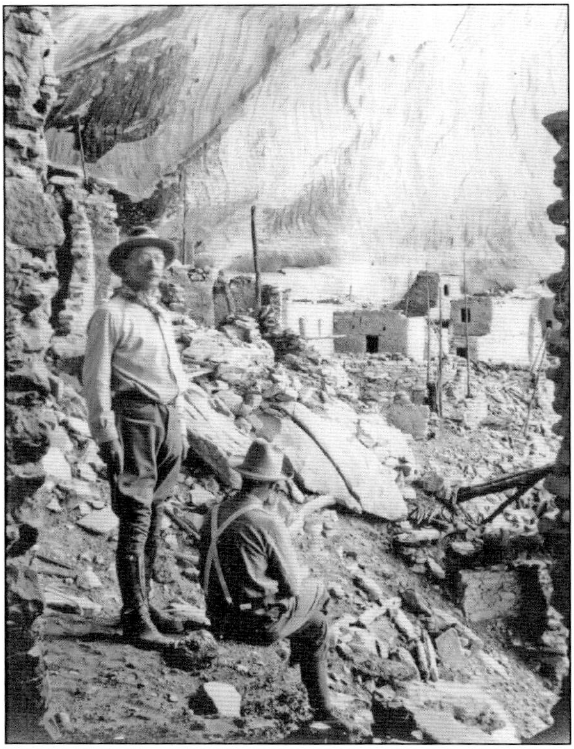

Charles Leopold Bernheimer, pictured at Keet Seel in 1922, was a wealthy New York businessman who came under the spell of the slickrock country around Kayenta. He was a benefactor of the American Museum of Natural History and gathered valuable collections for that institution on his nearly annual trips with John Wetherill between 1920 and 1931. Although he was well liked by his Anglo and Navajo guides, he was a strange contrast to them with his slight frame and formal eastern manners, his red sleeping cap, and smelly 5¢ cigars. He carried a suitcase for dress clothes and always changed for dinners. The Bernheimer expeditions, led by John Wetherill, traveled into regions north of Kayenta that were unexplored by white men. There were no trails, and the area was a bewildering maze of slickrock and often-impenetrable chasms. Where a route was impassable, sometimes dynamite, TNT, and black powder were a last resort for forward progress.

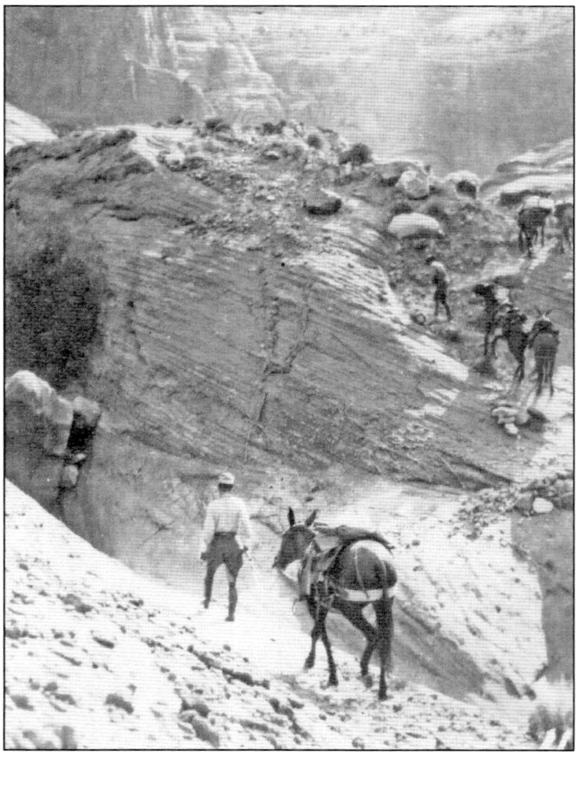

A surveyor standing on a ledge at the top of a canyon looks over the desolate and wild country north of Kayenta in this 1909 photograph.

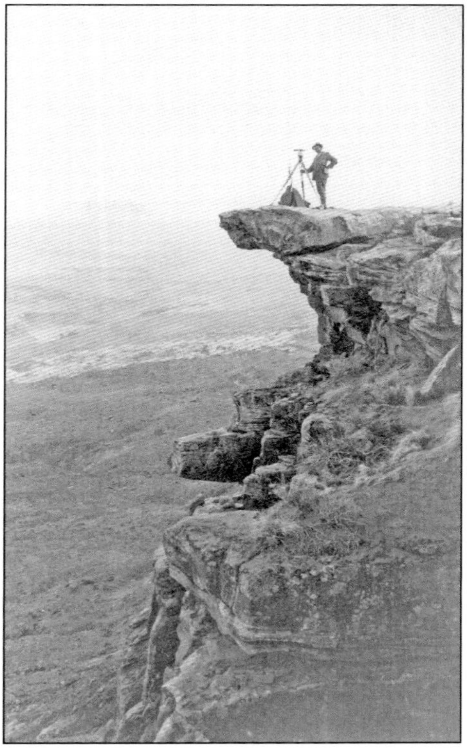

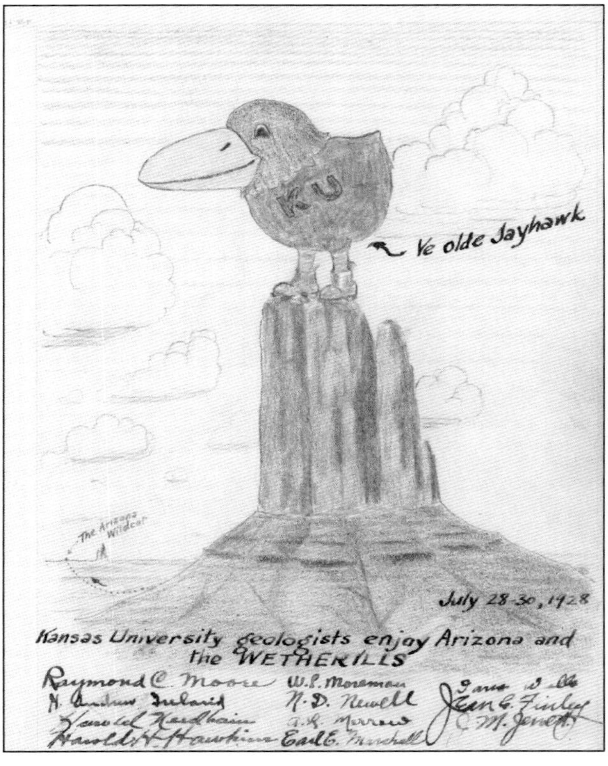

Prof. Raymond Moore brought a group of geology students from Kansas University to study the unique landscape of the Kayenta area in 1928. Moore coauthored *Geology of the Kaiparowits Region* with Herbert E. Gregory of Yale, another of the eminent scientists to visit Kayenta. Many groups of scientists from museums and universities traveled to Kayenta to base their summer field schools and expeditions.

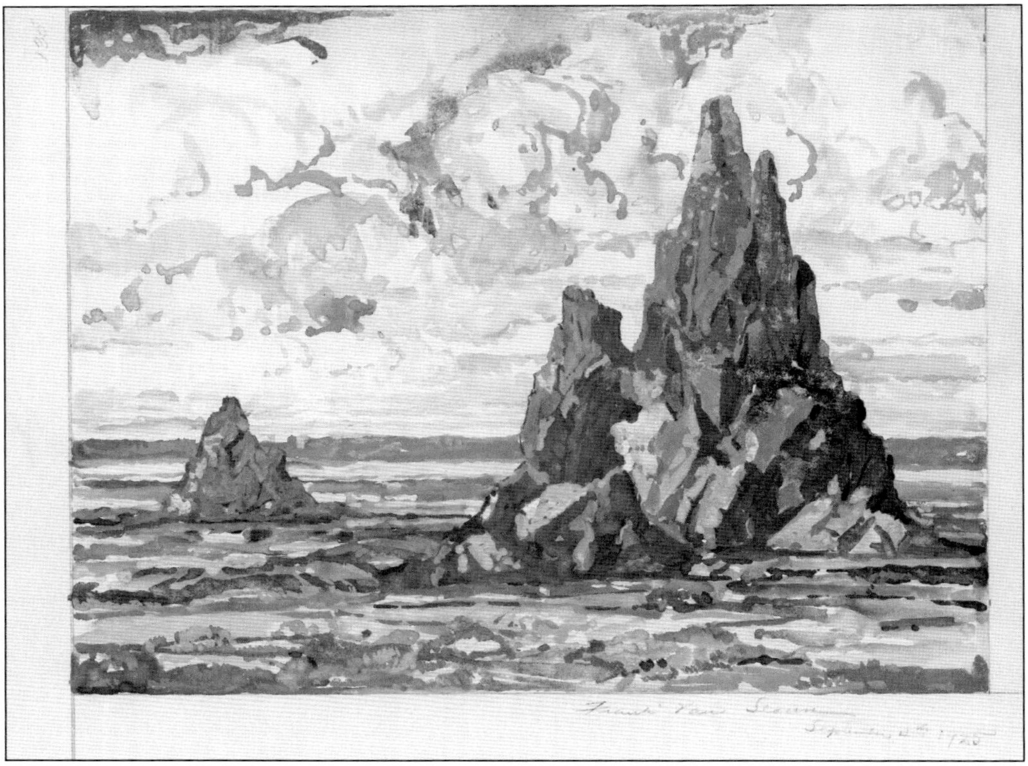

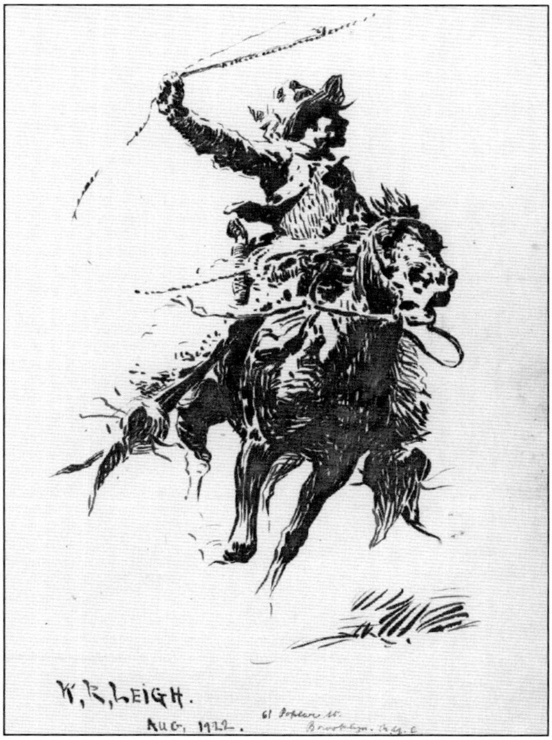

California artist Frank Van Sloun painted Agathla Peak on a page in the Wetherills' guest book during a 1925 trip to Kayenta. Van Sloun was known as an American realist, and he was commissioned by the State of California to paint murals in several of the state's public buildings.

William Robinson Leigh visited Kayenta in August 1922 with his good friend and fellow artist Maynard Dixon. Although Leigh was from the east, William H. Simpson of the Santa Fe Railroad sponsored his trips to the west in return for several of his paintings. Leigh eventually was known as the "Sagebrush Rembrandt."

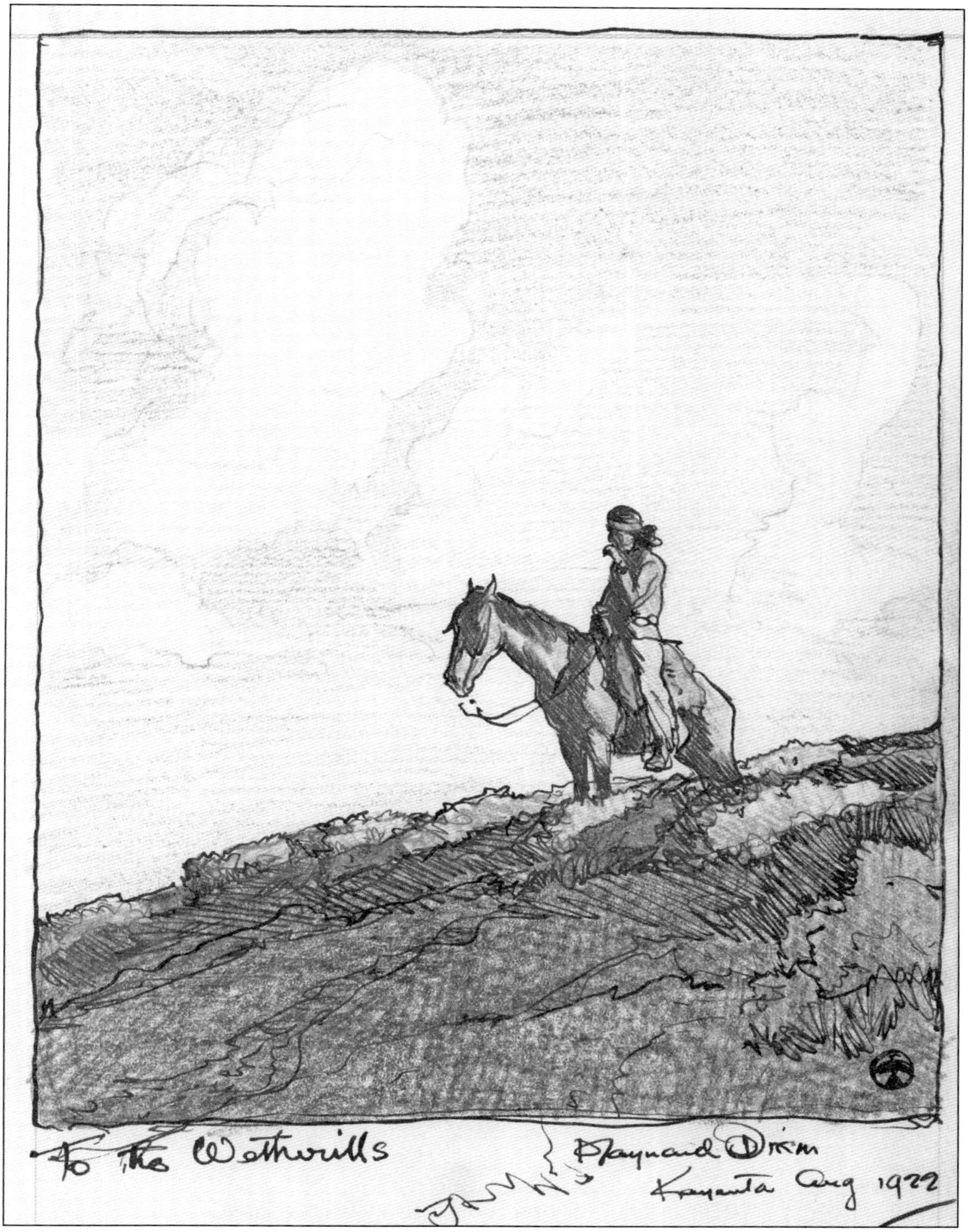

The famed artist Maynard Dixon created this color sketch of a silhouetted Navajo rider in August 1922. His painting in the Wetherill's guest book is dedicated "To the Wetherills." Dixon has been called the "Painter of the West."

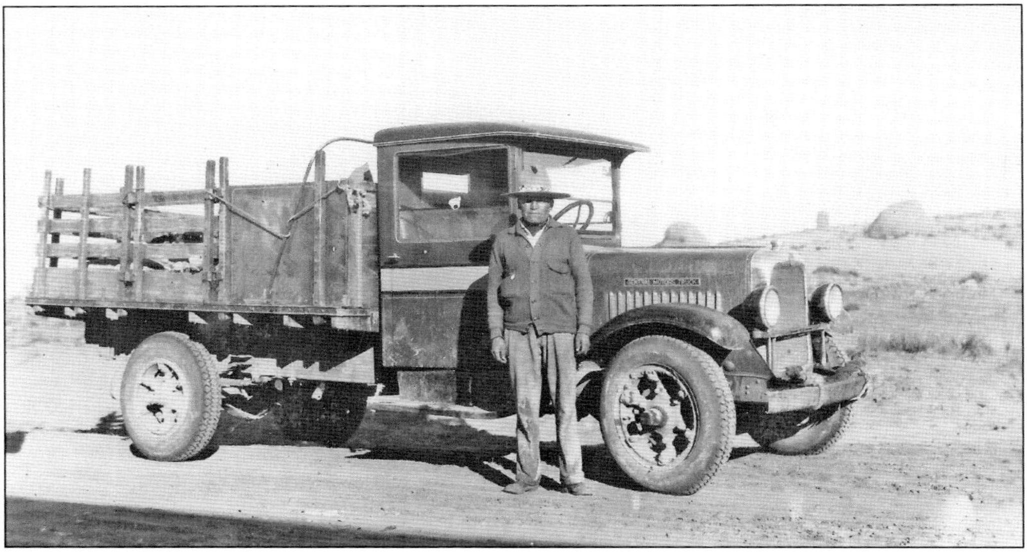

Edwin Kaywayumptewa, a Hopi, drove the mail truck on the Kayenta and Tuba City route around 1935. The mail truck came to Kayenta once a week on Tuesdays.

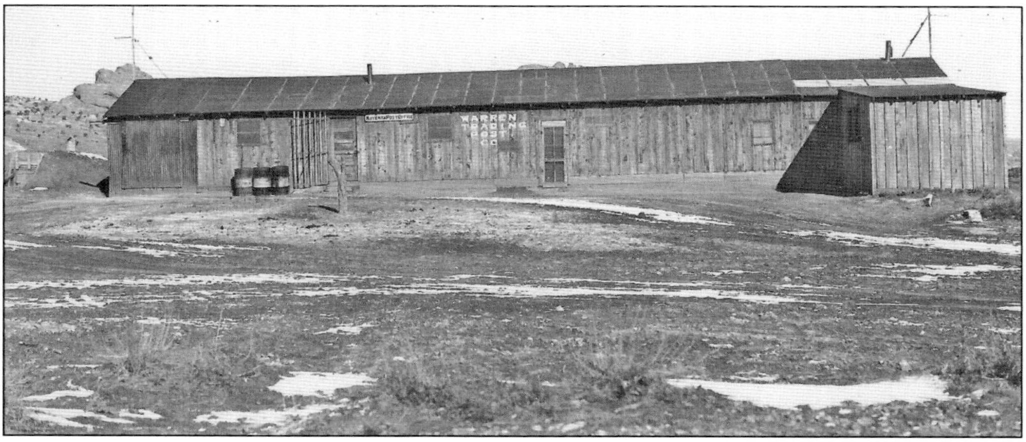

Warren Trading Post was built in 1927 by H. K. Warren, who operated it with his wife, Hazel, for three years. They sold a partial interest to the Babbitt family in 1930 but stayed on to run the store. The trading post was located about a quarter-mile west of the Wetherill and Colville Trading Post. The post office was also located at Warren's for several years. Nothing remains of the site today.

Presbyterian minister Hugh Dickson "Shine" Smith (1881–1966) was appointed missionary to the Kayenta church in 1921. Smith is in the center of the photograph taken about that time, and Tom Holiday is on the right. The man on the left is unidentifed. Smith was a champion of the Indian but was eventually removed from official church duties by administrators who thought he should be eradicating Indian religion in favor of conversions to Christianity. Even though he was removed from official church membership, Smith stayed in Navajo country and often worked at trading posts in the area.

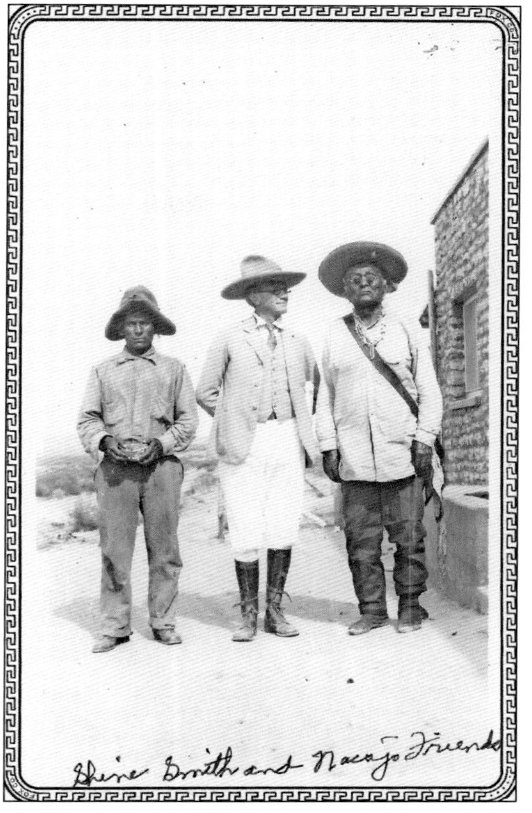

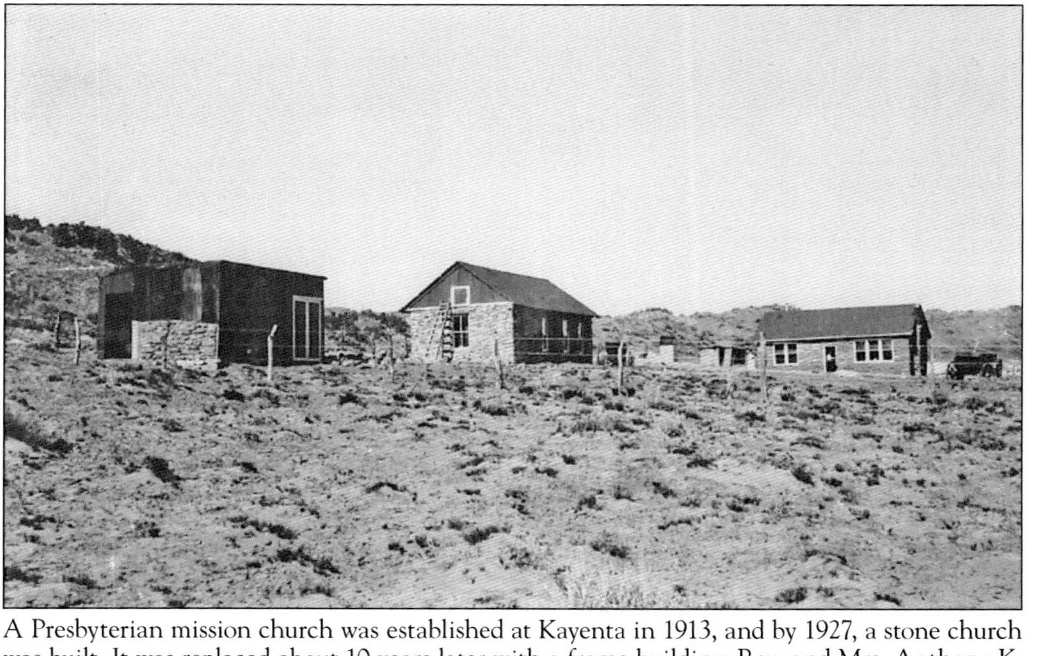

A Presbyterian mission church was established at Kayenta in 1913, and by 1927, a stone church was built. It was replaced about 10 years later with a frame building. Rev. and Mrs. Anthony K. Locker were the first missionaries at the church. (Courtesy of Ken Douthitt.)

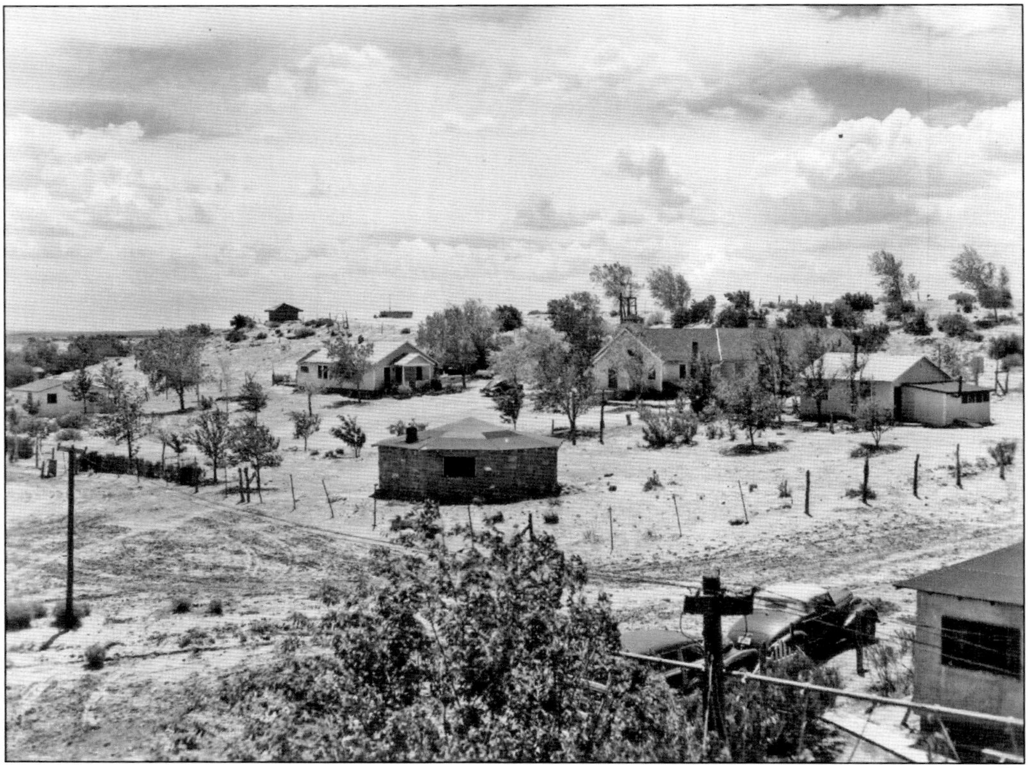

The stone church was replaced in the late 1930s. The interpreter's house is at right, and the parsonage is the building to the left. The large hogan in the center of the photograph was used for housing visitors and for meetings. (Courtesy of Ken Douthitt.)

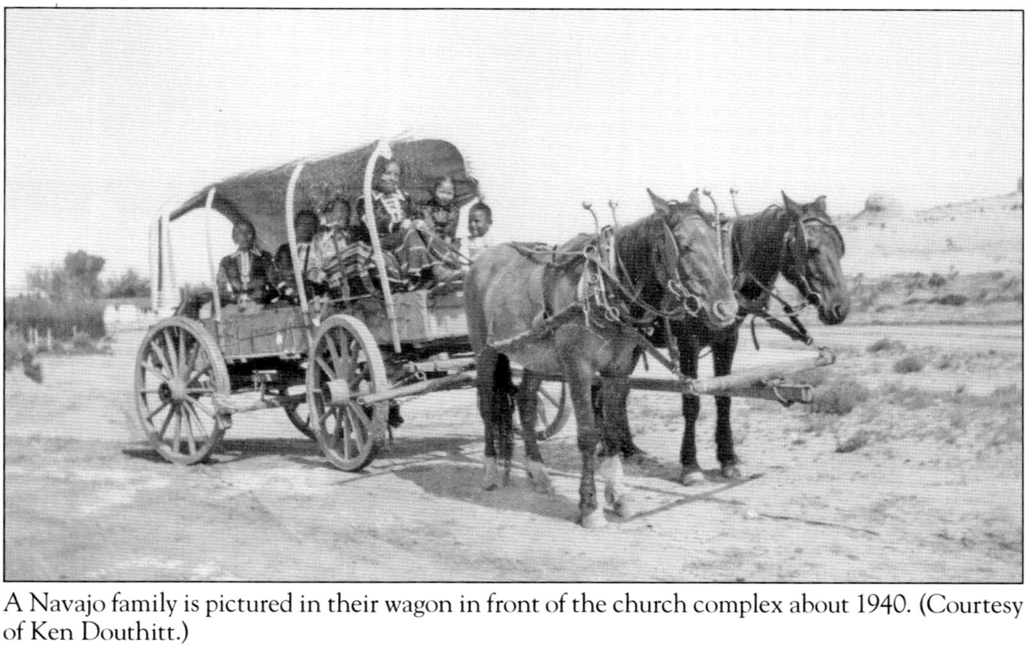

A Navajo family is pictured in their wagon in front of the church complex about 1940. (Courtesy of Ken Douthitt.)

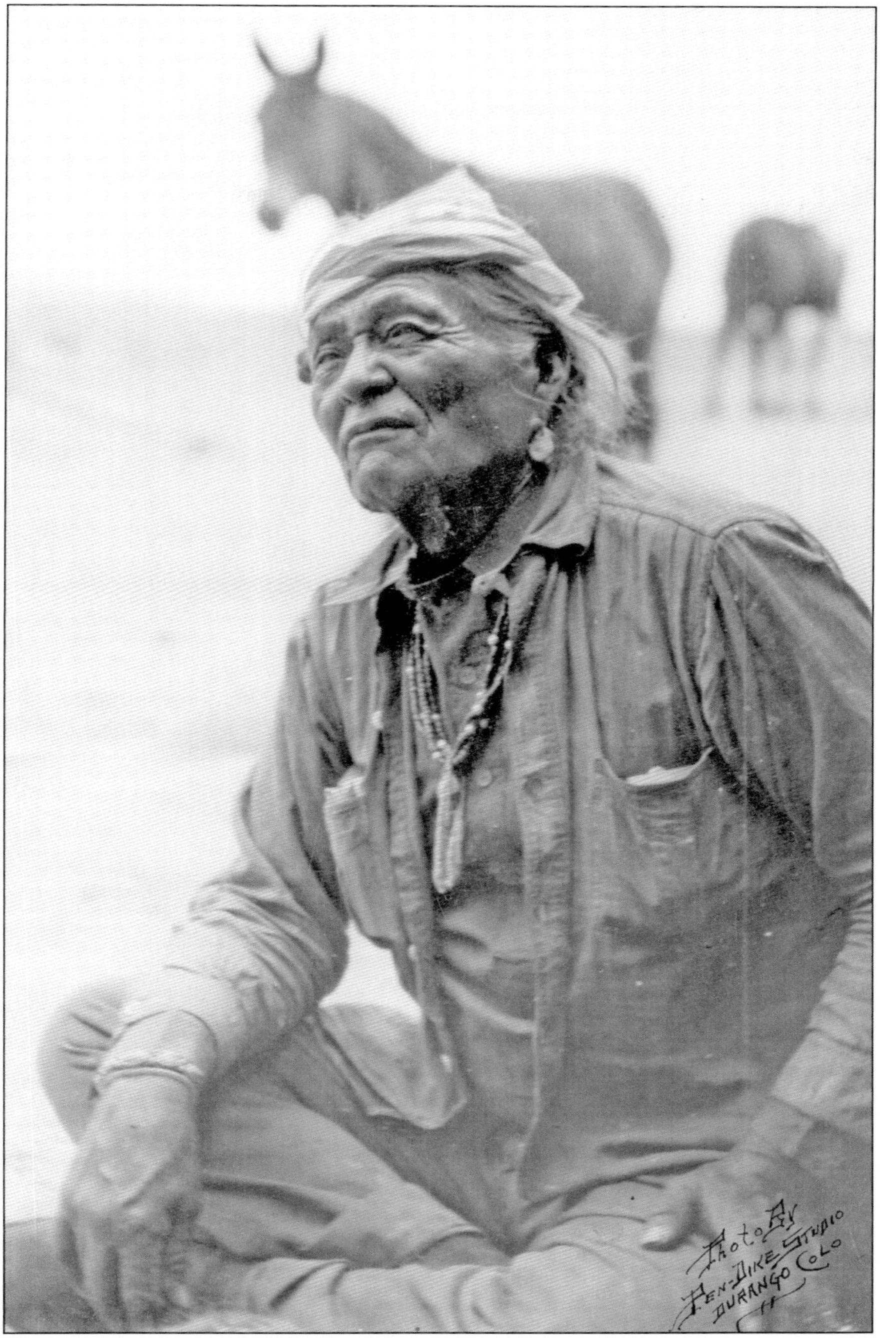

Wolfkiller was a shepherd who had vast knowledge of plants and their use by traditional Navajos. Wolfkiller worked for the Wetherills, and he shared his ancient wisdom with Louisa Wetherill, who recognized that he had a unique depth of character. The traditional lore that he had learned from his mother and grandfather helped him through hardships in his life. Louisa wrote down his words, and his story was eventually published in the book *Wolfkiller: Wisdom from a Nineteenth-Century Navajo Shepherd.*

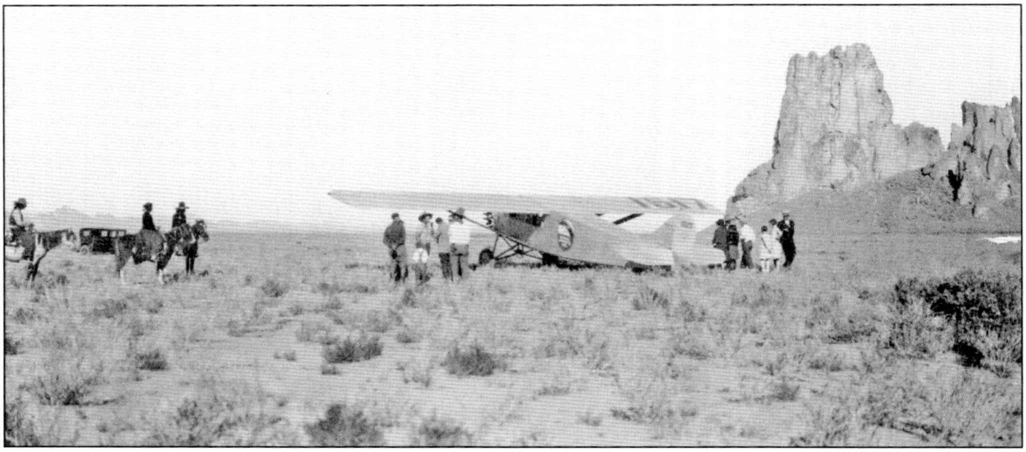

The first record of an airplane in the Kayenta area was in 1926, when famed *Life* magazine photographer Margaret Bourke White visited Monument Valley. The following year, J. Parker Van Zandt landed his Scenic Airway No. 1 Stinson near Church Rock just east of Kayenta. Van Zandt recorded in the Wetherill guest book, "A perfect terminus for a marvelous flight." The Scenic Airways group stayed in Kayenta, and John Wetherill guided them to Rainbow Bridge and Monument Valley. Soon afterward, Wetherill built a landing strip in anticipation of more airplane visits from eastern tourists.

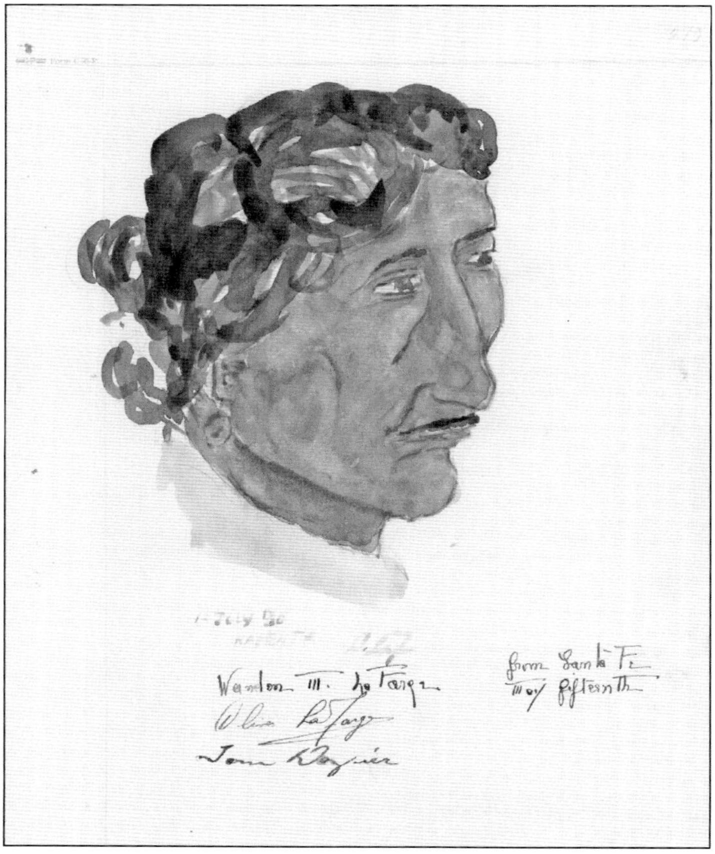

When Oliver La Farge visited Kayenta in 1930 with his wife, Windon, he had just won the Pulitzer Prize for his novel *Laughing Boy*. He was one of the many writers, artists, and other notable people to visit the area. La Farge sketched this head in the guest book and signed his name underneath.

After a visit to Kayenta, author Erna Fergusson wrote, "When the first council of the Navajos met, in 1923, there was a long delay in getting started. Many of the Navajos would not enter the meeting until a certain white woman came. Government officials, Indian agents, important gentlemen from Washington fretted about it, but nothing could be done. Washington has had to wait before and since, until the Indian thinks that the moment has come. When the white woman came, they said they could begin. She was Mrs. John Wetherill, of Kayenta, Ariz., wife of an Indian trader at the post farthest from the railroad." Another writer, Pulitzer Prize–winning journalist Ernest "Ernie" Pyle, was similarly impressed with Louisa Wetherill during his 1939 visit. As they discussed the arduous journey over the dirt road leading to Kayenta, Pyle asked if Wetherill had ever been over that route. "Her mouth opened slightly, her expression did not change, only from somewhere came that devastating chuckle. 'Have I? By wagon, horseback, afoot, by truck.' You could live in the desert 40 years, and still be a tenderfoot beside Mrs. John Wetherill."

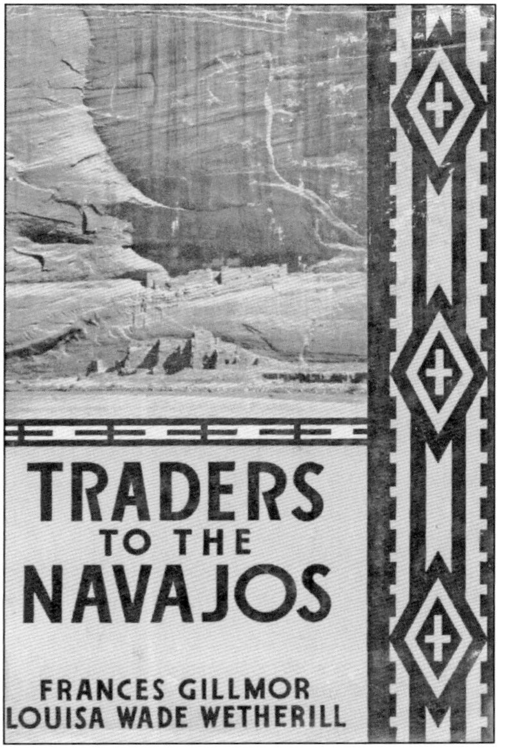

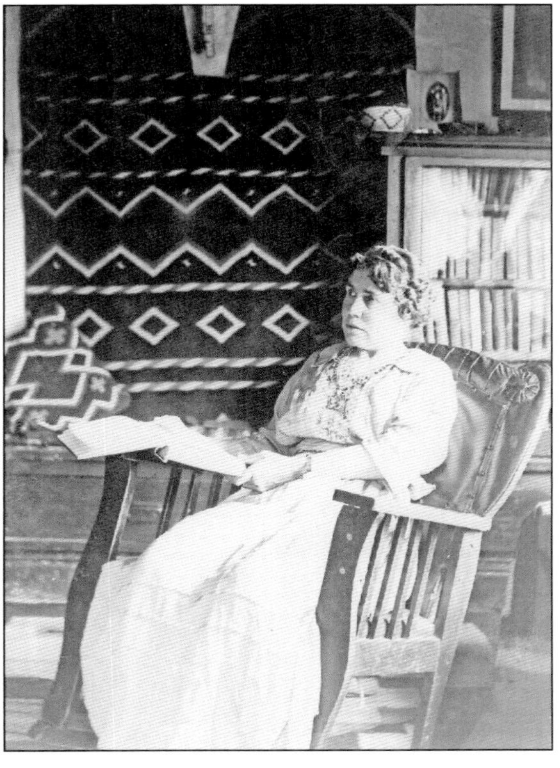

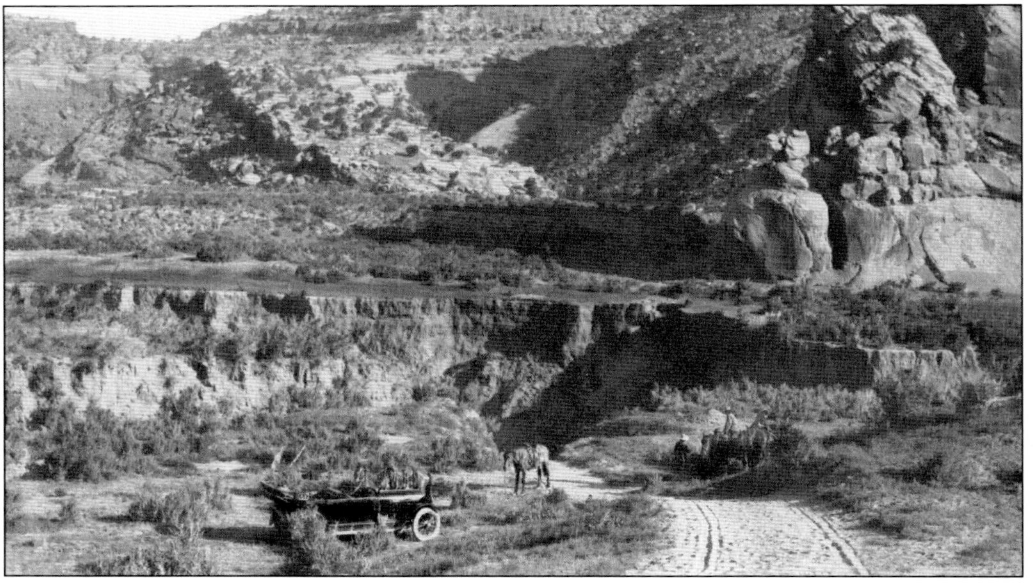

Laguna Creek was the end of the road for automobile travel. The group of travelers above is transferring from their touring car to horseback to continue their journey across and beyond Laguna Creek. Lacking automobiles in the early years, most Navajos continued to travel by the more practical means with horses and wagons.

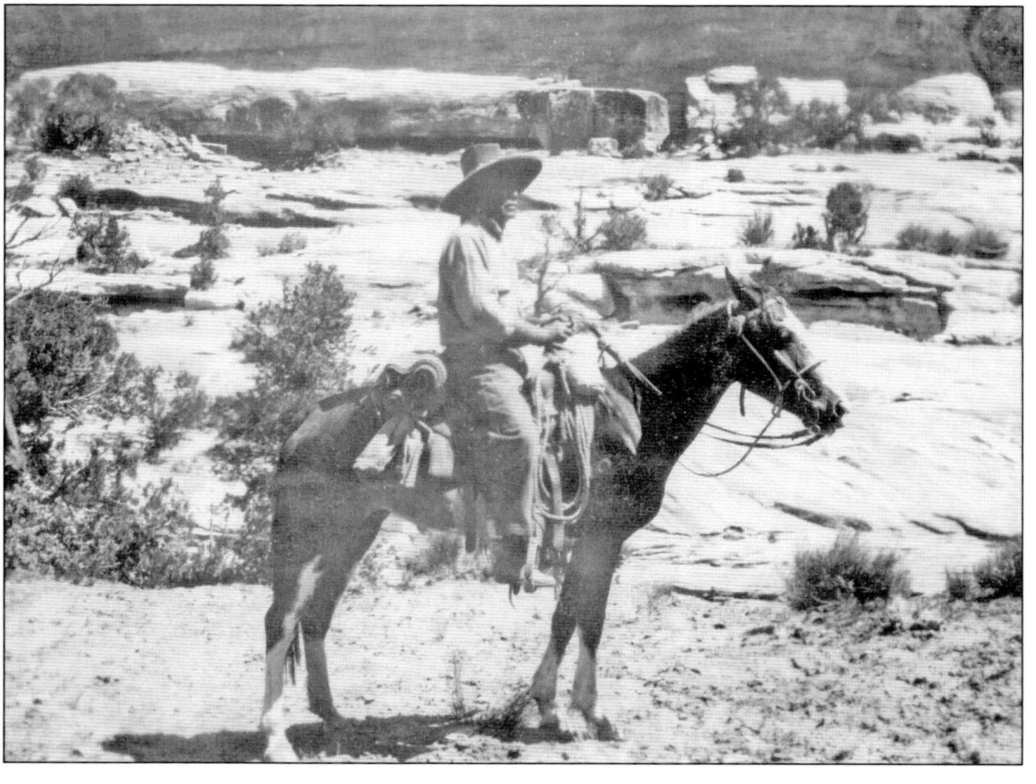

Shorty Gahn was a Navajo man who lived in the Kayenta area. His photograph was published on a postcard, and he became a local celebrity.

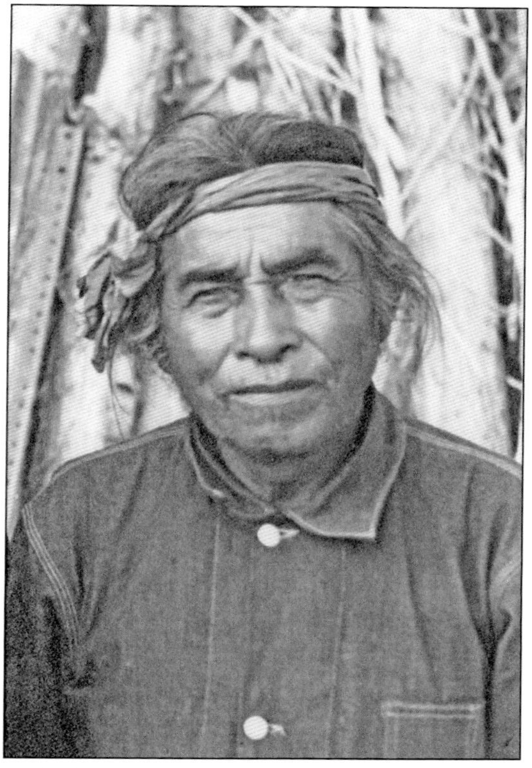

The 1925 silent movie *Vanishing American* was based on a Zane Grey novel. It was directed by George B. Seitz and starred Richard Dix, Lois Wilson, and Noah Beery. Louisa Wetherill was a technical advisor, and she also had a small role, as did the emerging actor Gary Cooper. The film was important in that it portrayed the plight of the American Indian. It was the first movie filmed in the area and was responsible for bringing the landscape of Kayenta and Monument Valley to national attention.

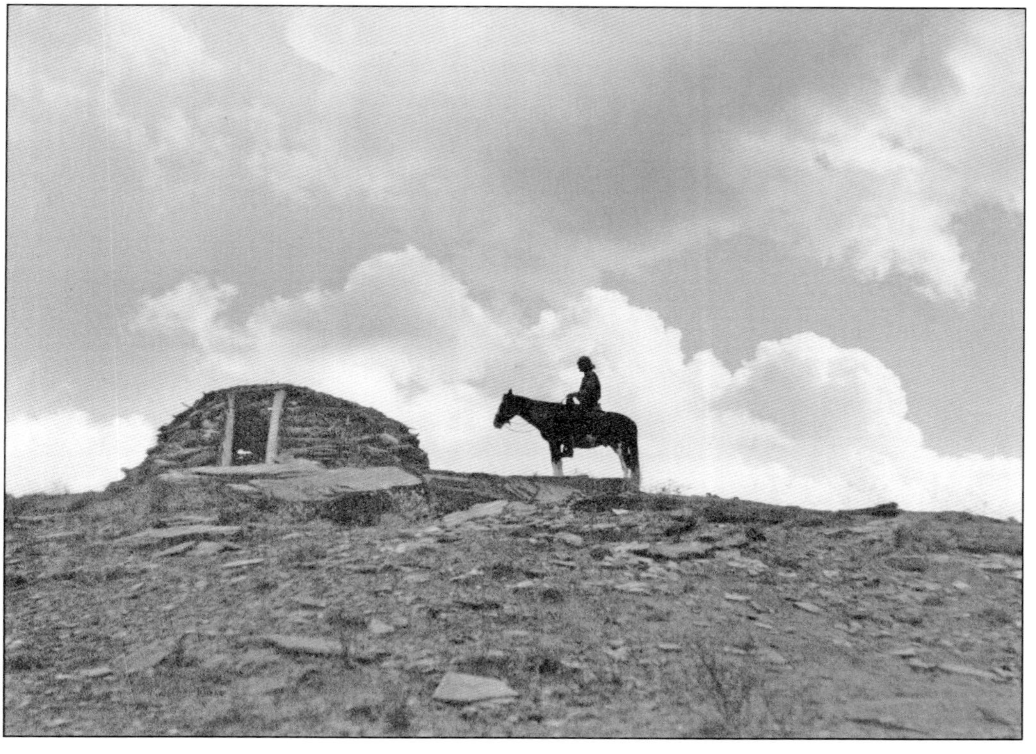

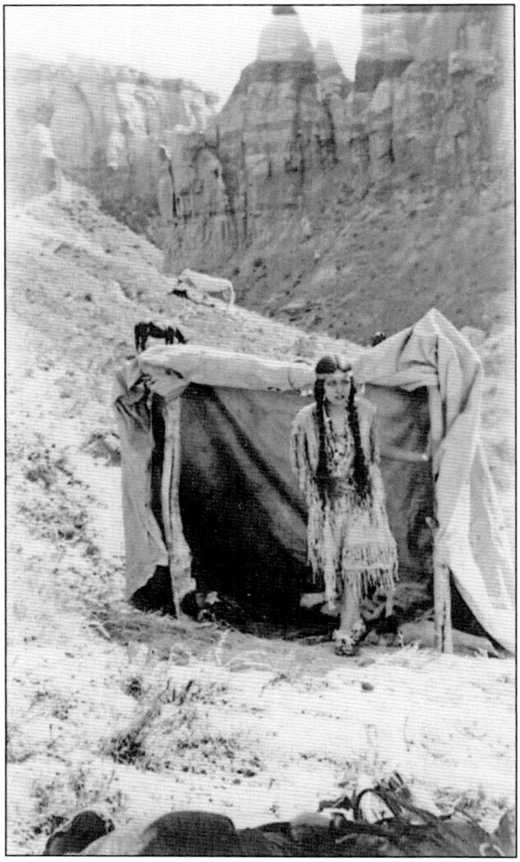

In 1928, Dorothy Janis (left) and Fred Thompson (below) starred in the silent film *Kit Carson*. Janis was only 18 when she starred as Sings-in-the-Clouds, and she only made movies for two more years before marrying and retiring from film. She died in Arizona in March 2010 at age 100. Thompson died of tetanus on Christmas day 1928, just months after the filming of *Kit Carson*; he played the title character in the movie. (Both, courtesy of Mary May Bailey.)

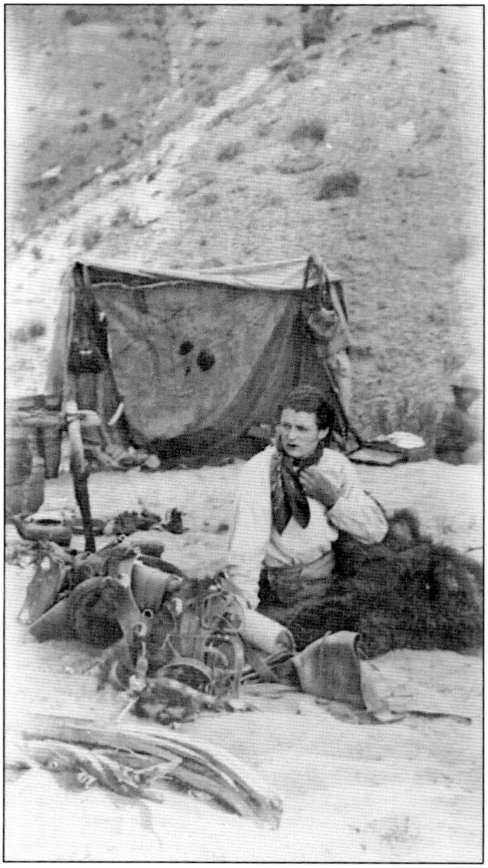

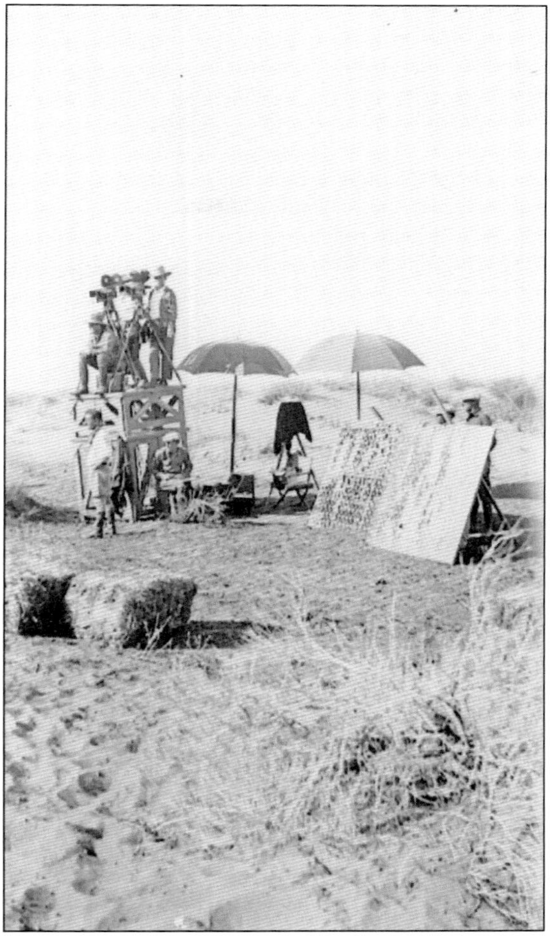

The producers of the 1928 silent movie *Kit Carson* hired many local Navajos for the film. The movie was filmed southwest of Kayenta near Coal Mine Canyon and Tuba City. (Both, courtesy of Mary May Bailey.)

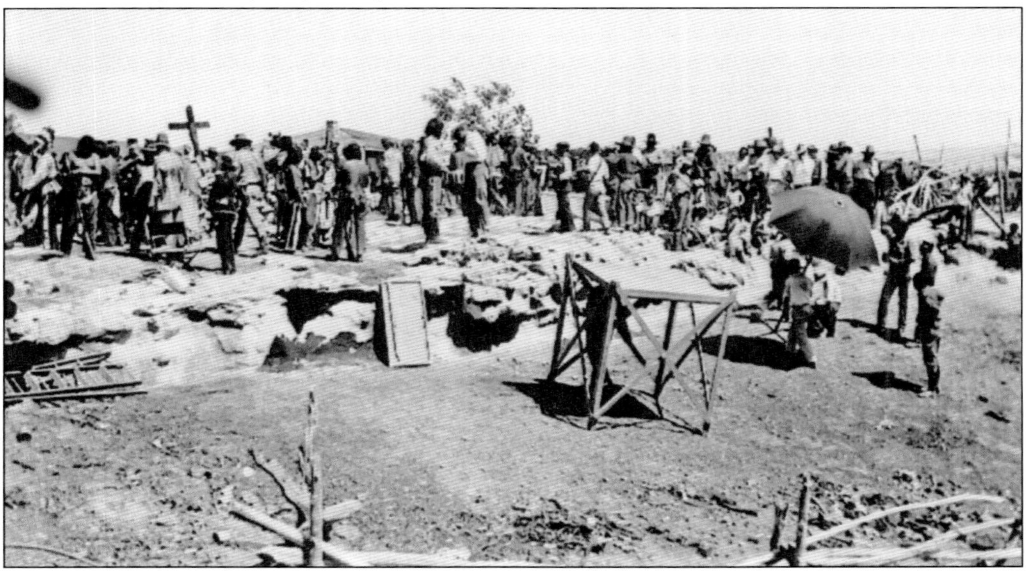

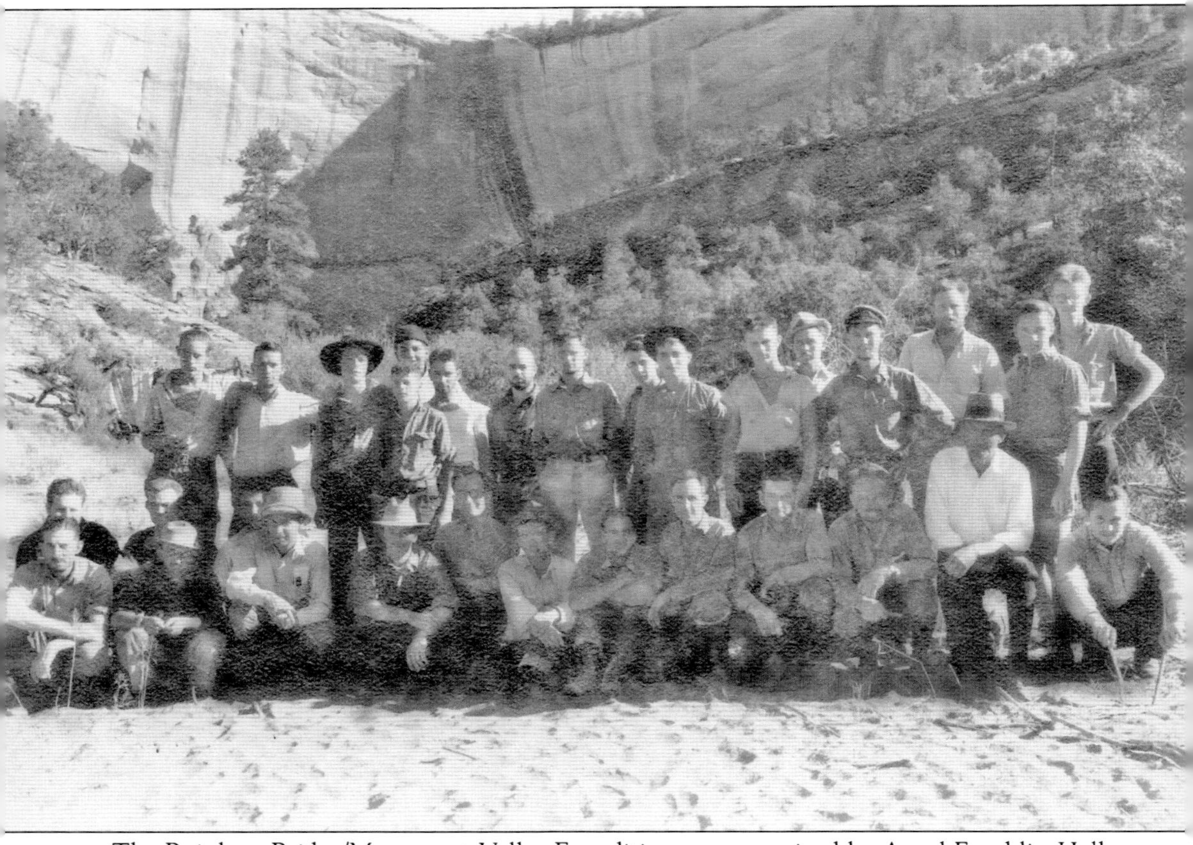

The Rainbow Bridge/Monument Valley Expedition was conceived by Ansel Franklin Hall, a National Park Service administrator. His plan was for a multiyear expedition from 1933 to 1938 encompassing a range of individuals from academic sciences to study the natural wonders and prehistoric ruins and cliff dwellings of the Kayenta area. It was the largest multidisciplinary expedition in the United States. The expedition staff of 50–75 each summer included archaeologists, botanists, geologists, doctors, cooks, packers, guides, and students. In this 1934 photograph of the expedition crew, the legendary Everett Ruess can be seen in the back row wearing a black hat. Young Ruess was an artist who wandered the Southwest on foot, leading his burro. He disappeared in the canyon country north of Kayenta in the fall, after he visited with the expedition members. (Courtesy of Andrew L. Christenson and Dan Cassidy.)

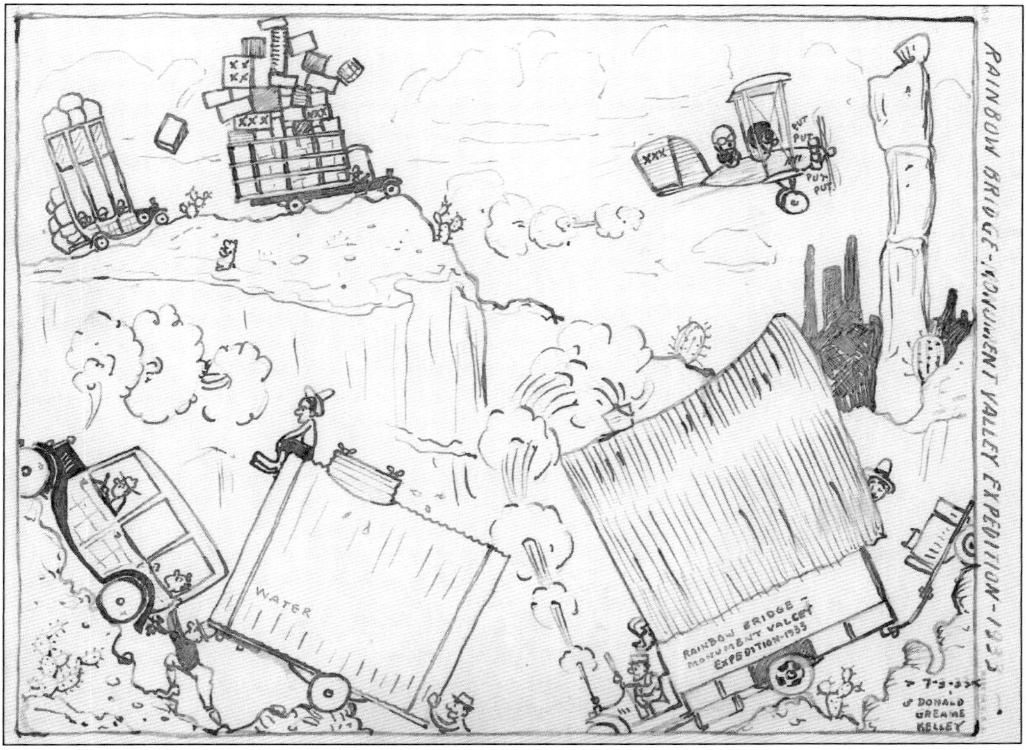

Crew member Donald Greame Kelley depicted the treacherous travel of the 1933 Rainbow Bridge/ Monument Valley Expedition in this delightful sketch in the Wetherill guest book. Kelley later was editor and art director of *Pacific Discovery*, a magazine published by the California Academy of Sciences. Kelley also designed the bear on the California bear flag.

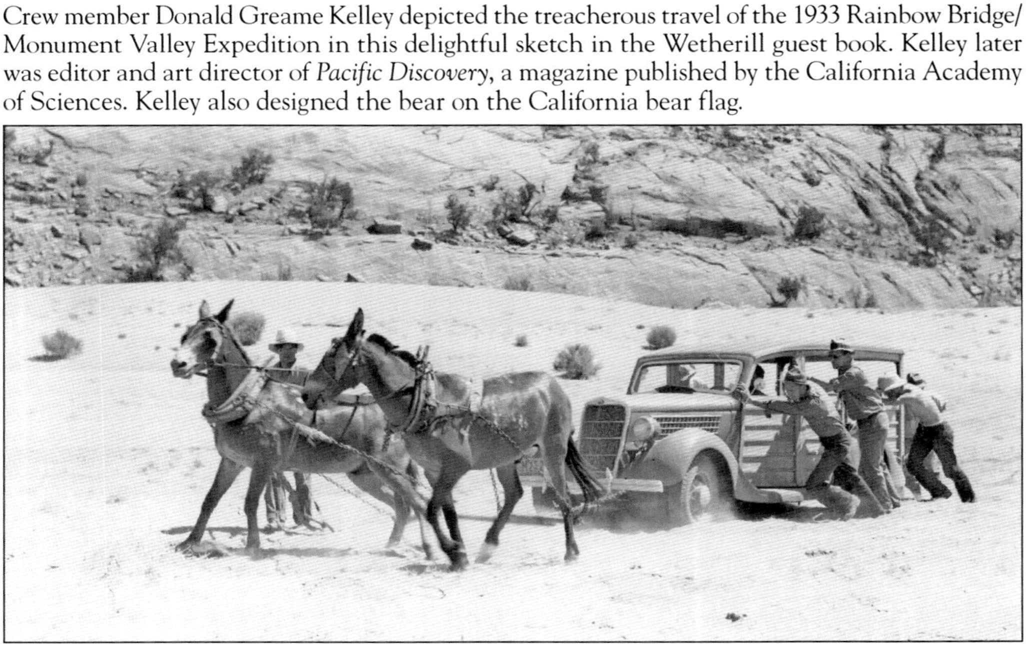

Ford Motor Company donated a fleet of trucks and station wagons to the Rainbow Bridge/ Monument Valley Expedition. The first expedition staff arrived in Kayenta in the summer of 1933 after a grueling trip through deep sand; the 100-mile trip took eight hours. (Courtesy of Andrew L. Christenson.)

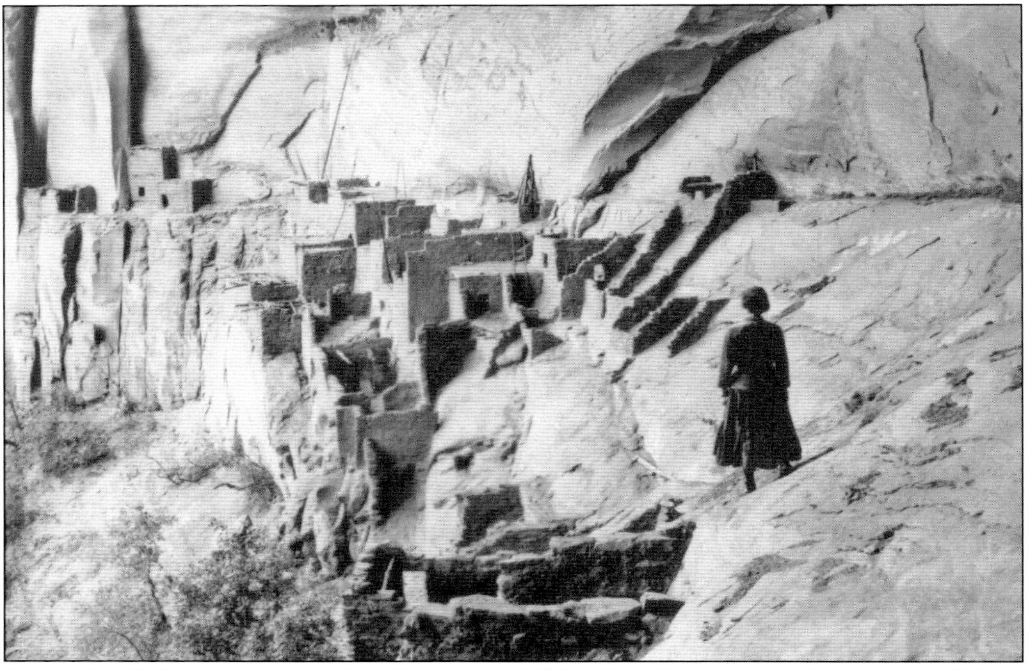

An unidentifed tourist contemplates Betatakin cliff dwelling. Kayenta was the jumping-off place for people from all walks of life to come and experience the frontier, including the ways of the ancient Indians.

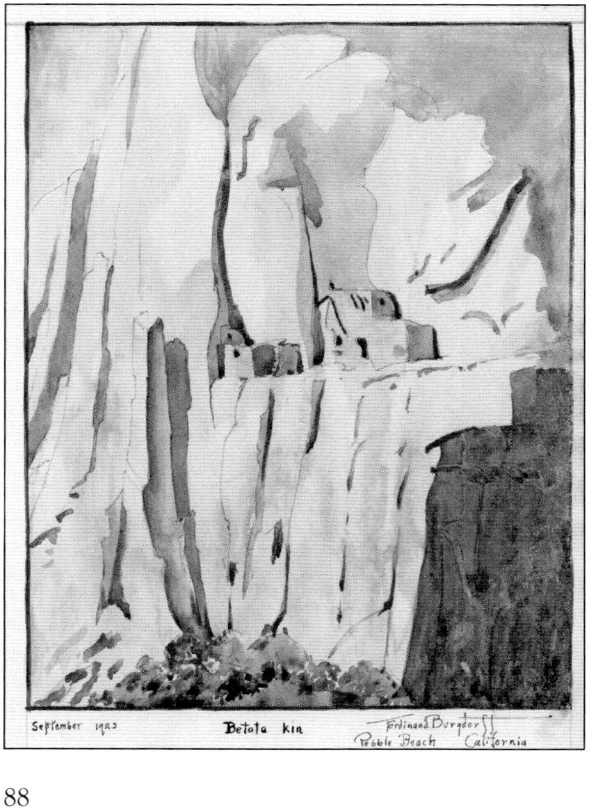

In September 1923, John Wetherill led artist Ferdinand Burgdorff on a pack trip to see the magnificent cliff house Betatakin. The ruin is the second largest cliff dwelling in Arizona. Today it is part of Navajo National Monument and is visited by thousands of tourists annually. Burgdorff painted this image of "Betata kin" in the Wetherill guest book.

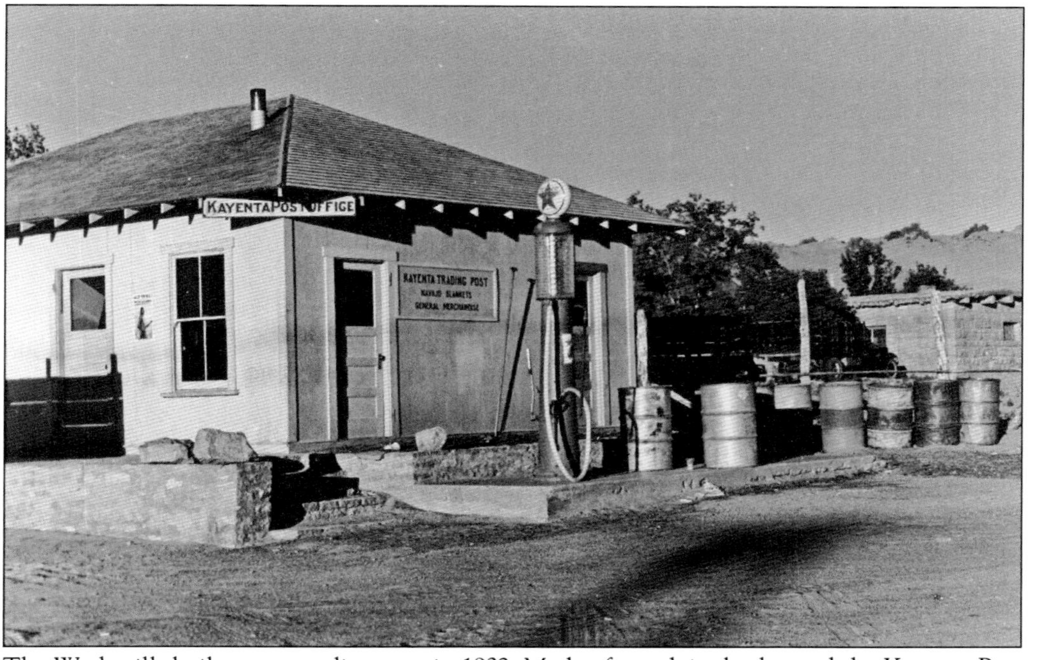

The Wetherills built a new trading post in 1932. Made of wood, it also housed the Kayenta Post Office. Mail came once a week. The sign on the front of the building advertised Navajo blankets and general merchandise. (Courtesy of Billy Crawley.)

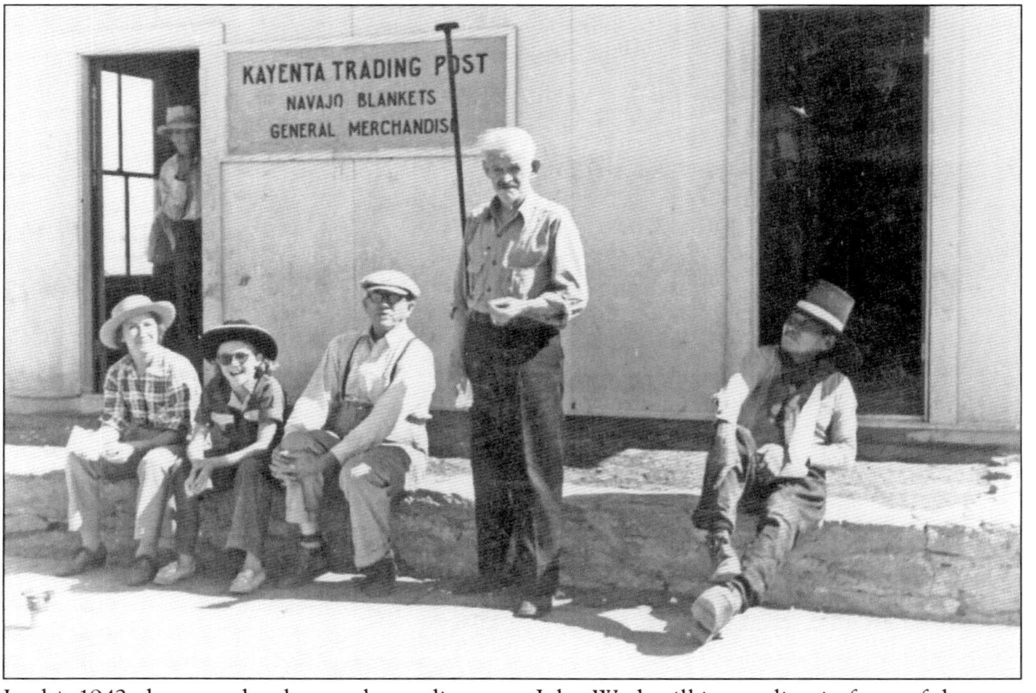

In this 1942 photograph taken at the trading post, John Wetherill is standing in front of the step, Hugh "Shine" Smith is seated to the left, and Wetherill's granddaughter Johni Lou Kilcrease is next to Smith.

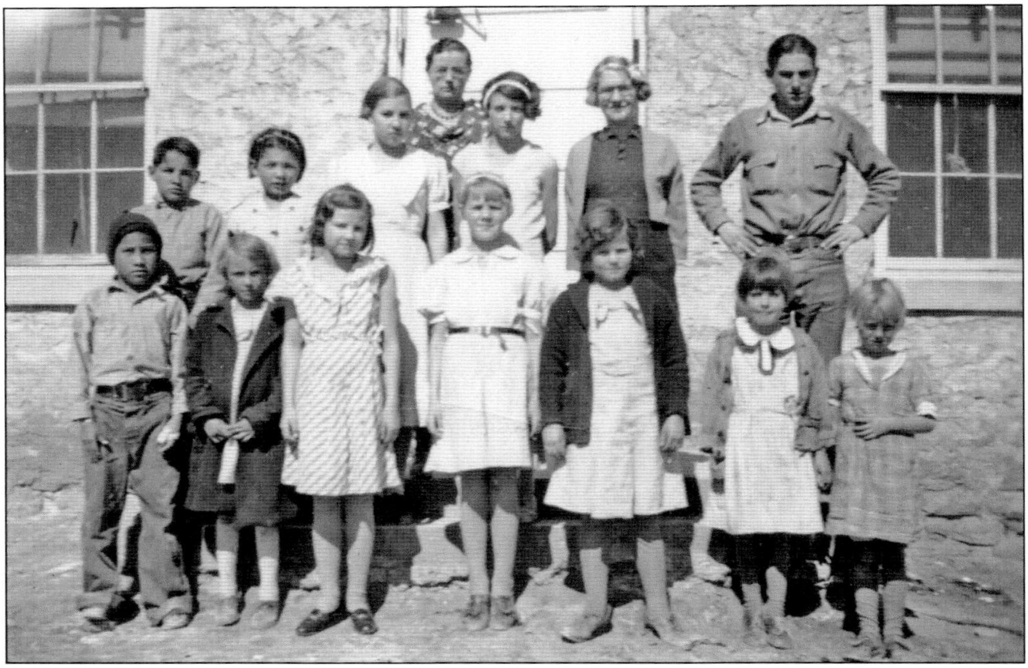

The old stone schoolhouse was built in 1913, and in 1934, the teacher, Cordelia Dunaway (above), posed with her class. Her husband worked for the government; his job was to maintain the wells and windmills all over the western reservation. From left to right are (first row) Frank Bradley, three unidentified, Dorothy Kilcrease (the Wetherills' granddaughter), and two unidentified; (second row) Frank's siblings Lee and Sarah Bradley, Jessie Taylor, Tiny Taylor, Omega Mangum, and Jack Taylor. The Bradleys' grandmother was Sue Bradley, the weaver.

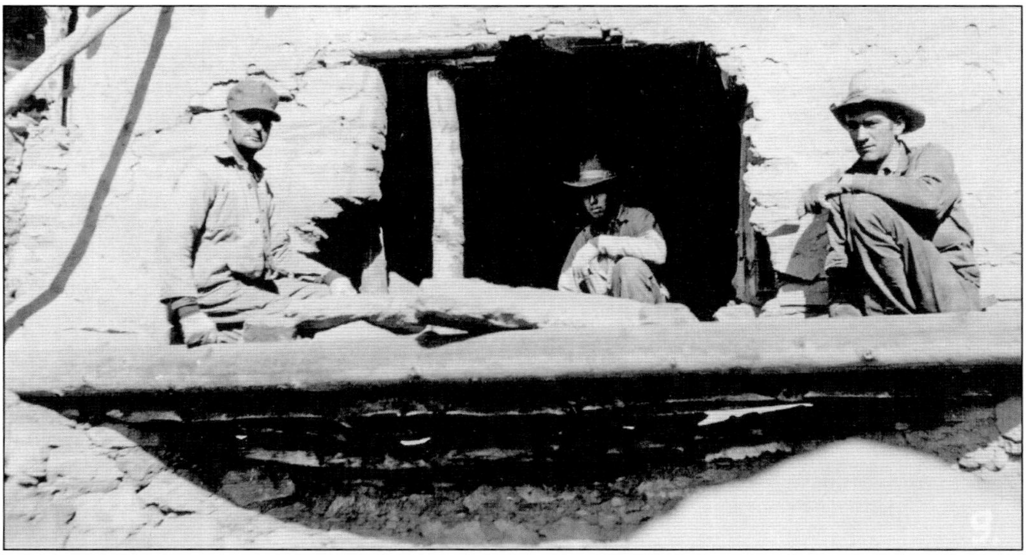

Henry Carmack (left), Tom Bowen (center), and Marion Perkins (right) worked on a Civilian Conservation Corps project at Keet Seel at Navajo National Monument in 1934. The men rebuilt a retaining wall and stabilized the cliff dwelling, and one young archaeologist, Julian Hayden, kept a historically valuable journal of the job and camp while working on the project.

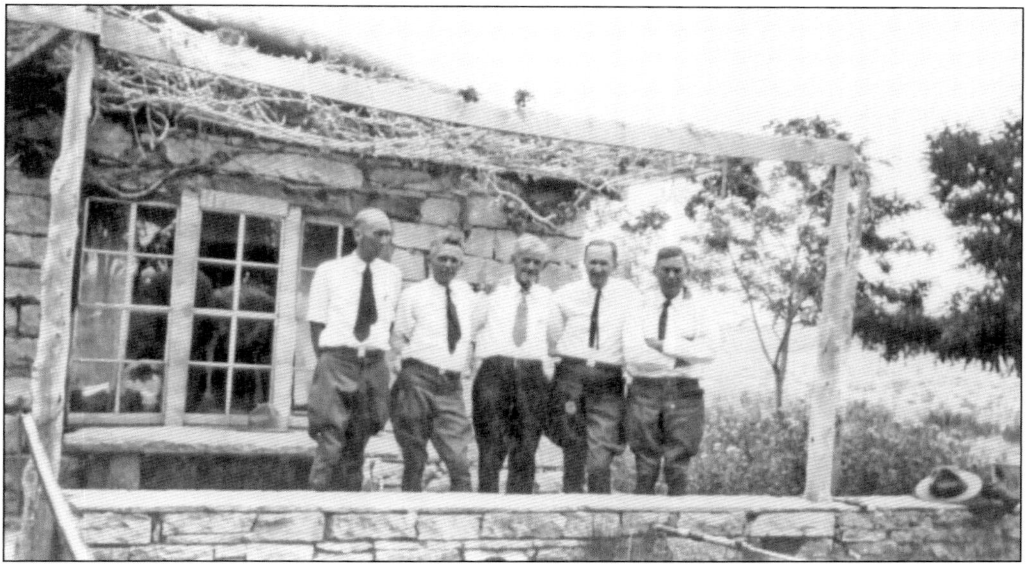

On June 30, 1932, there was a meeting in Kayenta to discuss the establishment of Navajo National Park, which would have covered the area from Monument Valley to Rainbow Bridge. The men are, from left to right, Frank "Boss" Pinkley (superintendent of the Southwestern National Monuments), Horace Albright (director of the National Park Service), John Wetherill (custodian of Navajo National Monument), M. R. Tillotson (superintendent of Grand Canyon National Park), and Marshall Finnan (superintendent of Mesa Verde National Park). The park never became a reality.

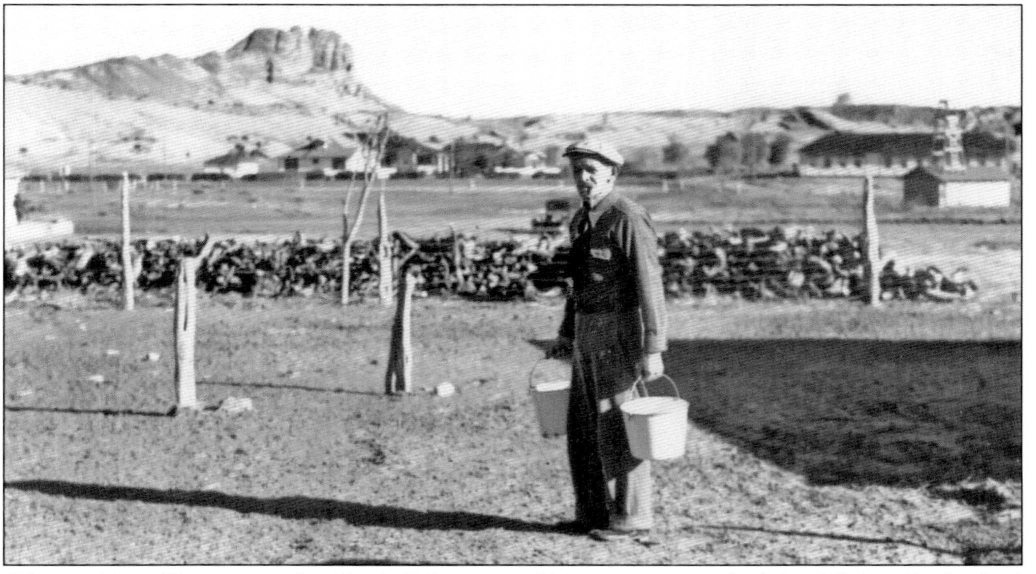

After a visit to Kayenta, author Ernie Pyle wrote of his great respect for John Wetherill, who had "more to do with the discovery of archeological ruins in the Southwest than any scientist. . . . It was John Wetherill who, in 1913 led Teddy Roosevelt on the long pack into Rainbow Bridge, for John Wetherill was the only person who knew how to get there. . . . He smokes cigarettes, wears a white shirt and tie, and overall. After supper each evening he has to jump up and go milk a cow."

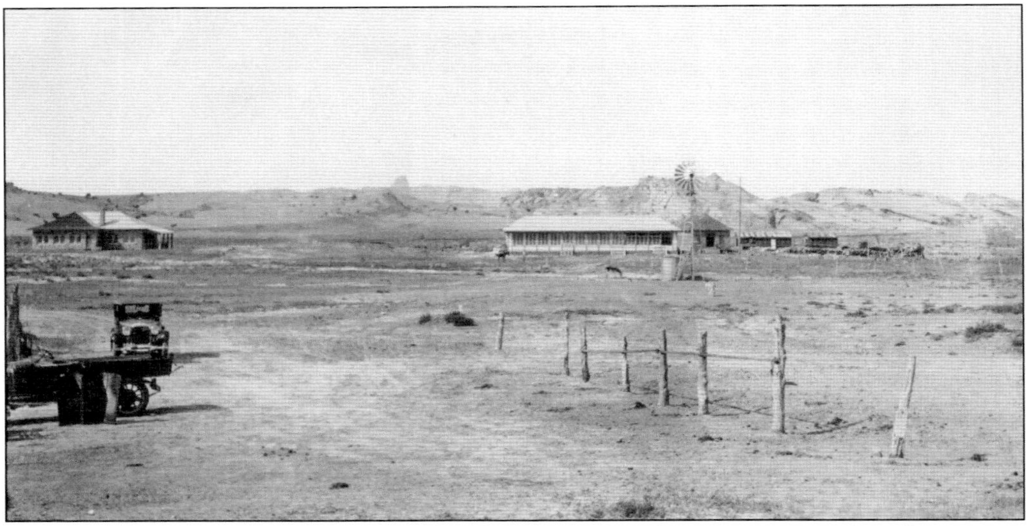

Kayenta resident Lillian Smith recalled that the first resident doctor came to work at the Kayenta hospital in 1928. About 1934, it was converted to a tuberculosis sanitarium. Because many children had tuberculosis, they lived at the hospital. During the 1930s, movies were shown in the meeting room on Saturday nights, and church was held there on Sundays. The hospital is on the right, and the doctor's quarters are at left.

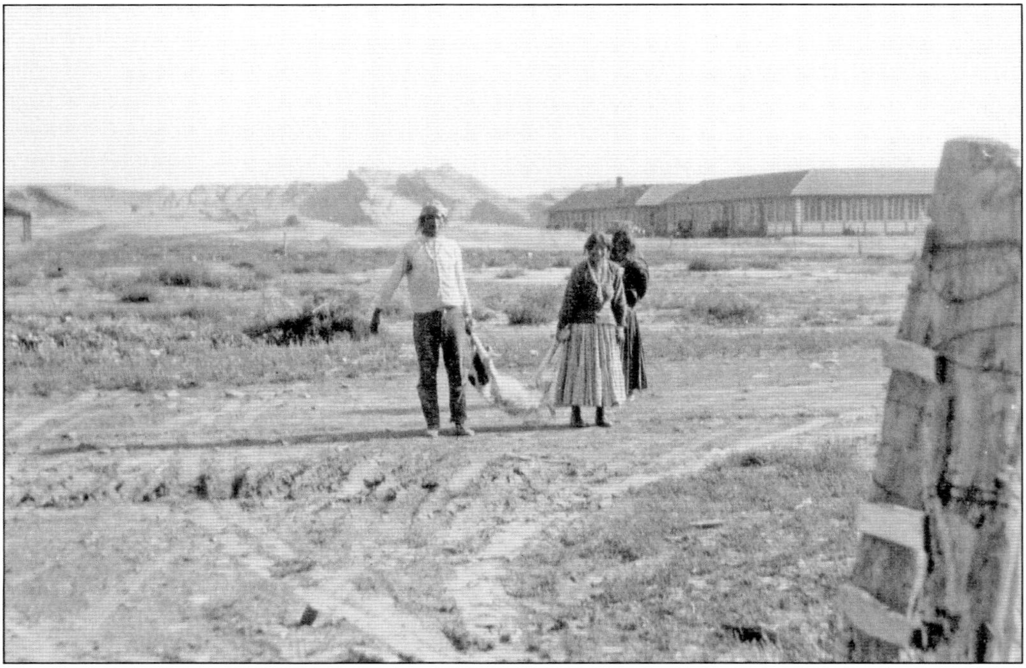

These Navajo visitors are bringing a sheep that they could trade for commodities such as sugar or coffee to the gate of the trading post. The government hospital is the building in the background.

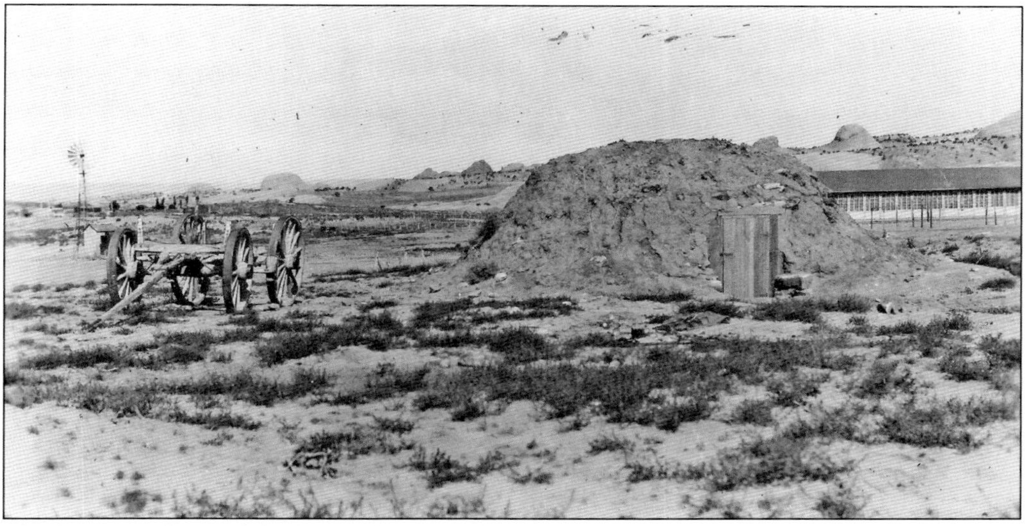

The hogan in front of the hospital was for the use of families who traveled from their distant hogans to visit relatives at the hospital.

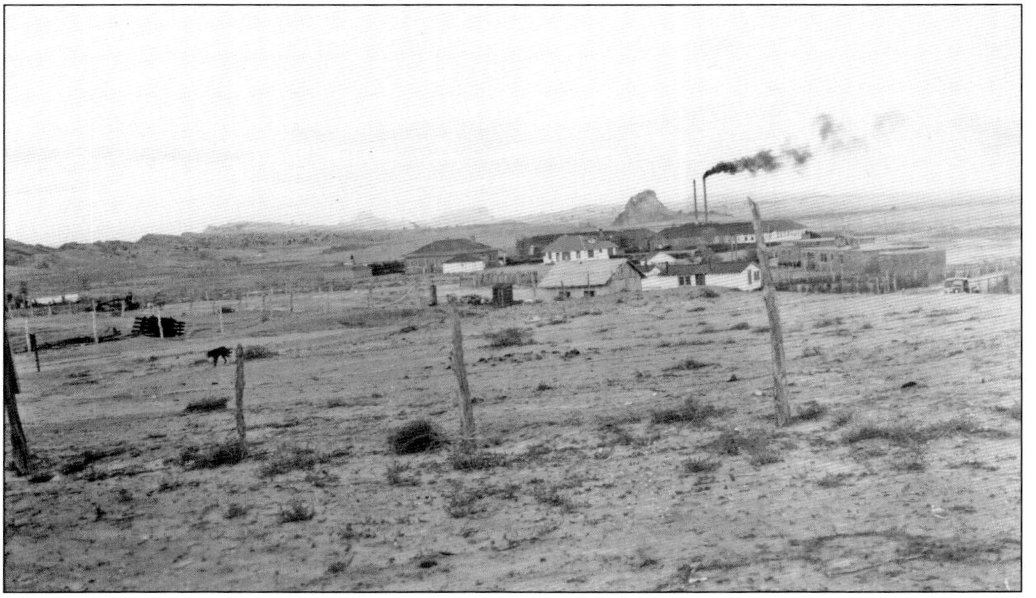

The government hospital and sanitarium at Kayenta was closed in 1944 because all the doctors and medical personnel had been called away during the war. The sanitarium complex is in the center of the photograph, and the government day school is the large building to the right. Katherine and Andrew McGaffin came to Kayenta in 1940. Reverend McGaffin was the minister at the Presbyterian church for 17 years. Katherin McGaffin was a nurse, and after the hospital closure, she was asked by the government to dispense medicine to the local people. (Courtesy of Ken Douthitt.)

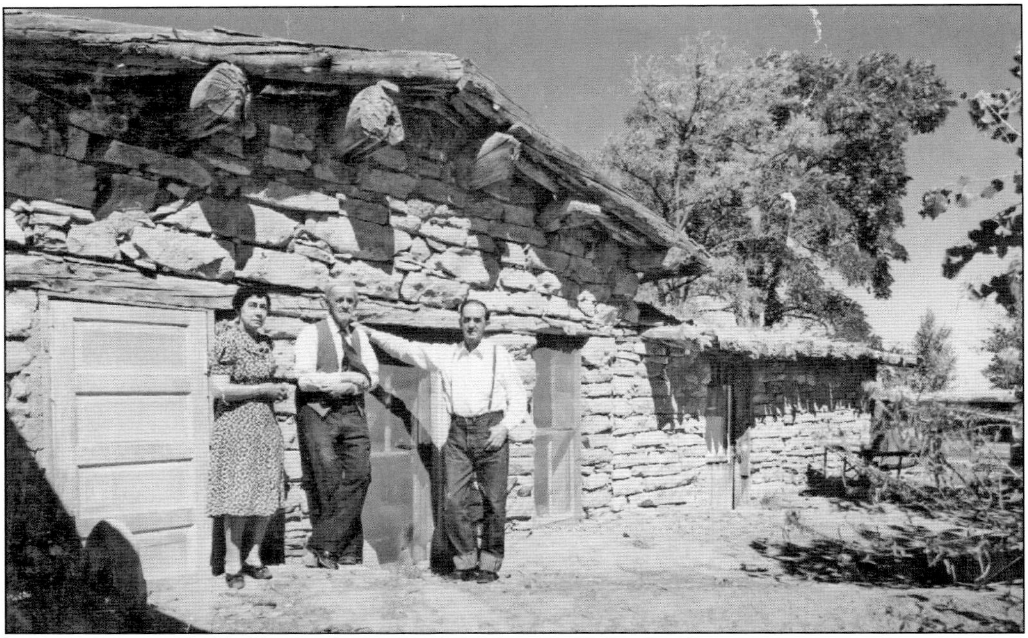

Louisa and John Wetherill, along with Clyde Colville, operated the Wetherill and Colville Trading Post until John's death in November 1944. Clyde died four months later in March 1945, and Louisa sold the post to Babbitt Trading Company before her death in September 1945. In less than a year, the three companions of over 40 years were gone, and with them went the legacy of the Wetherills: the trading post, the deep friendships with the Navajos, and the grand exploring adventures in the canyons and ruins.

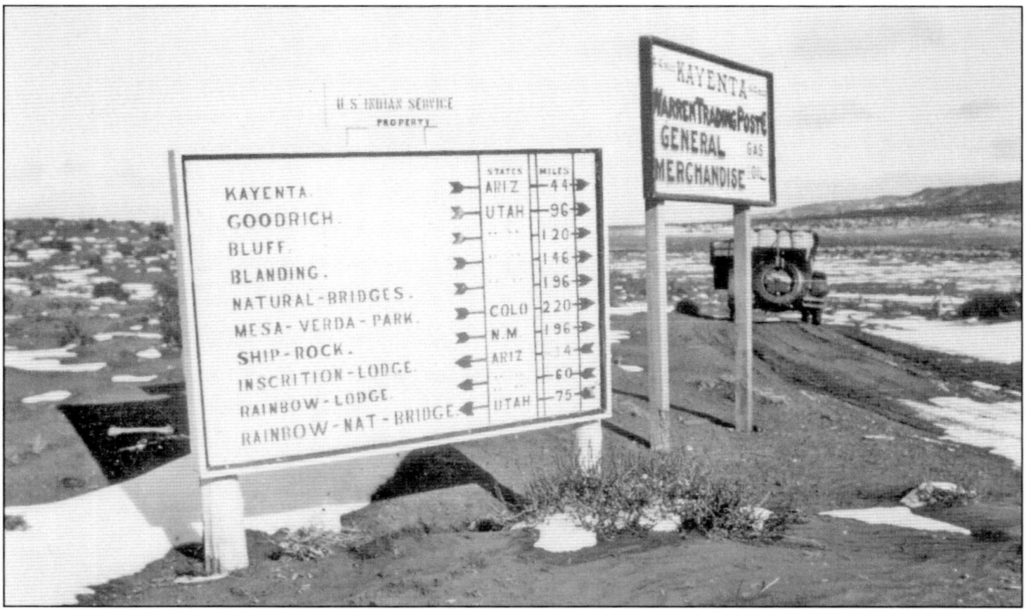

As more tourists traveled to northern Arizona, signs were posted to assist travelers in the sparsely populated area. The unpaved road to Kayenta, shown here in a December 1930 photograph, would have been a challenge in winter weather.

Five

Monument Valley

Monument Valley, located 20 miles north of Kayenta, straddles the Arizona and Utah borders and is a part of the Colorado Plateau. About 100 square miles of the desert country were designated a Navajo tribal park on July 11, 1958. Navajos call it Tsé Bii' Ndzisgaii, or "Valley of the Rocks." Because of Monument Valley's dramatic landscape, dotted with red sandstone spires, mesas, and monoliths, some rising 1,000 feet above the valley floor, the area is one of the most recognizable areas in the country, as it has been the setting for hundreds of international movies and commercials. In early times, the country was inhabited by western Navajos and Paiutes and was a part of what was known as the Paiute Strip. Later the government designated the land as public domain, but in 1934, it was formally given to the Navajo Reservation by an act of Congress.

Over the years, visitors have written lyrically of the area. Zane Grey toured Monument Valley in 1913, and "the shifting sands, the red looming walls, the purple sage, and the towering monuments" so impressed him that he featured the area in his 1917 novel *Wildfire*. That Monument Valley made a searing impression on Grey is apparent in the description that he wrote: "My first sight of Monument Valley came with a dazzling flash of lightning. It revealed a vast valley, a strange world of colossal shafts, and buttes of rock, magnificently sculptured, standing isolated and aloof, dark, weird, and lonely. When the sheet lightning flared across the sky showing the monuments silhouetted black against that strange horizon, the effect was marvelously beautiful."

Silent films became popular in the 1920s, and Zane Grey's *The Vanishing American* was filmed in the Kayenta area in 1925. Within a decade, producer John Ford was filming his classic movies in Monument Valley, with the result that the unique landscape has become instantly recognizable to people around the world. The Kayenta and Monument Valley country is a timeless landscape, with a compelling, mystical beauty, eternally thrilling to each new generation that sets eyes upon the craggy pinnacles and towers and the soaring mesas.

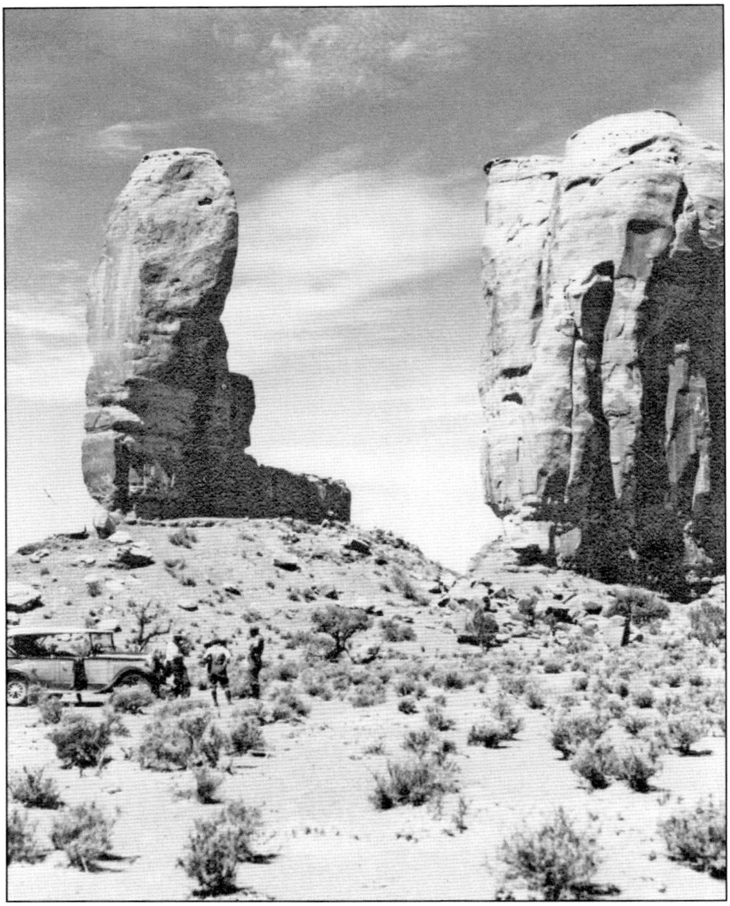

The Navajo people consider Monument Valley to be an immense hogan or spiritual dwelling, but while many of the stone landforms have religious meaning, the valley is still homeland for many Navajo families. Even though Navajos live in the area and may be accustomed to the buttes and spires, visitors are always awestruck by the dramatic landscape. Zane Grey visited Monument Valley and wrote, "I rode down the sweet-scented sage slopes under the shadow of the lofty Mittens and around and across the valley. And when I had completed my ride a story had woven itself into my mind." The Mittens that Grey wrote about in his novel *Wildfire* are pictured in the photograph below.

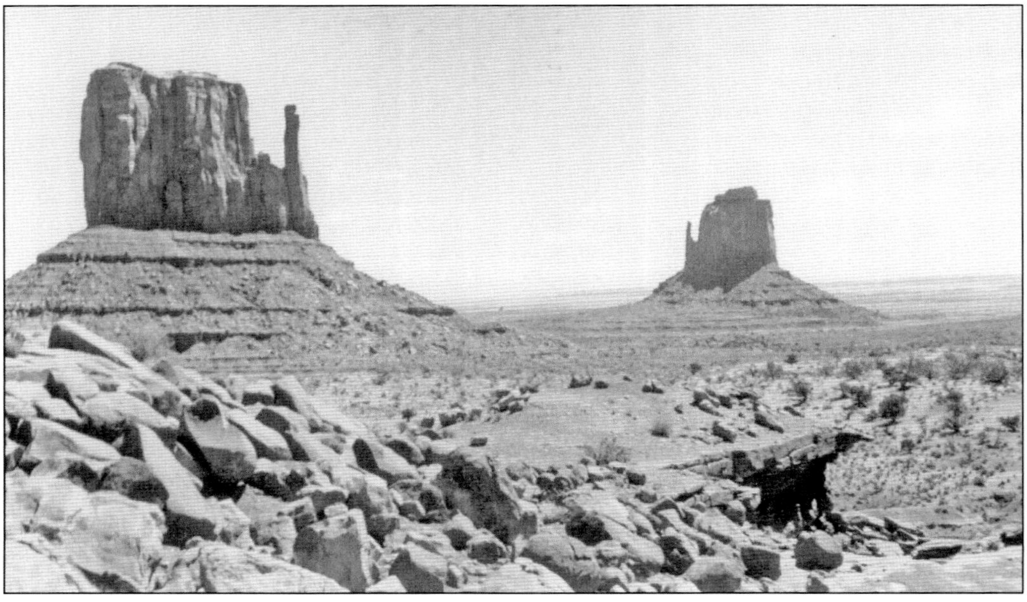

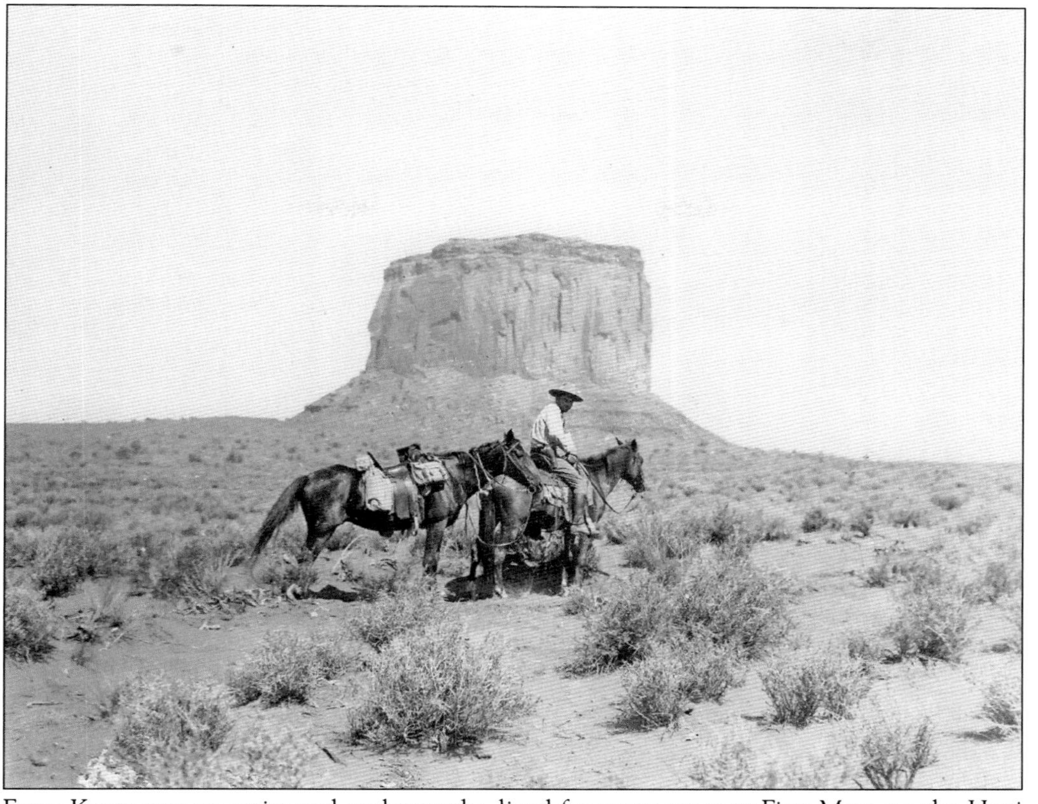

Emry Kopta was an artist and sculptor who lived for many years at First Mesa on the Hopi Reservation. He visited Kayenta and signed the Wetherills' guest book in 1920 before setting off on a camping and painting trip into Monument Valley. (Courtesy of Ed Mell.)

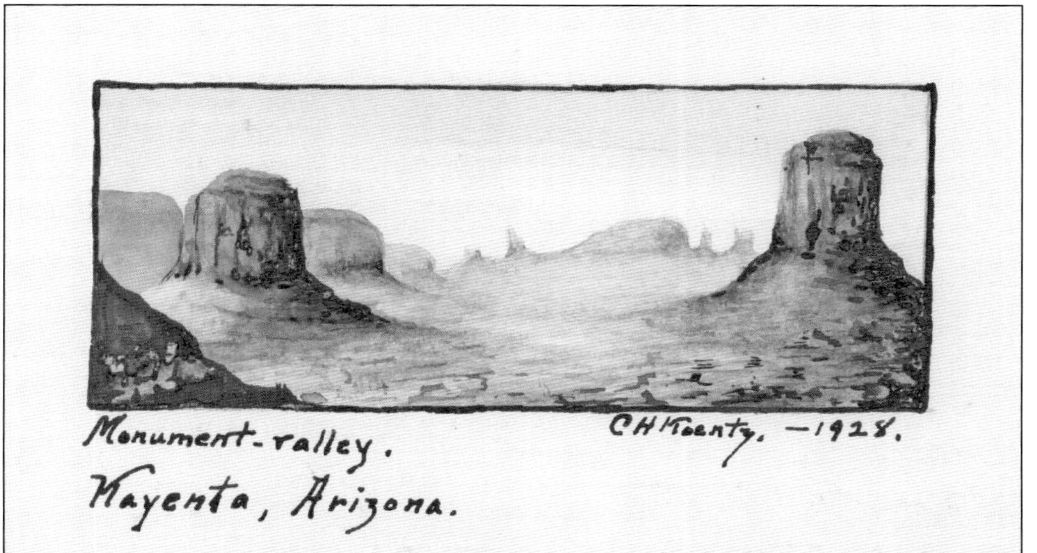

Dr. C. H. Koentz, a local doctor in Kayenta, painted a landscape of Monument Valley in the Wetherills' guest book in 1928.

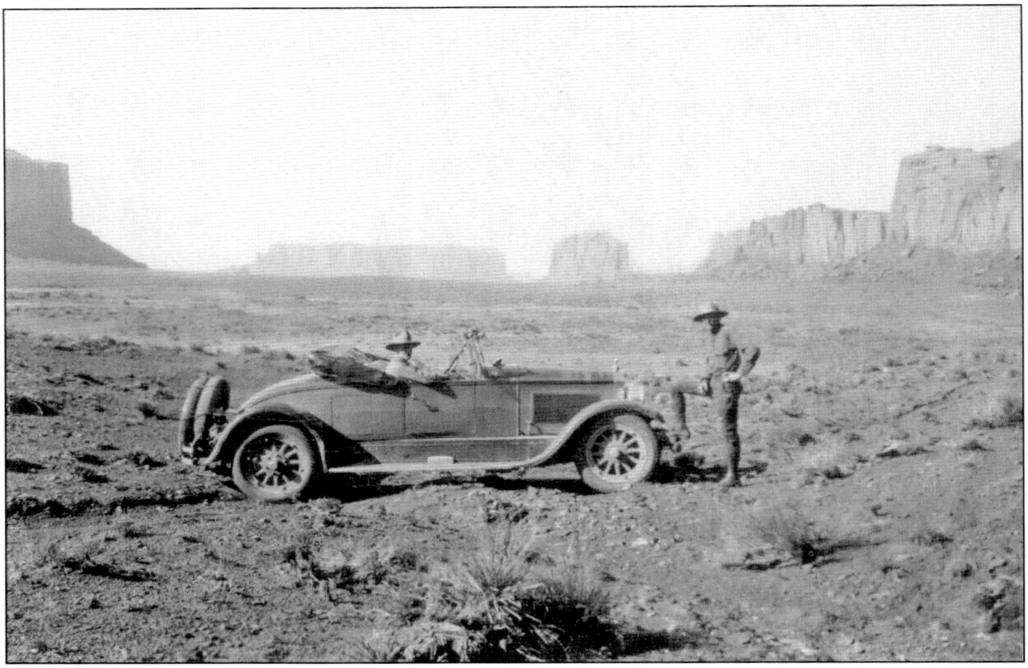

John Wetherill, above, guided tourists through Monument Valley, sometimes in an automobile, other times by horseback. The photograph below was taken by Wetherill and published in a 1929 edition of *Encyclopedia Britannica* with the caption, "View across a section of Monument Valley, in the northeastern part of Navajo County, showing some of the ruins in the distance."

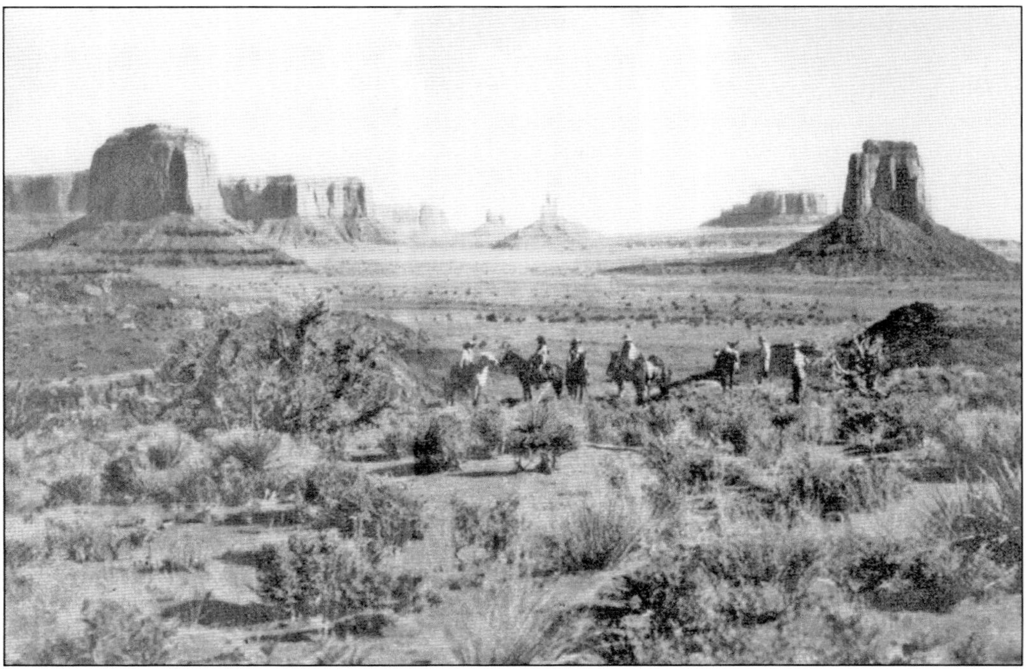

In 1923, Harry and Leone "Mike" Goulding came to Monument Valley, where they first began trading with the local Navajo people, selling goods from the back of a wagon. They eventually built a trading post and lodge at the base of a towering mesa. In 1938, the Gouldings traveled to California, taking along a portfolio of photographs of the majestic Monument Valley area in an effort to interest filmmakers in the beautiful Monument Valley country. Within a month of meeting director John Ford, filming was scheduled for the classic western *Stagecoach*. In these Joseph Muench photographs, Harry and "Mike" Goulding are posed against a corral fence in the early 1950s. The Goulding Trading Post and Lodge looks across the valley to the craggy mesas of Monument Valley. (Both, courtesy of Nathan LaFont and Goulding's Trading Post and Lodge.)

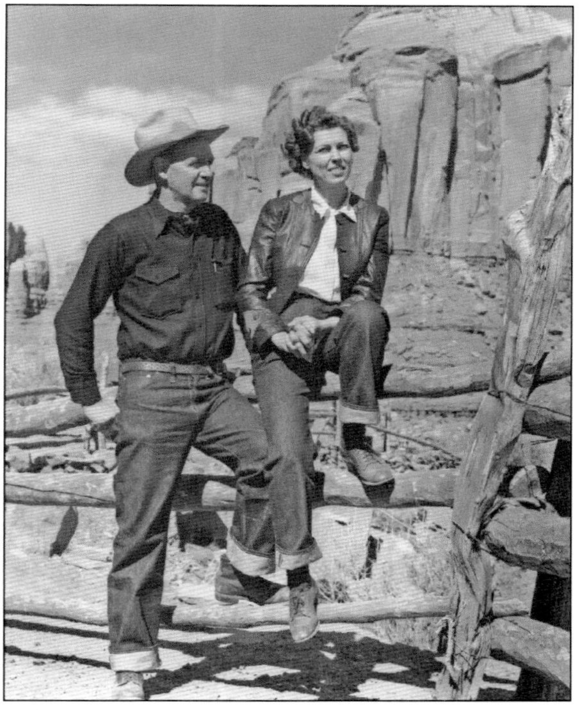

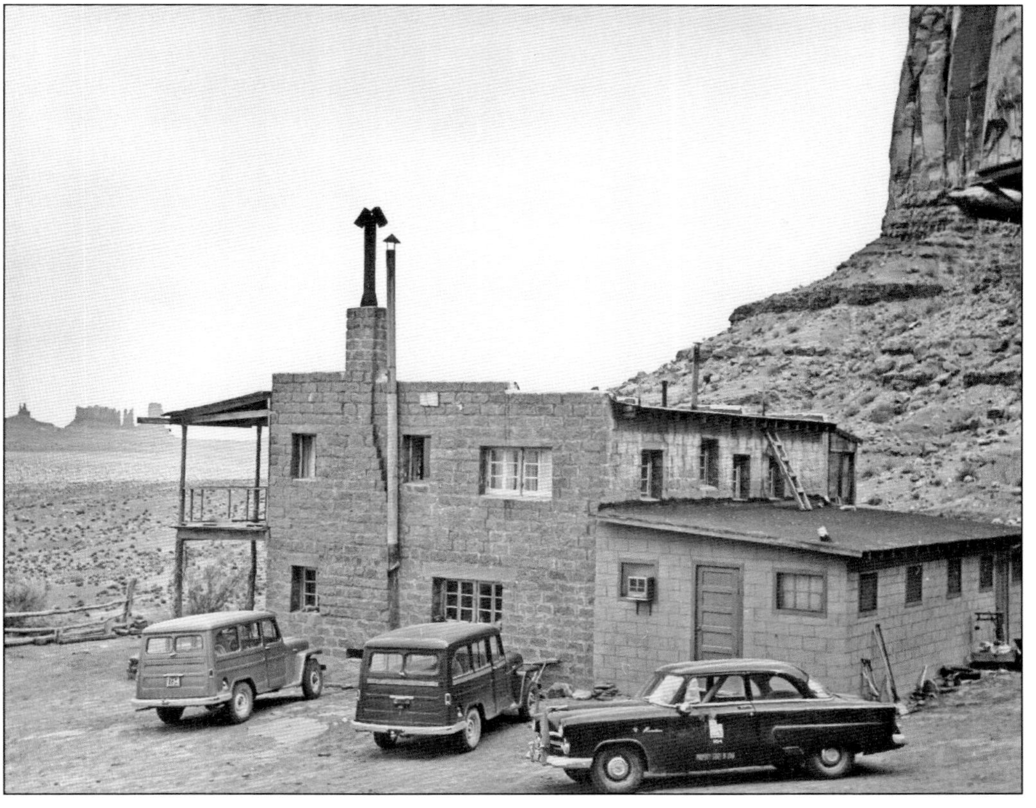

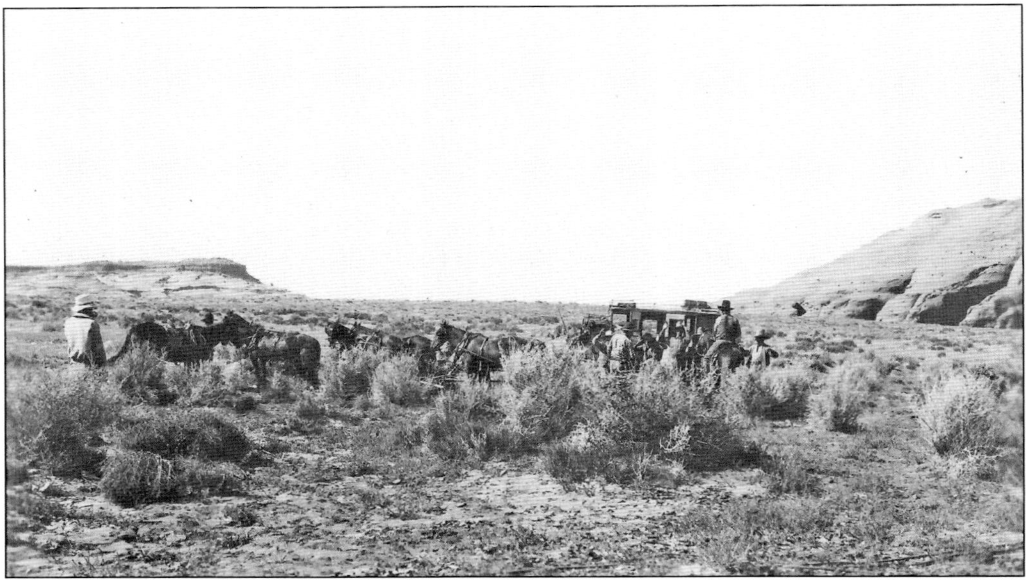

Director John Ford filmed *Stagecoach* in 1939, featuring the emerging actors Claire Trevor as Dallas, a prostitute, and John Wayne as the Ringo Kid, a professional outlaw. With the backdrop of Monument Valley, *Stagecoach* has been called the perfect western, and the American Film Institute has ranked it in the top 10 of all films in the western genre. Speaking for the millions of visitors who have been awed by the spectacular landscape of Monument Valley, John Wayne, on his first sight of the country, is reported to have said, "So this is where God put the West."

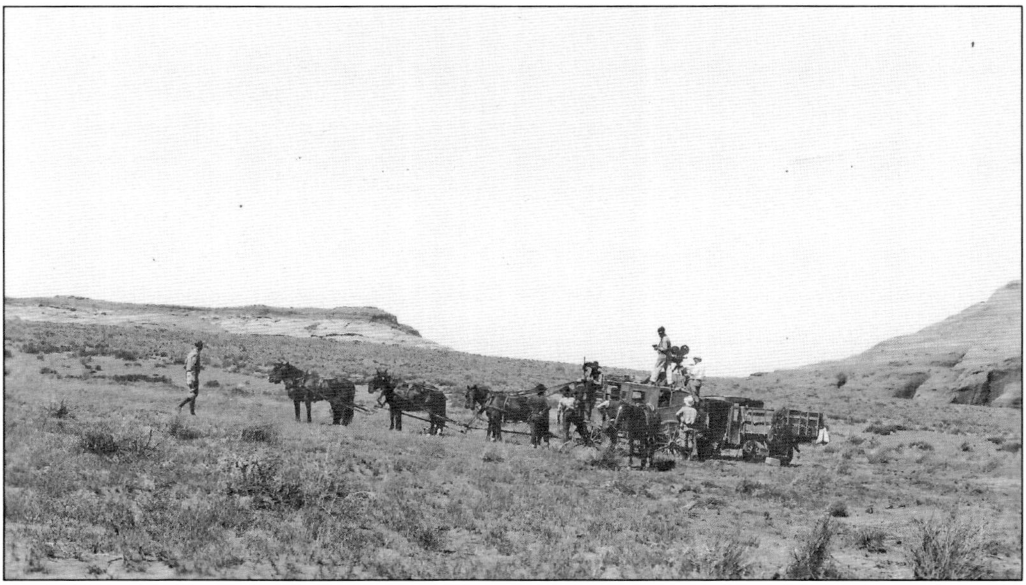

Famed actor John Wayne fell in love with the spectacular Monument Valley country and returned many times to film as well as to vacation. From left to right are John Wayne, John Ford, Harry Brendon (standing), Harry Goulding, and Ward Bond. The man at the right with a white hat is one of the film crew members. (Courtesy of Nathan LaFont and Goulding's Trading Post and Lodge.)

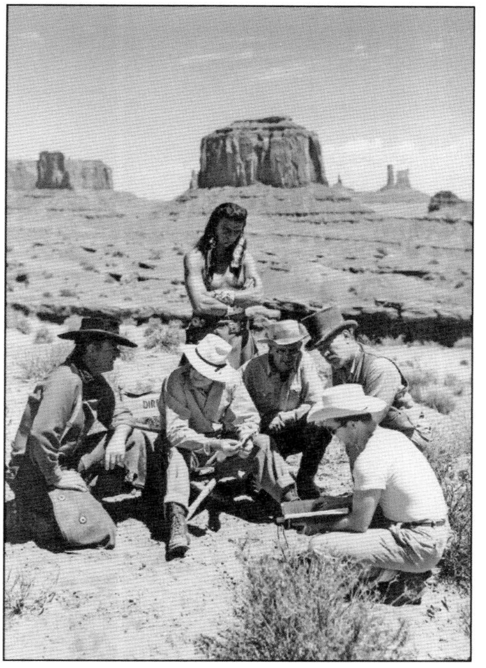

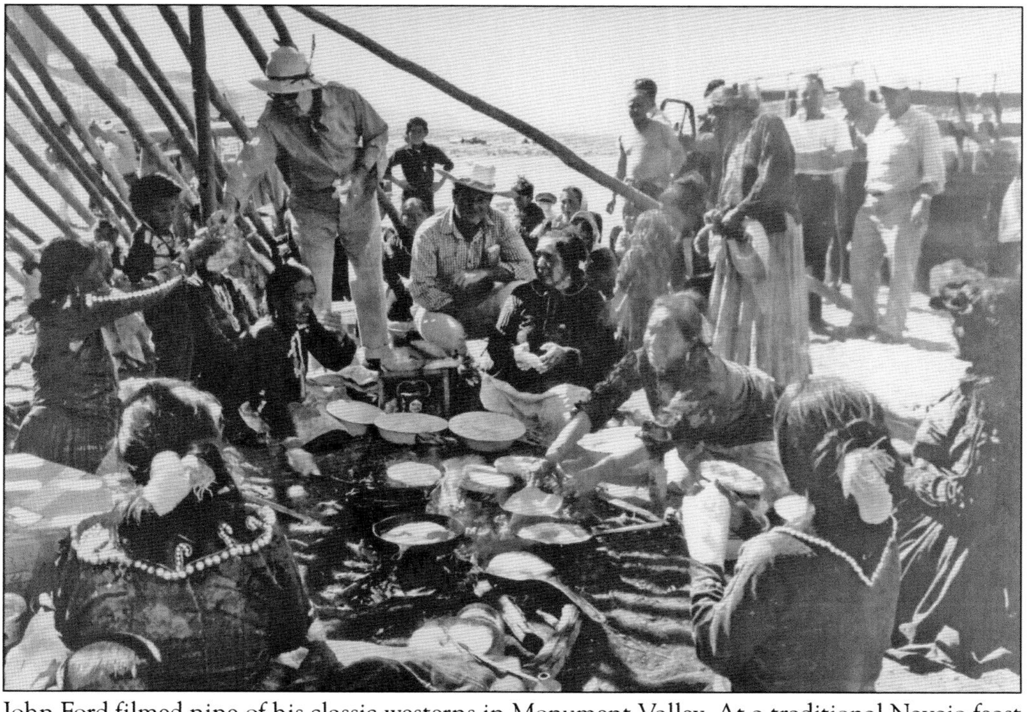

John Ford filmed nine of his classic westerns in Monument Valley. At a traditional Navajo feast for the film crew and Navajo friends, John Ford, standing, made fry bread. The crew took a break from filming *The Searchers*, a 1955 movie that has been ranked as 12th by the American Film Institute in a list of the 100 best films and the best western ever made. (Courtesy of Nathan LaFont and Goulding's Trading Post and Lodge.)

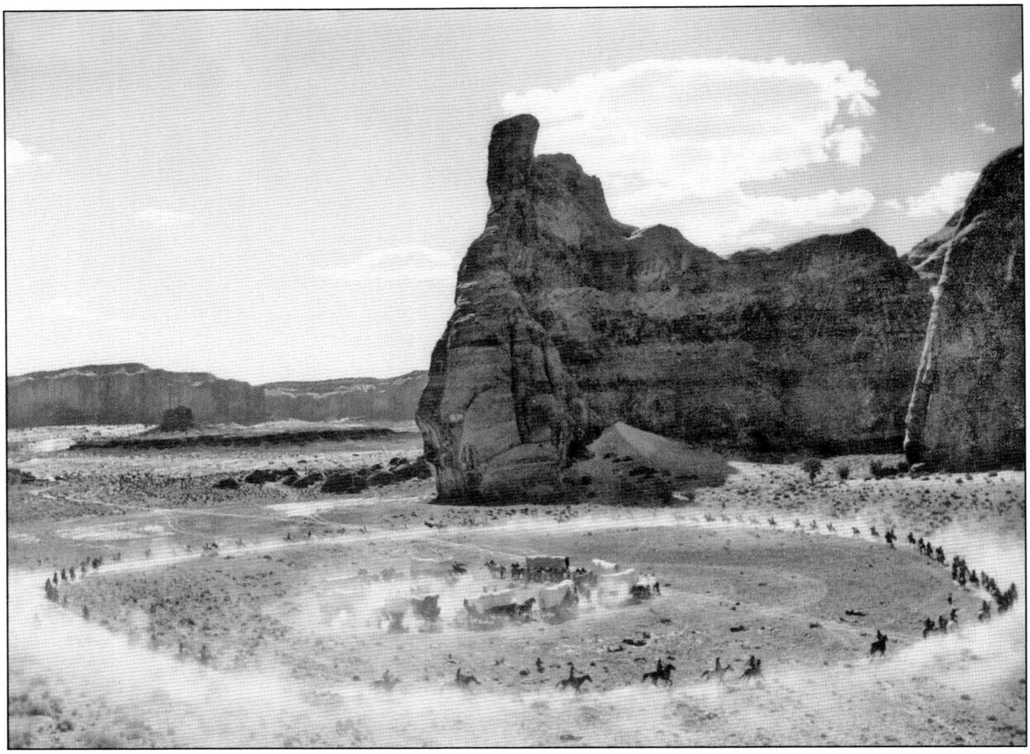

George B. Seitz, who directed *The Vanishing American* near Kayenta in 1925, returned to Arizona 15 years later to direct *Kit Carson*. The 1940 movie was filmed in Monument Valley and told the story of trapper Kit Carson, played by Jon Hall; John C. Fremont, played by Dana Andrews; and their men, who are attacked by Indians as they journey to California. While the movie was historically inaccurate, the Monument Valley scenery contributed to the appeal of the picture.

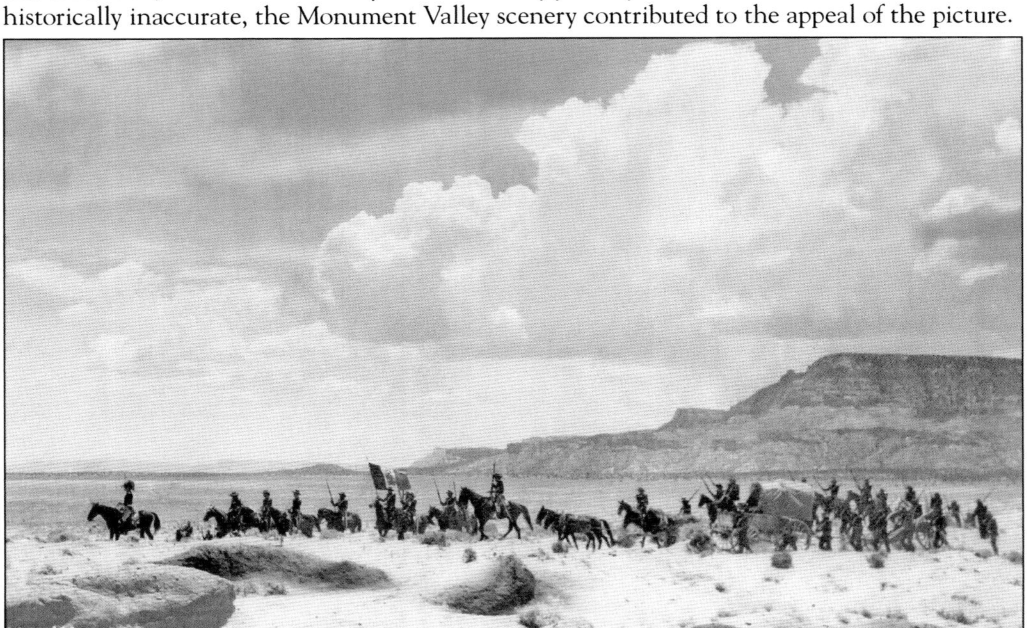

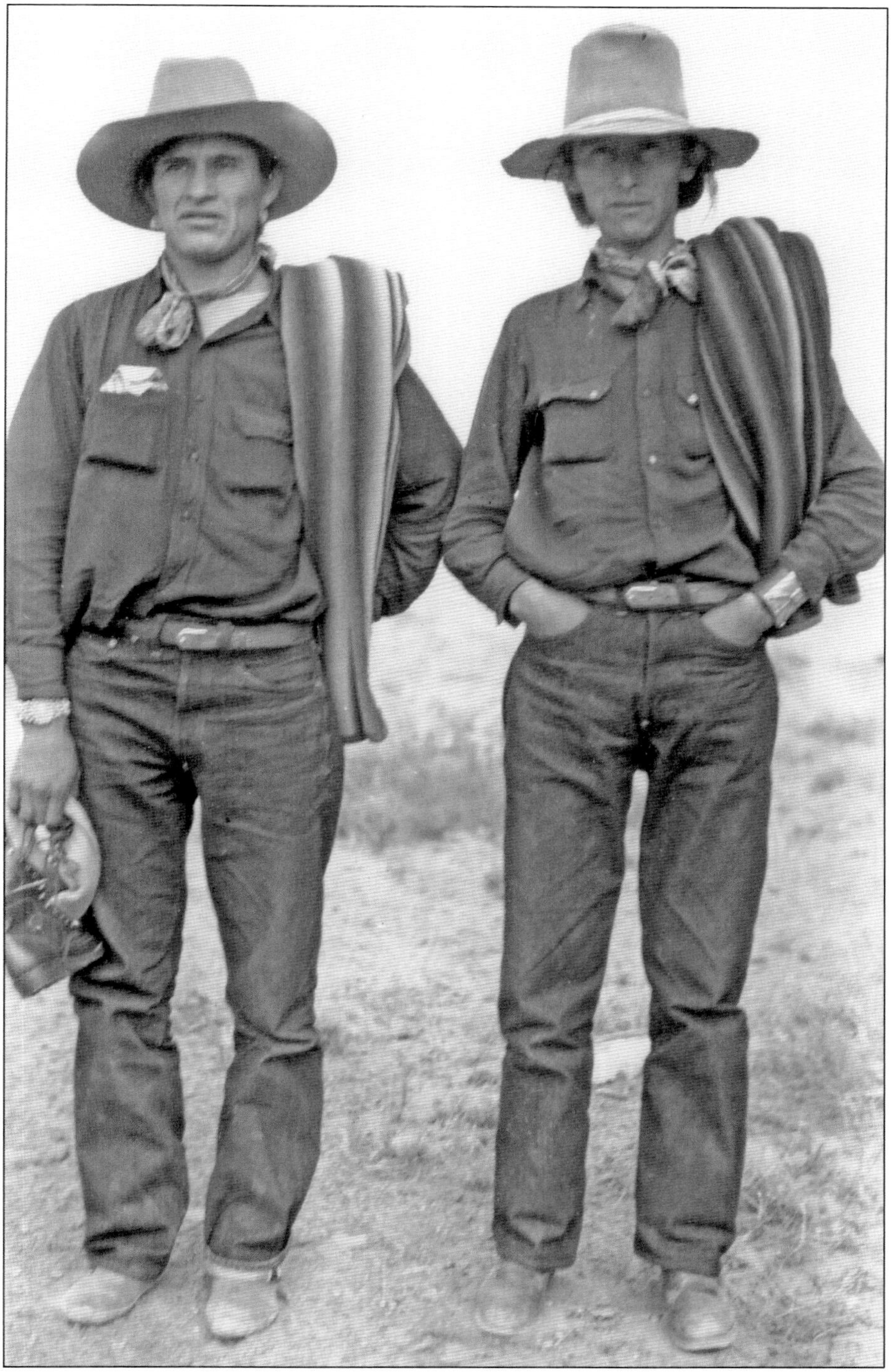

Billy Yellow, on the left, appeared in several John Ford movies; at the right is his son, who was known as "Kid Diné." Billy Yellow, a Navajo who lived in Monument Valley, is wearing homemade leather moccasins and holding a pair of commercially manufactured boots. Perhaps the moccasins were more comfortable, or maybe he was just saving wear on the more expensive store shoes.

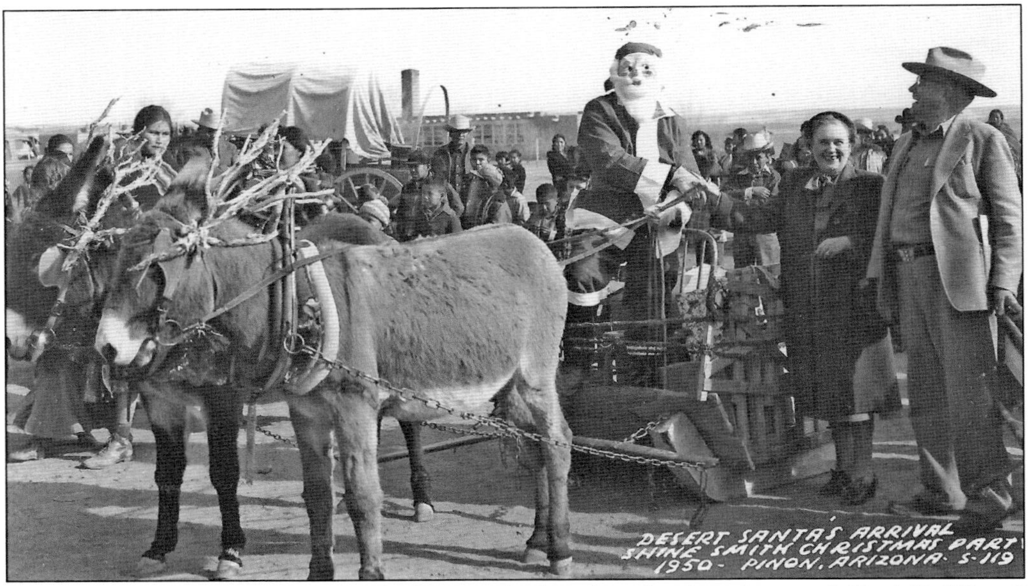

Christmas is celebrated here with a donkey on which stick antlers have been tied. Hugh D. "Shine" Smith became minister of the Kayenta church in 1921. Smith was later expelled from the church because he supported too many traditional Indian practices at a time when the church and the government were trying to eradicate Indian language and religion. When Smith performed a marriage for a Navajo couple, he would ask a Navajo medicine man to also perform the ceremony according to Navajo tradition. Smith remained on the reservation in spite of attempts by church officials to have him barred and worked at various trading posts. He later became well known for the huge Christmas parties he held around the reservation with support and donations from people around the country. One notable Christmas, Barry Goldwater flew to Monument Valley to play Santa for the Navajo children. (Both, courtesy of Nathan LaFont and Goulding's Trading Post and Lodge.)

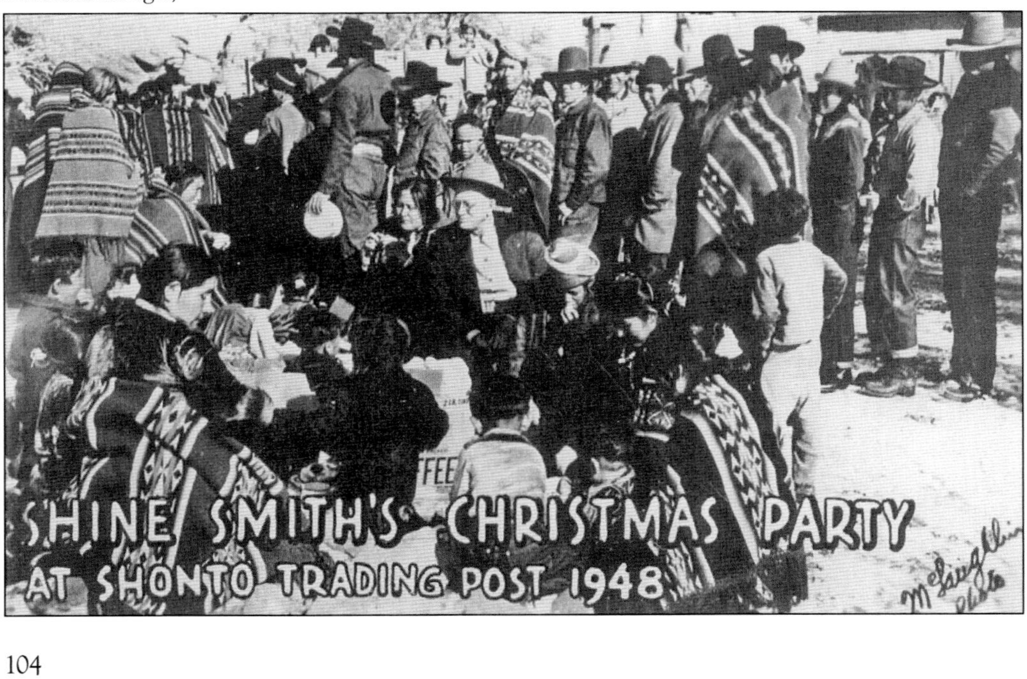

In 1976, Kiowa author and poet N. Scott Momaday wrote of Monument Valley, "The valley is vast. When you look out over it, it does not occur to you that there is an end to it. You see the monoliths that stand away in space, and you imagine that you have come upon eternity."

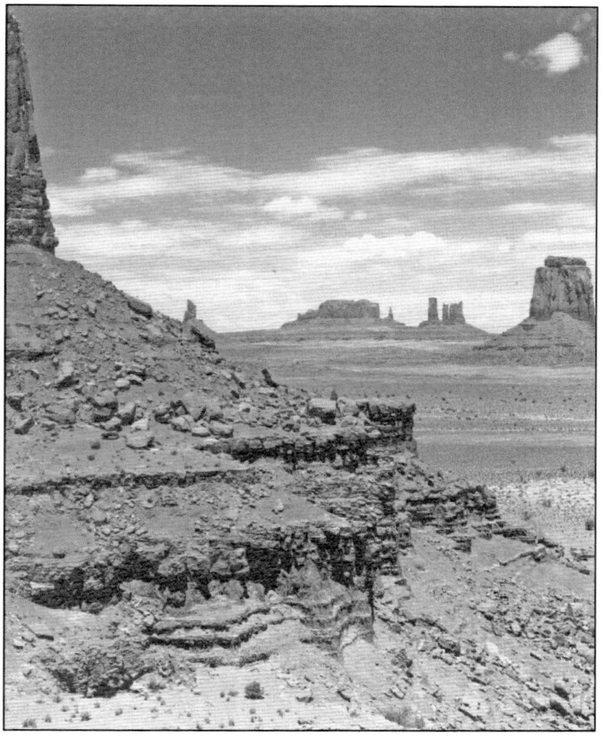

John Wetherill, seated on a rock, took archaeologist Neil Judd to Monument Valley in 1908. Years later Judd described his first sight of the valley: "We saw no living thing, no sign of life. There were no trees on the sandy plain; no shrubs worth of the name. The valley was empty and silent." But to Judd, Monument Valley had a mystical beauty, and he described it as a "fairyland."

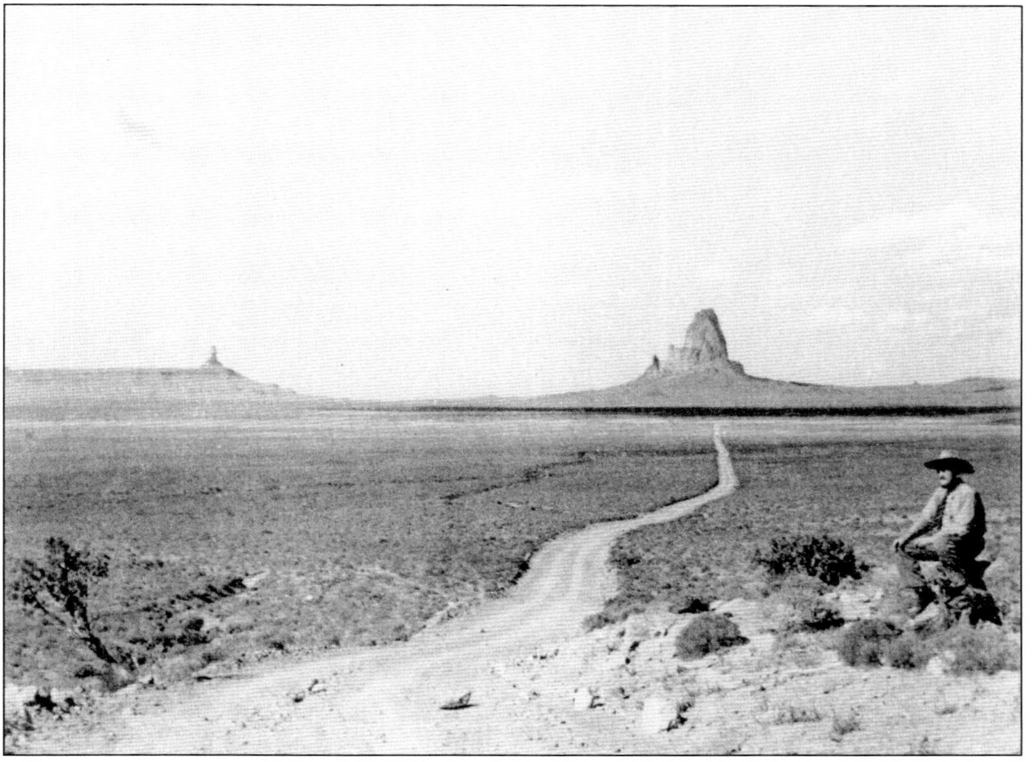

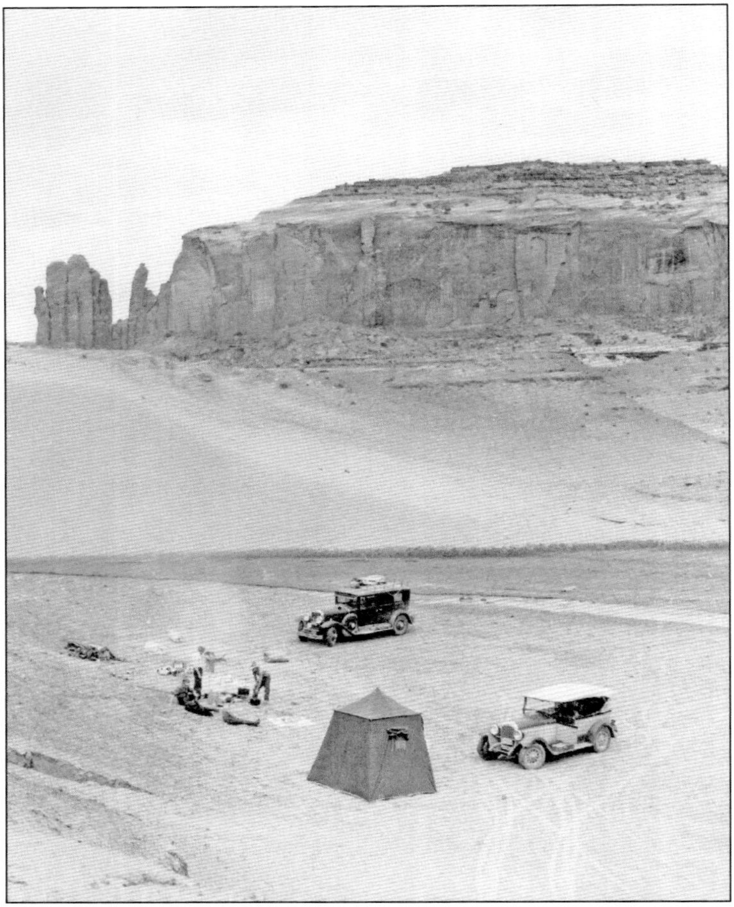

Since John and Louisa Wetherill began trading at Kayenta in 1910 and Harry and Mike Goulding arrived in 1923, tourists have been discovering and visiting Monument Valley. In the photograph at left, a group of tourists are camping below a mesa, and below, a couple enjoys a picnic lunch at a picturesque spot in the valley.

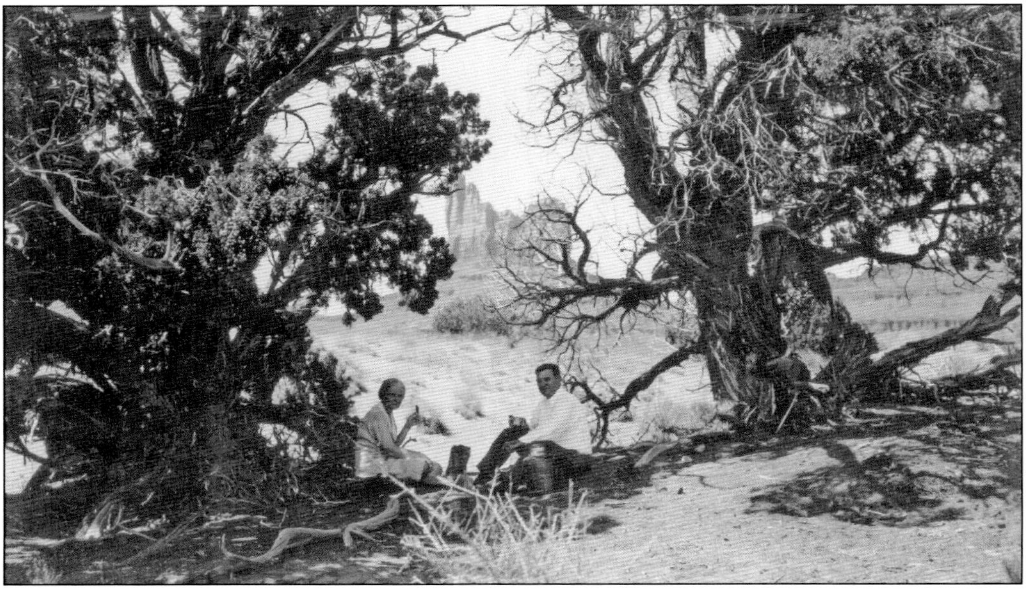

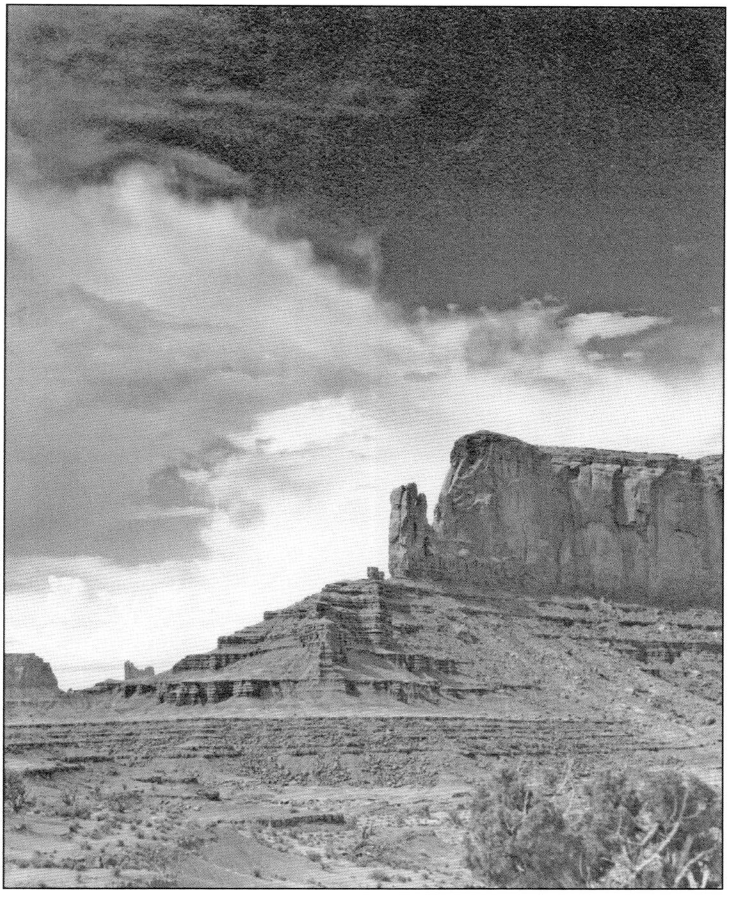

Each year, Monument Valley's fame spreads as more people come to view the area. This couple is examining dinosaur tracks in a photograph taken about 1940. Another ancient trace of the dinosaurs that once walked through the valley are the gastroliths or dinosaur gizzard stones that are strewn across the ground. The shiny smooth gizzard stones gleam in the sunlight as they erode up through the sandy earth.

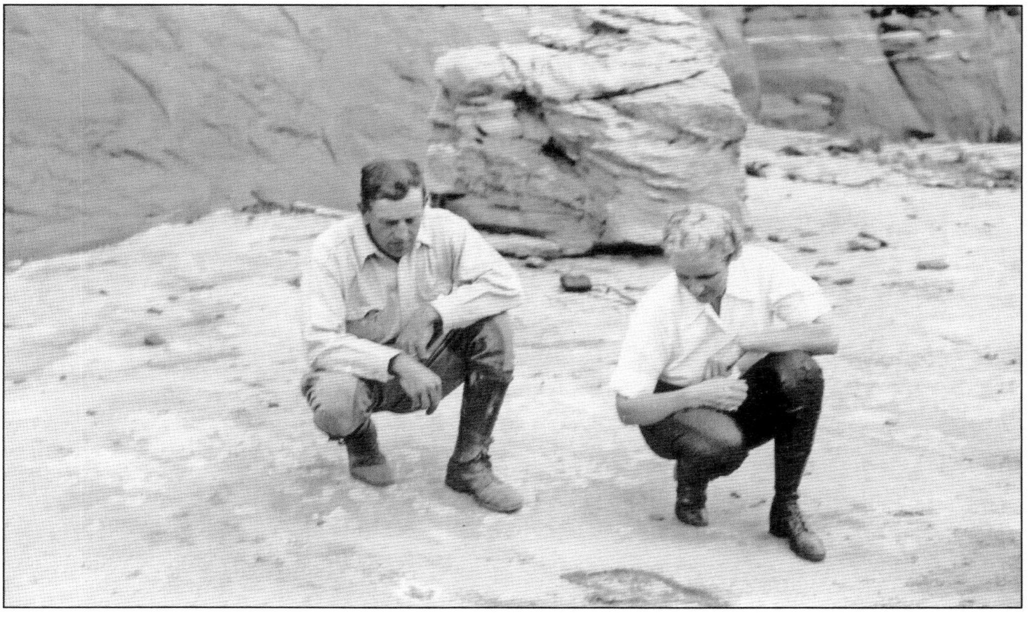

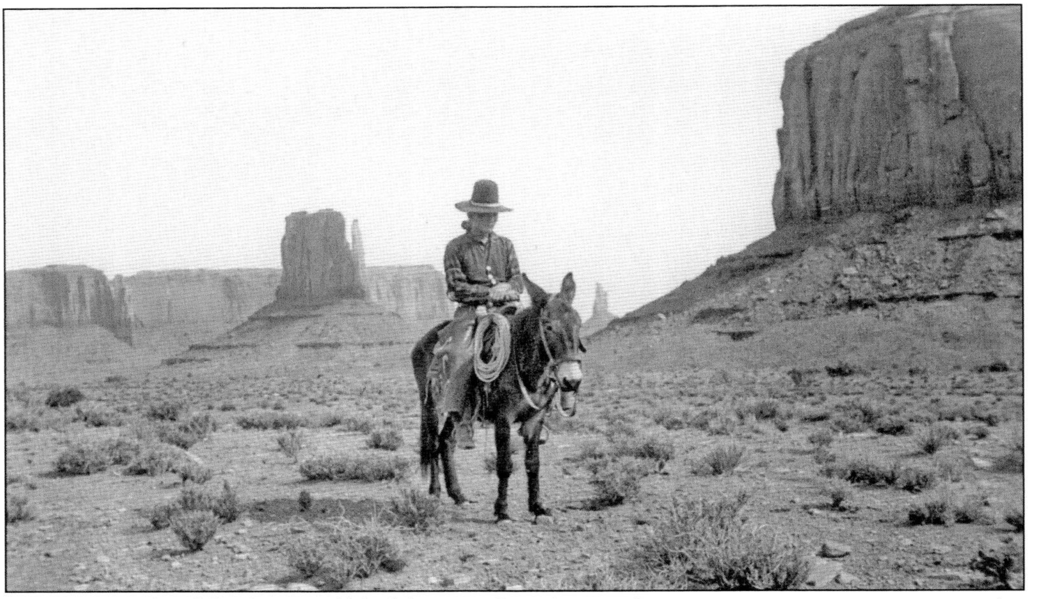

High-crowned and flat-brimmed black hats, such as the one this man is wearing, were very popular with Navajo men, though nowadays they are seen less often. This Navajo man is riding his mule in Monument Valley; one of the Mittens can be seen behind his right shoulder.

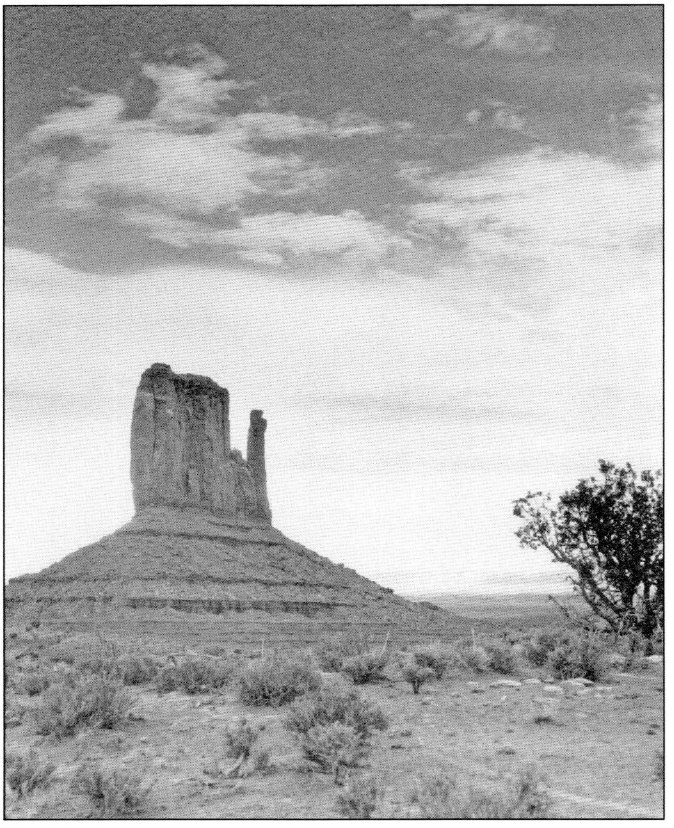

Author George Wharton James visited Monument Valley in 1915, and he wrote the following eloquent words to describe the buttes and towers he had seen: "In the brilliant vividness of the red sandstone they seemed like glorified homes of angels of light."

The Yei Bi Chai and Totem Pole formations are rock features on the 17-mile unpaved road that runs through Monument Valley Navajo Tribal Park.

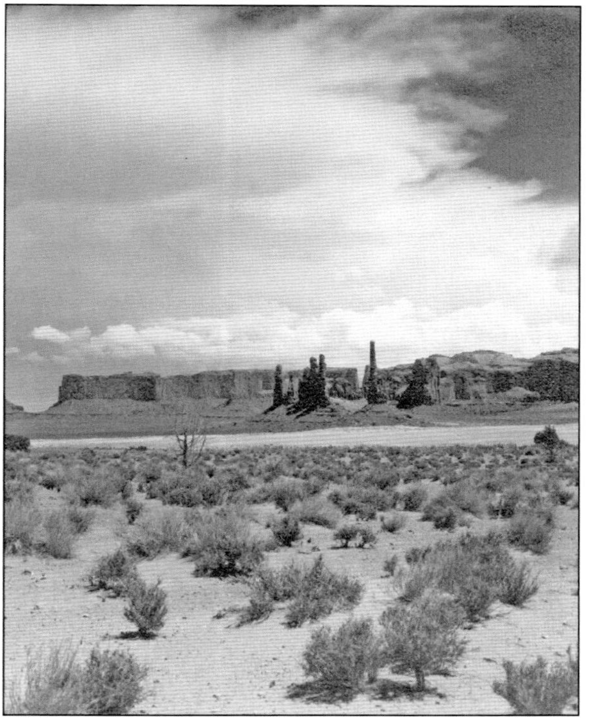

These two lovely Navajo girls were photographed by tourists in the 1950s. It was thought that they had been herding sheep, but it was more likely, given the amount of silver and turquoise they were wearing, that they were earning money by posing for tourists. One woman wrote, "We were dazzled by their jewelry." (Courtesy of Nathan LaFont and Goulding's Trading Post and Lodge.)

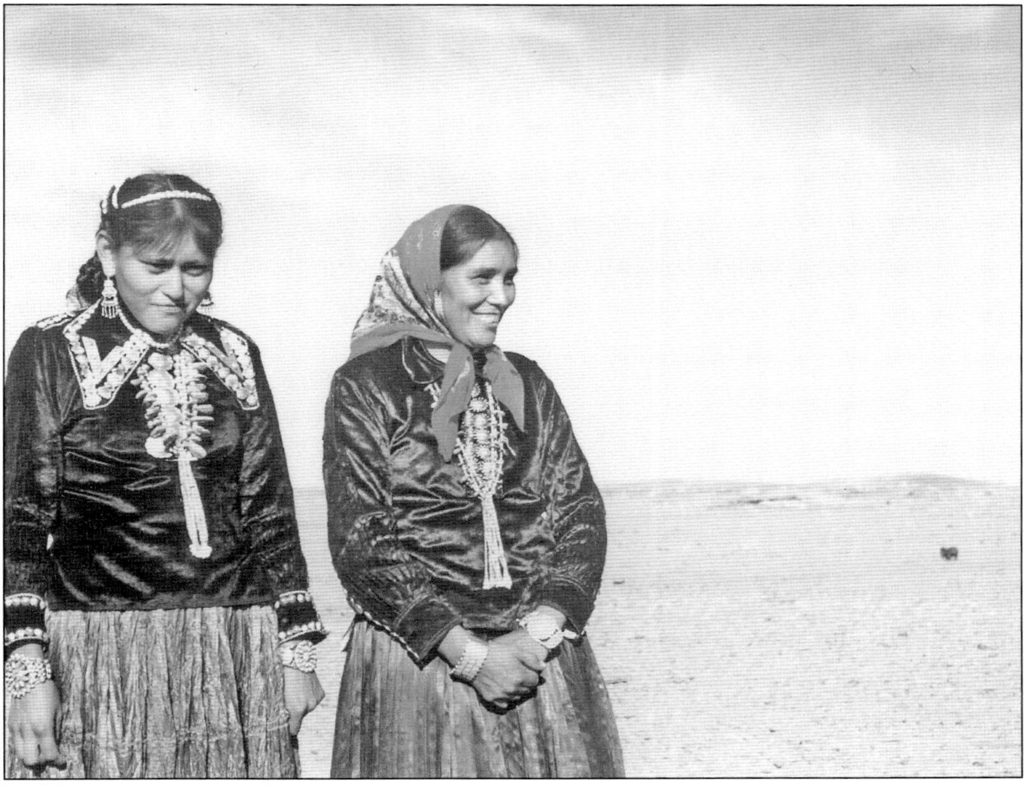

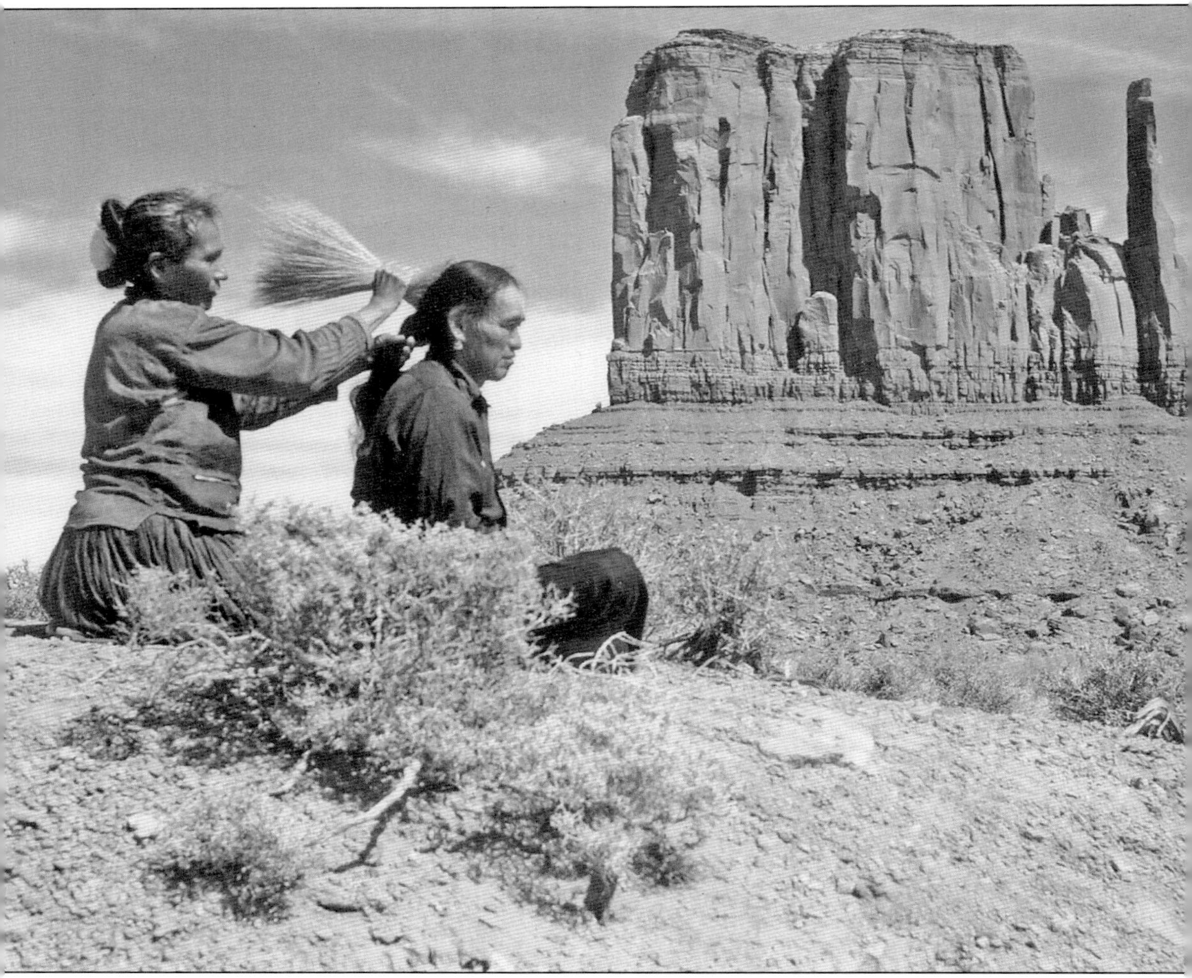

Happy and Willie Cly lived in a hogan in Monument Valley near the Mittens; they were good friends of Harry and Mike Goulding. In the 1950s, Willie worked in the uranium mines in the area, and Happy earned money by posing for photographs when tourists came to Monument Valley. Consequently, she also appeared in many national magazines. She was a weaver and was always willing to give lessons to visitors. One woman recalled that when she tried to tamp down the yarn with a weaving comb, Happy just "cracked up" at her ineptness. Willie Cly died from uranium poisoning contracted during the years he worked at the uranium mines. (Courtesy of Nathan LaFont and Goulding's Trading Post and Lodge.)

Six

Kayenta Today

John and Louisa Wetherill passed away in the mid-1940s, and new stores and businesses were established as Kayenta grew. Local people became more active in state and national politics, and now the community is unique in the Navajo Nation in that it is governed by a local township council. Kayenta is the only Navajo community on the reservation with a municipal-style government. Established in 1985, the township is managed by an elected five-member board and a township manager. Kayenta is also considered a chapter, the typical political division within the Navajo Reservation.

The years of World War II brought changes to the area as young men went away to serve in the armed forces. Some became Navajo code talkers, using their Navajo language to pass secret communications in a code that was never broken by enemy forces. Others joined different branches of the service and traveled to distant countries. Upon their return, Kayenta, like many isolated communities, began to change and integrate into the modern world.

The Kayenta township established a taxation commission, and the income collected provides for local self-leadership as well as services for the community. Leases for homes and businesses can also be granted. Kayenta township includes land in Arizona as well as in Utah, and the population is about 5,000. The average annual income for a Navajo family is $32,500. Employment is scarce in the Kayenta area, and many families still continue traditional Navajo lifestyles, raising sheep and cattle and living in remote areas of the western reservation. In 1921, a visitor wrote, "Kayenta is the last outpost of civilization in the United States." While Kayenta is still remote, today it is the crossroads for hundreds of thousands of tourists who visit Monument Valley, the Four Corners area, and the Grand Canyon each year, and each year those numbers increase as more people visit these pristine places that are too quickly disappearing. But the Navajo people and the landscape endure, and as another early visitor to Kayenta wrote, "The blackness, the orange hills, the swinging lights, the shouts, the listening stillness of the desert—that will always be Kayenta to me."

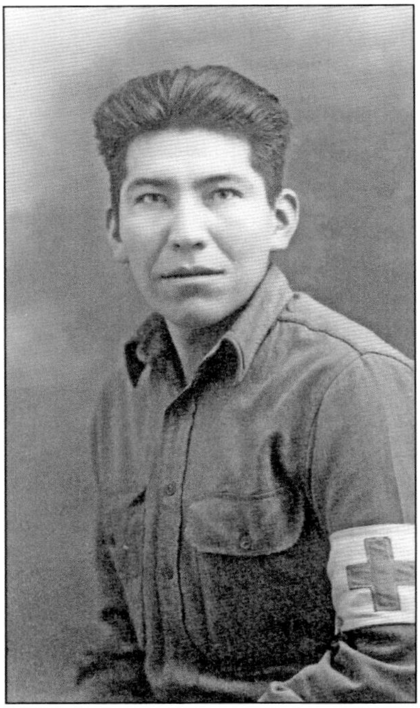

Boyd Haskan served as an army medic during World War II. In later years, he was active in local Kayenta politics, and he also served on the Wool Marketing Council, an organization vital to marketing and economic development for local Kayenta residents. During World War II, many Navajo men performed honorable and brave service in the military, a tradition that continues today.

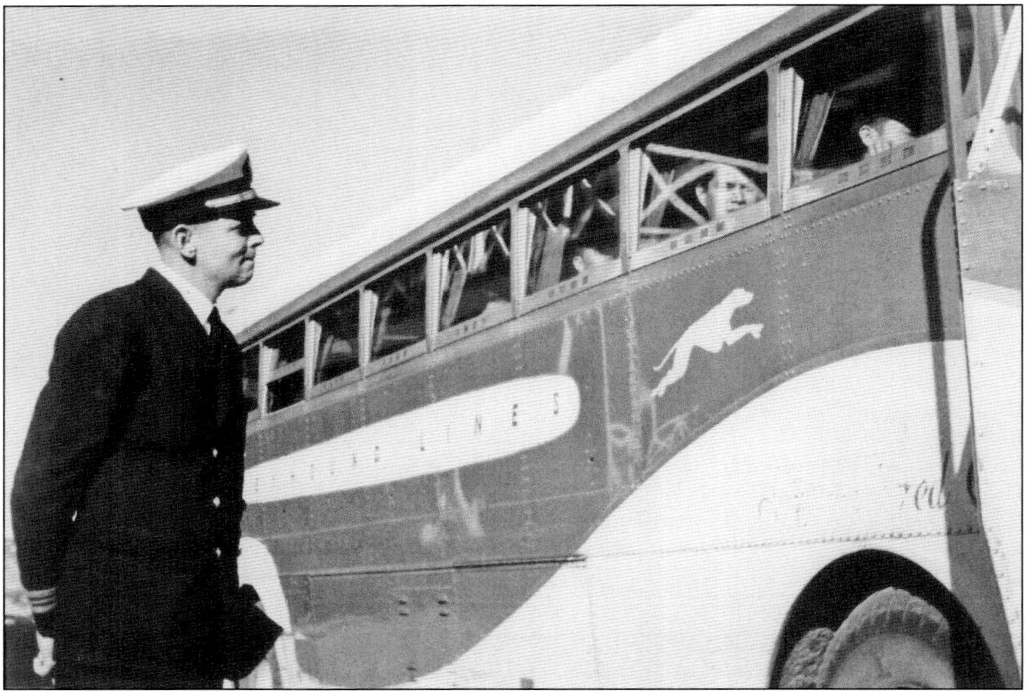

During World War II, about 400 Navajos who had joined the U.S. Marines were recruited to join a special unit that would use their traditional language as a secret code, enabling communications that would be indecipherable to the Japanese. These recruits are leaving on a bus for basic training and then Navajo Code Talkers Training School in 1942. (Courtesy of Richard Paul Mike and the Navajo Nation Museum.)

King Paul Mike was a Navajo code talker who served in Guam, Okinawa, Taiwan, and Guadalcanal. Mike, a bull rider in the rodeo, was given the name "King" after winning the Rodeo Cowboy Association championship in 1936. His athletic and outdoor skills served him well during the war. The Navajo code talkers were closely guarded during the war, and their code was never broken by the enemy. (Courtesy of Patty Mike.)

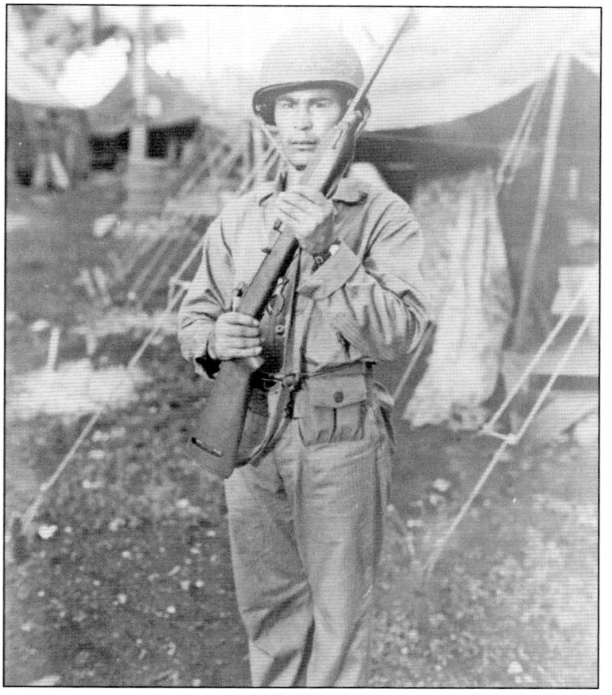

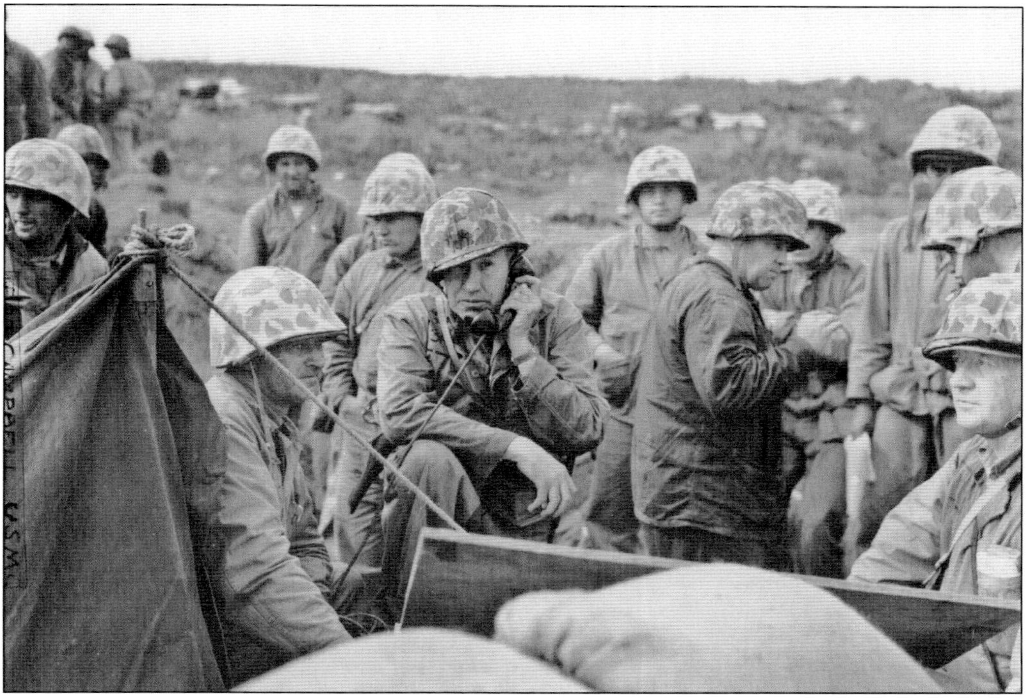

In this rare battlefield photograph, General Rocky is using the telephone to relay the latest information on troop movement on Iwo Jima. At right, Colonel Warner is giving a message to Navajo code talker Merrill Sandoval (far center right) and Thomas H. Begay (top right) to communicate in Navajo to the front. (Courtesy of Richard Paul Mike and Merrill Sandoval.)

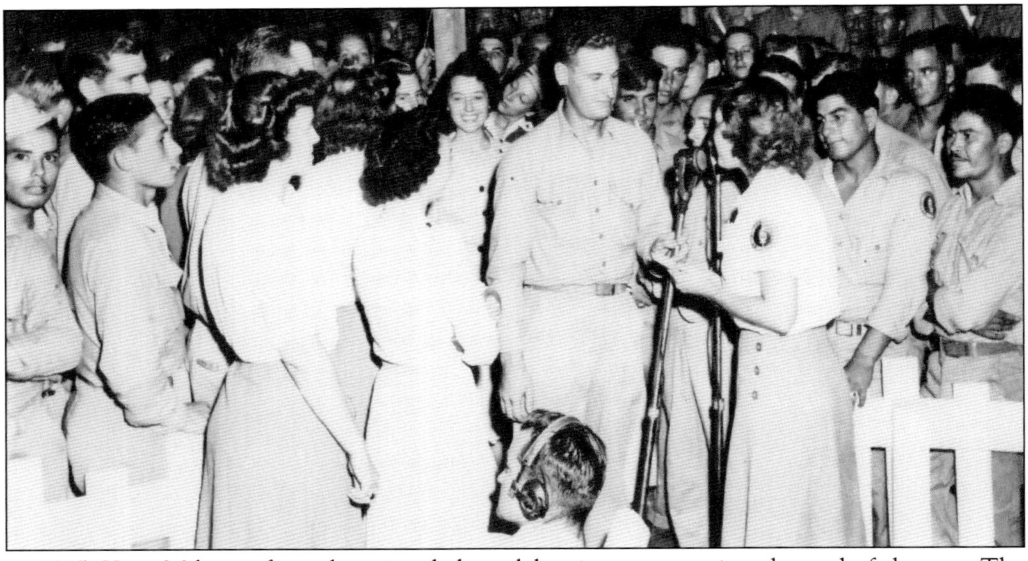

In 1945, King Mike, at far right, attended a celebration announcing the end of the war. The 6th Marine Division was in Tsingtao, China, where they were charged with the occupation of China. The soldiers and nurses assigned to the occupation were anticipating their return trip to the United States. (Courtesy of Patty Mike.)

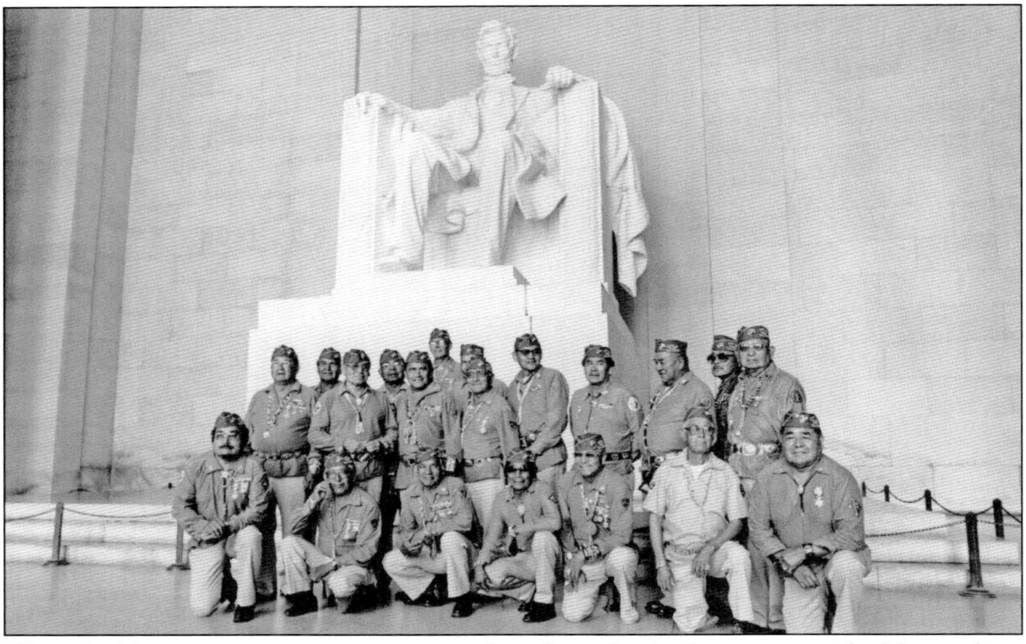

When the Navajos went away to government boarding schools, they were punished for speaking their language, but during World War II, a secret code was developed using Navajo words. The work of the code talkers was kept secret until the Navajo code was declassified in 1968, and in 1971, Pres. Richard Nixon officially commended the Navajo code talkers. These surviving code talkers were photographed at a commemorative event in Washington, D.C., in 1983. In the front row, Samuel Tom Holiday is fourth from left, and King Mike is second from the right in a light-colored shirt. (Courtesy of Kenji Kawano.)

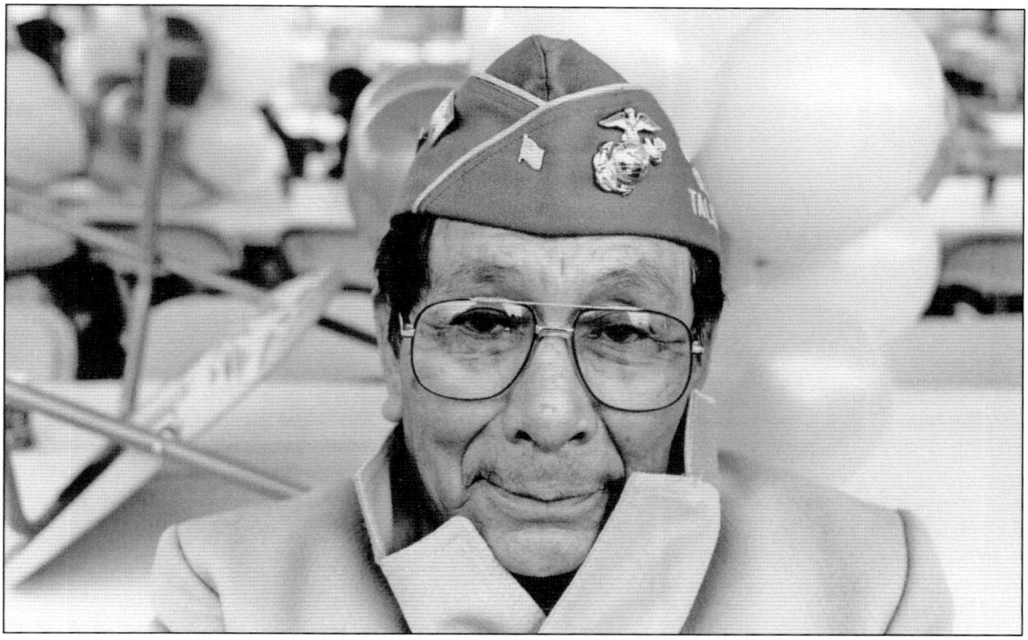

Samuel Tom Holiday was a Navajo code talker from Kayenta. He said, "My language became a secret weapon." Holiday served in Saipan, Iwo Jima, and Tinian. When he returned home, he never spoke of his war experiences, and even his family did not know about the secret code. Holiday humbly said that until the code was declassified in 1968, he did not realize the magnitude of their contribution but now is proud to say, "With a few words, we helped to win the war." (Courtesy of Kenji Kawano.)

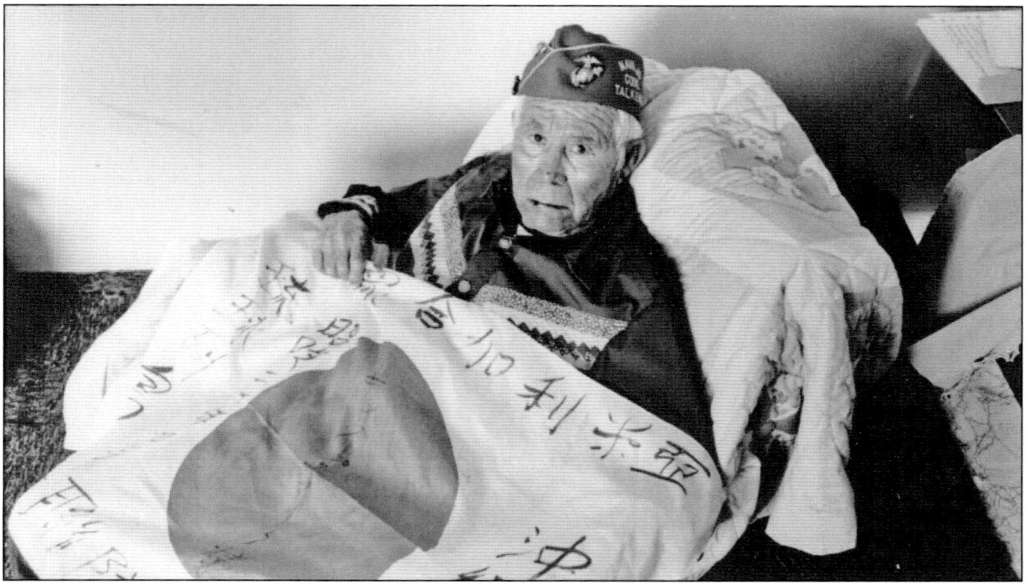

King Paul Mike was a code talker with the 6th Marine Division. While he was away, he wrote often to his wife, Patty, in Tuba City and sent her Japanese flags and other war booty right from the battlefield. Today those items are part of the Navajo Code Talker Museum in Kayenta, built by King Mike's son, Richard Paul Mike. (Courtesy of Kenji Kawano.)

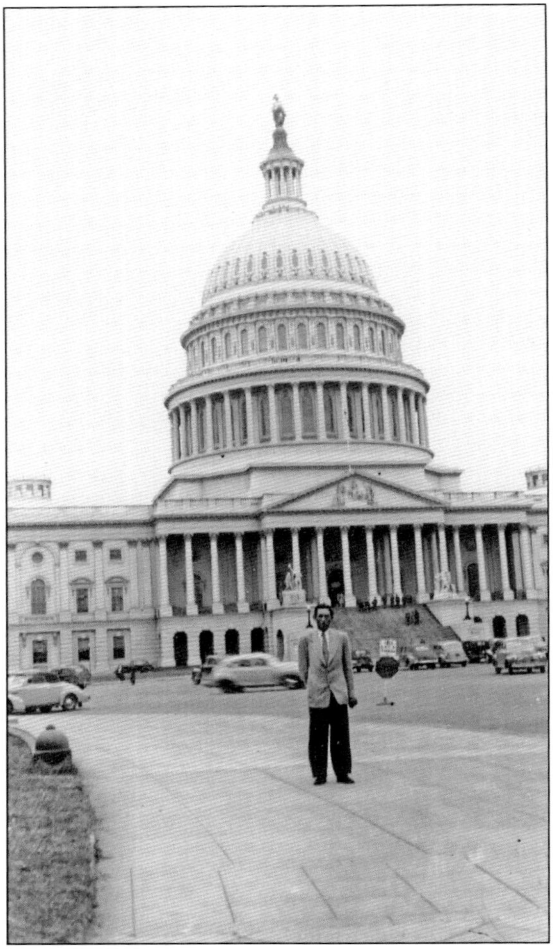

In 1946, Frank Bradley, accompanied by the Kayenta Presbyterian minister, Andrew McGaffin, and representing the Navajo Rights Association, traveled to Washington, D.C., to secure schools and a hospital for the people of the Kayenta area. (Courtesy of Ken Douthitt.)

A group of Kayenta residents met in 1943 to establish a Navajo constitution. It was decided not to proceed at that time out of fear that earlier treaty rights would be abolished. This photograph of the group was taken at the Kayenta Presbyterian Mission. (Courtesy of Ken Douthitt.)

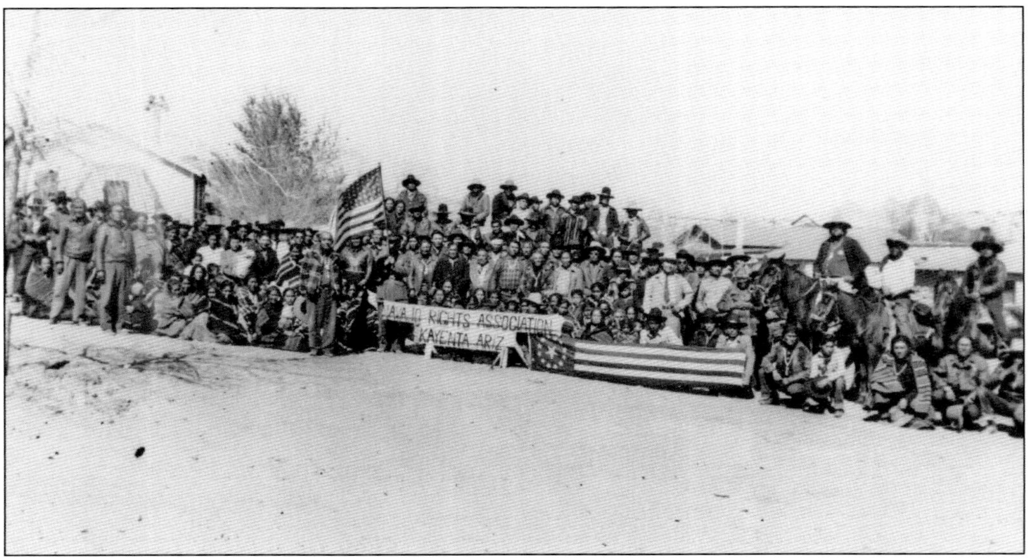

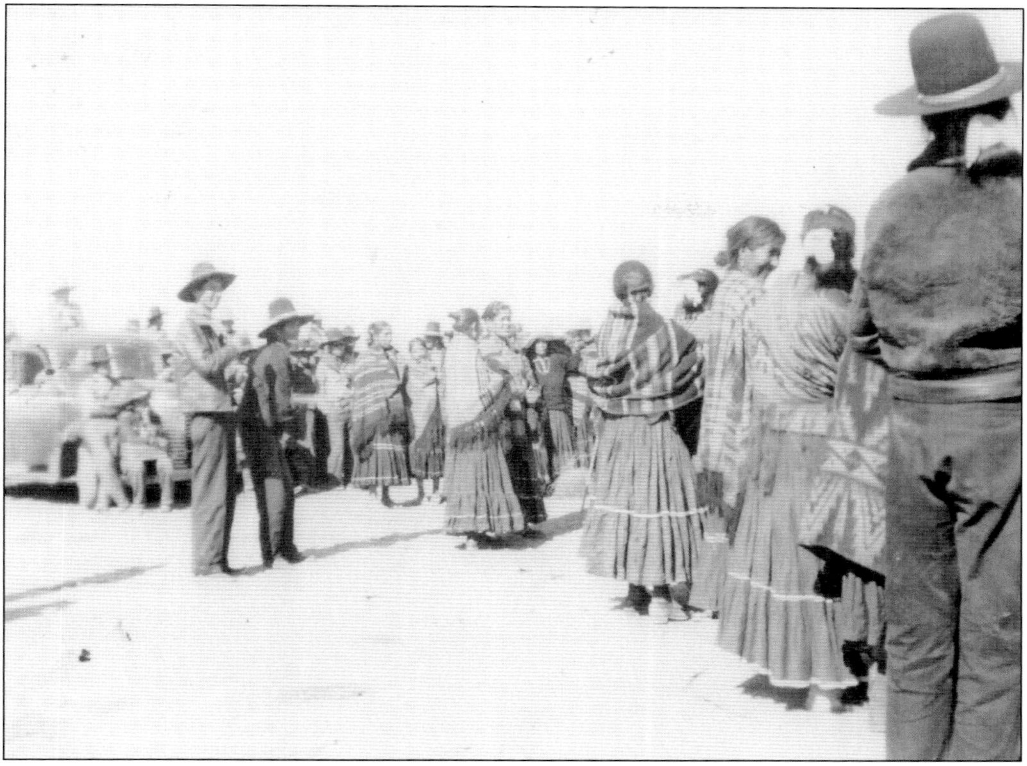

For many years, Kayenta residents gathered for a community day of visiting and feasting. Sometimes they were scheduled at the end of the school year, when parents would arrive by wagon and horseback from their distant hogans to pick up their children, who had spent the year at the boarding school. Known as Field Days, the festivities included races and rope pulls. Many families traveled at night in their wagons, arriving at dawn. They would then spend a day or two in Kayenta visiting and making their purchases at the trading post. (Both, courtesy of Richard Paul Mike.)

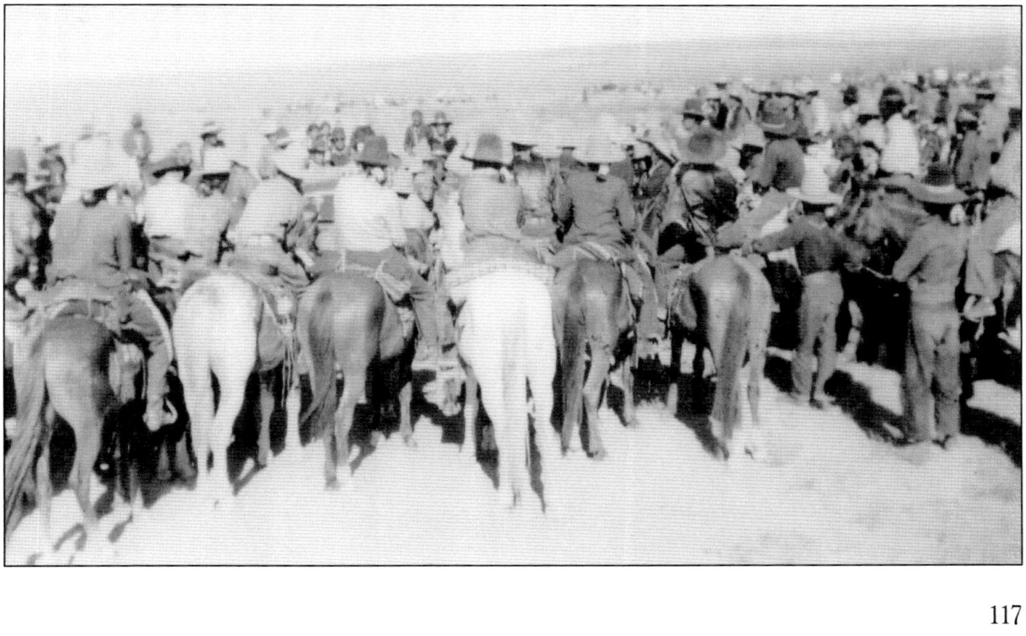

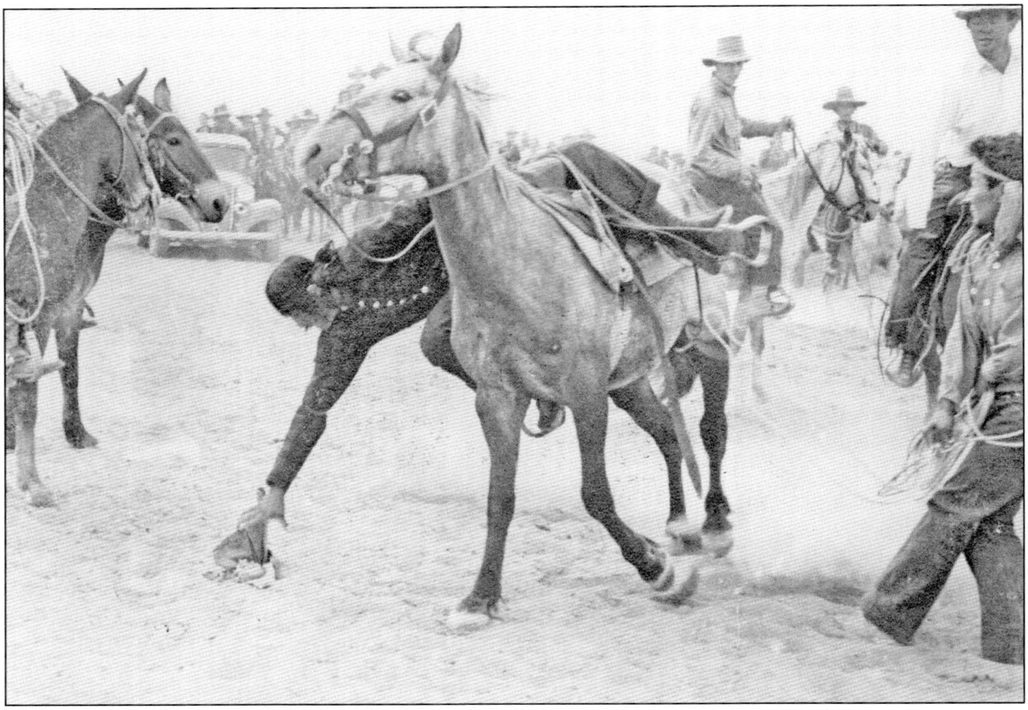

One of the events that took place during Field Days was a chicken pull. A bag of coins was partially buried in the ground, and riders, going as fast as they could, leaned over in their saddles and attempted to grab the neck of the bag and pull it out of the ground without slowing their horses. Some riders fell or were pulled right off their horses, but the successful horseman got to keep the money. (Courtesy of Dan Cassidy.)

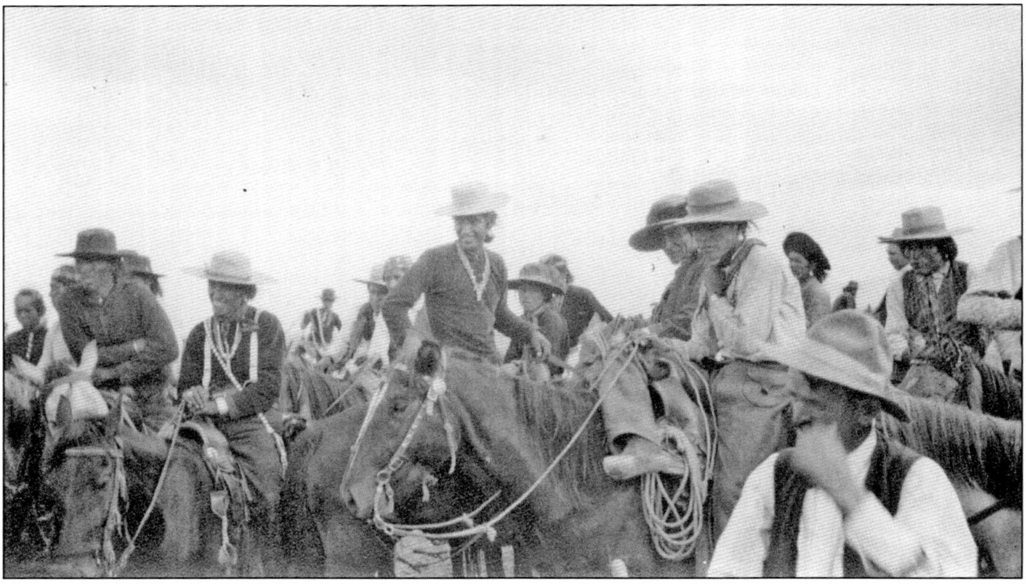

A group of Navajo horsemen visit at the trading post.

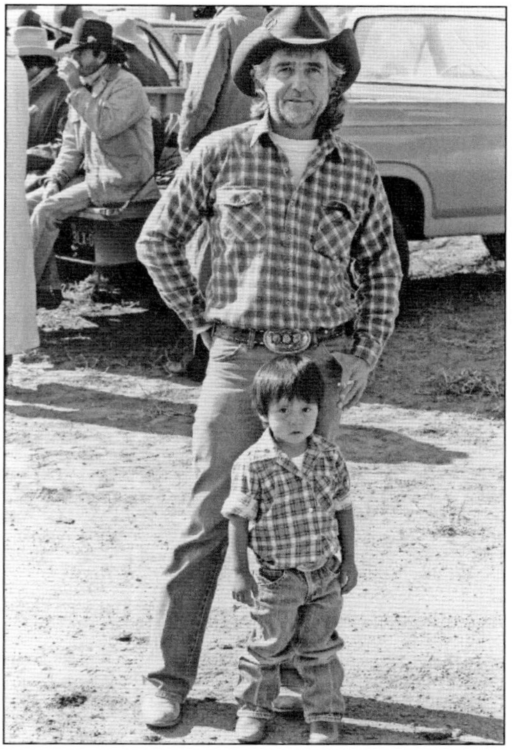

Billy Crawley, pictured here with his son Cooder, arrived in Kayenta in 1949 and has never left. His famous tour company not only guided tourists through Monument Valley but also facilitated companies filming movies and commercials in the area. Over the years, Crawley obtained permits from the Navajo tribe and provided vehicles, food, and lodging for the film companies. Movies that Crawley assisted with included *The Eiger Sanction*, in which Clint Eastwood climbed the Totem Pole in Monument Valley. Later, for an IBM commercial, a helicopter put a desk and computer on the top of the stone pinnacle. Parts of *National Lampoon's Vacation* with Chevy Chase were filmed in Monument Valley. Actress Claudia Cardinale, below, posed with a rifle in *Once Upon a Time in the West*. (Both, courtesy of Billy Crawley.)

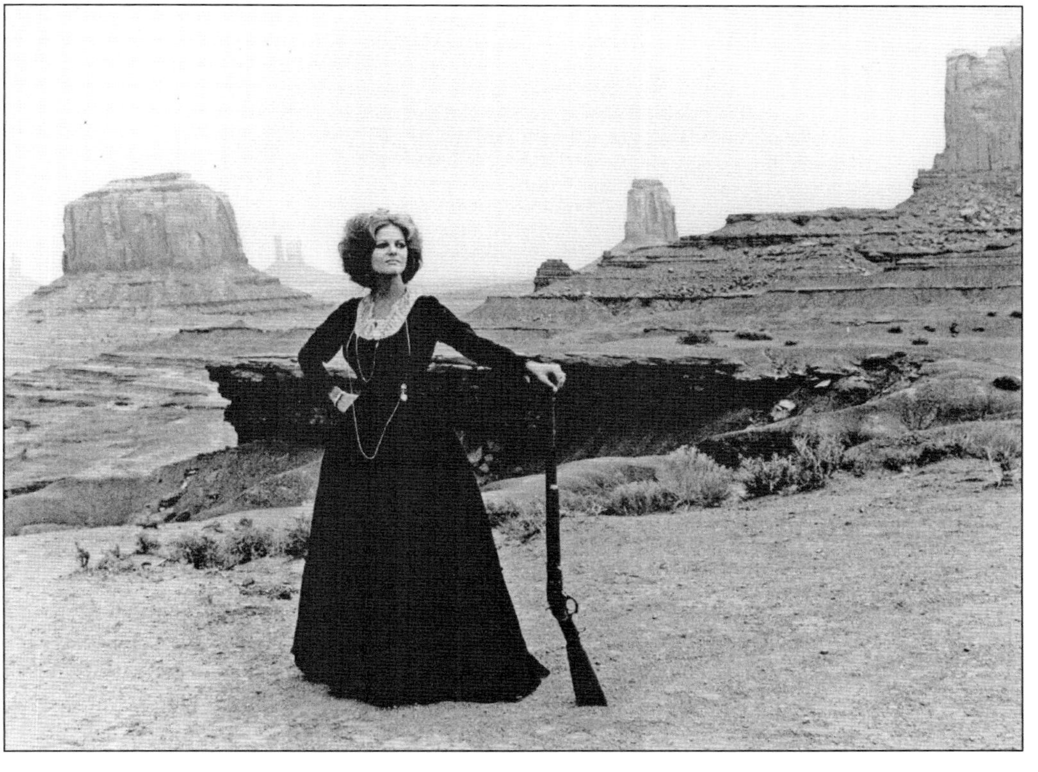

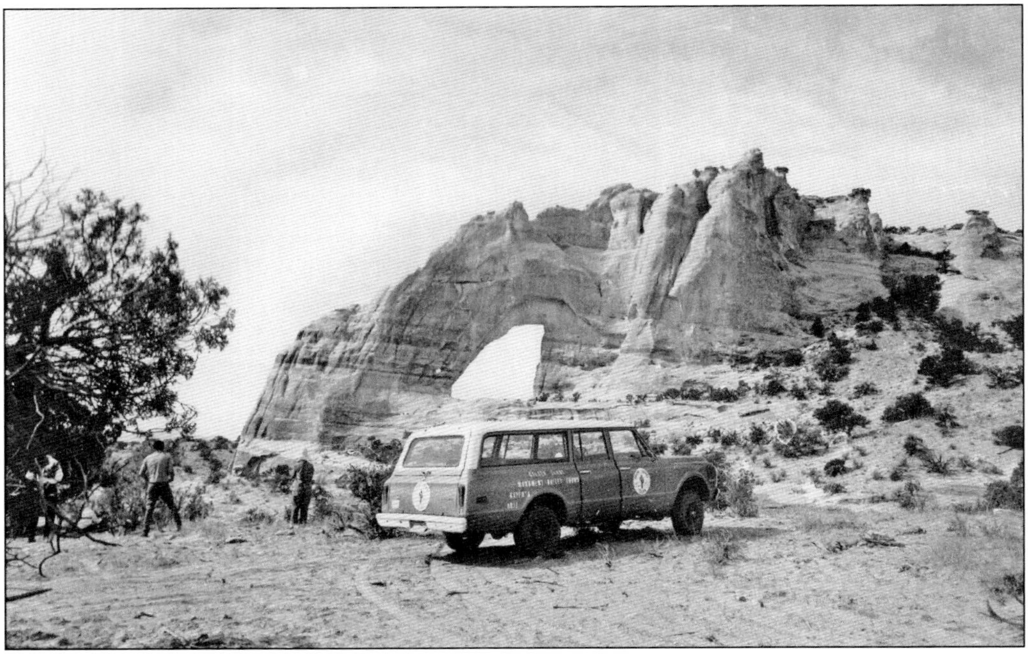

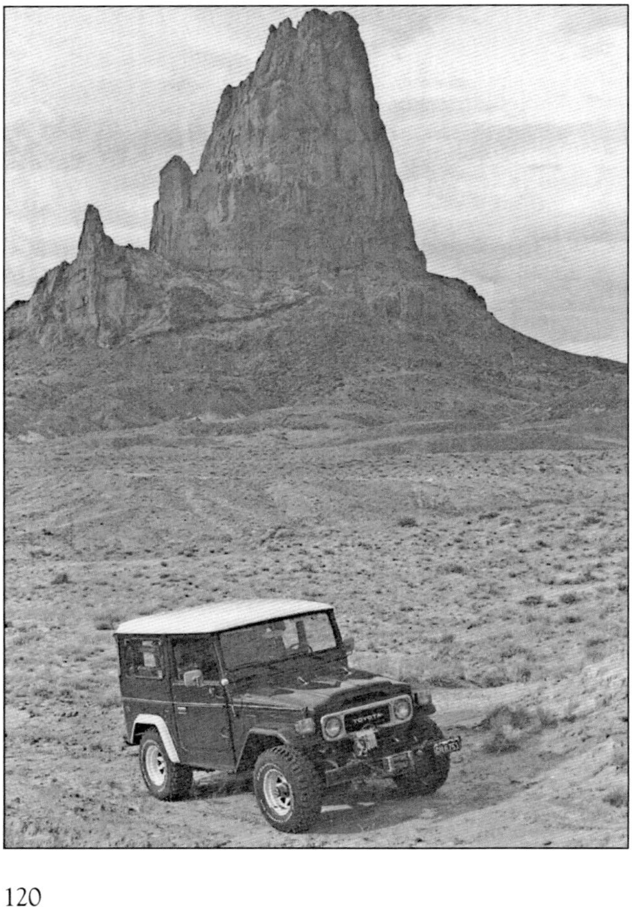

Crawley's Golden Sands Tours took visitors out to sights such as White Mesa Arch. In addition to movies, many commercials were filmed in Monument Valley. The Marlboro Man posed in front of a campfire in Monument Valley; the Clydesdale horses pulled a wagon advertising Budweiser beer; Yamaha pianos were helicoptered to the mesa tops; and Lamborghinis, Toyotas, and Harley Davidson motorcycles were all shown against the dramatic backdrop of the spires and pinnacles of Monument Valley. Even video games have used images from the valley landscape. (Both, courtesy of Billy Crawley.)

Tinker Yazzie Jr., son of one of Billy Crawley's employees, stands in front of one of the Golden Sands vehicles in this photograph from the 1960s. Tinker's hair is tied in a traditional hair knot. (Courtesy of Billy Crawley.)

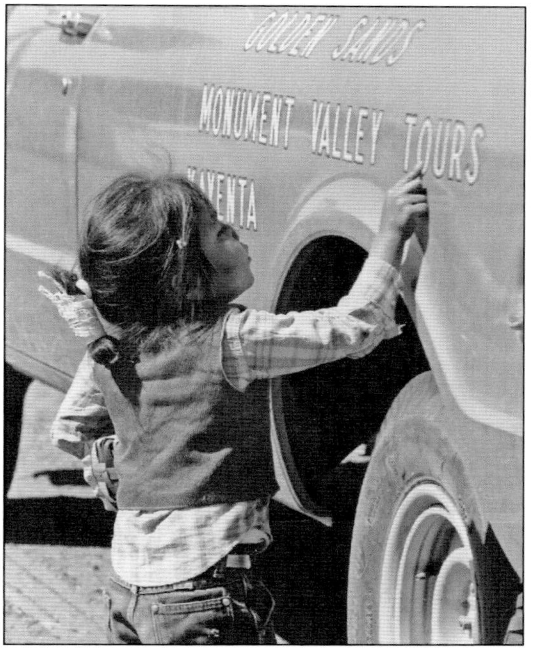

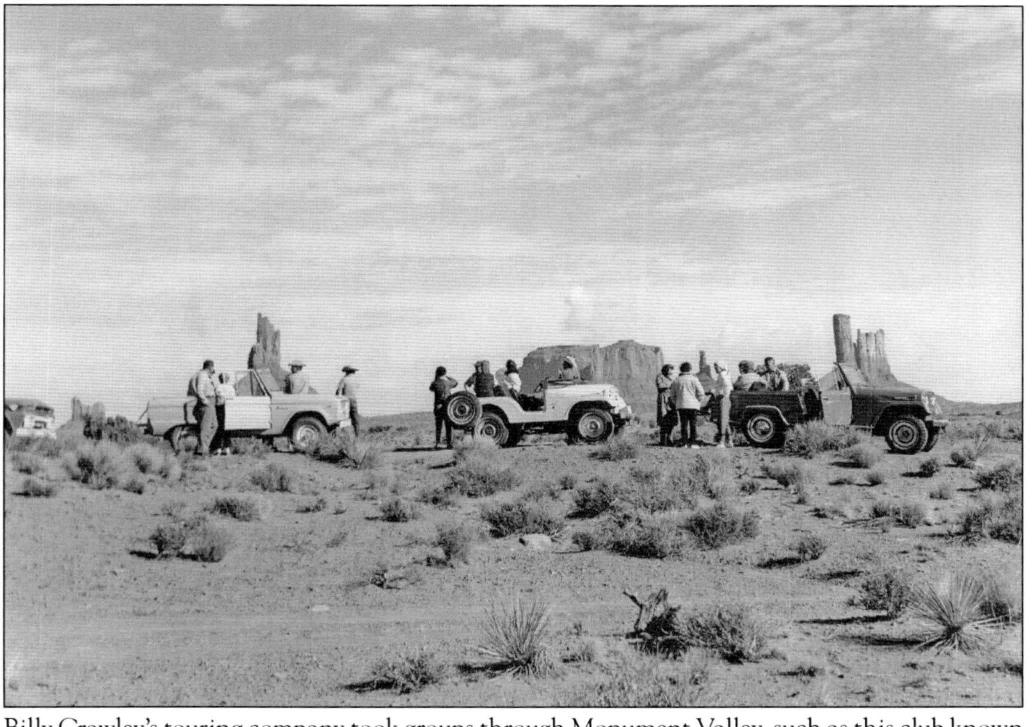

Billy Crawley's touring company took groups through Monument Valley, such as this club known as the Dons from Scottsdale, Arizona, who drove in four-wheel-drive jeeps through the sandy and rocky country. The Dons of Arizona began in the 1930s and continues today to preserve the history of the Southwest. Monument Valley was an appropriate destination for their tour. (Courtesy of Billy Crawley.)

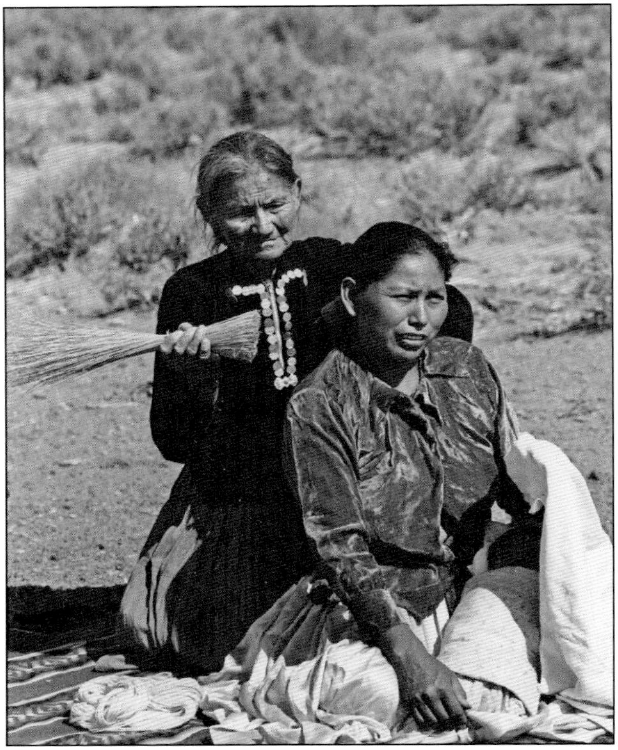

In this photograph taken at Monument Valley, Many Goats combs her daughter's hair with a traditional brush made of sweet grass tied in a bundle. The Navajo hairdo, called Ts'i Yéél' or "bundled hair," is worn by both men and women. Many Goats's daughter, Helen Salazar, is shielding her baby, wrapped in a cradleboard, from the sun. (Courtesy of Billy Crawley.)

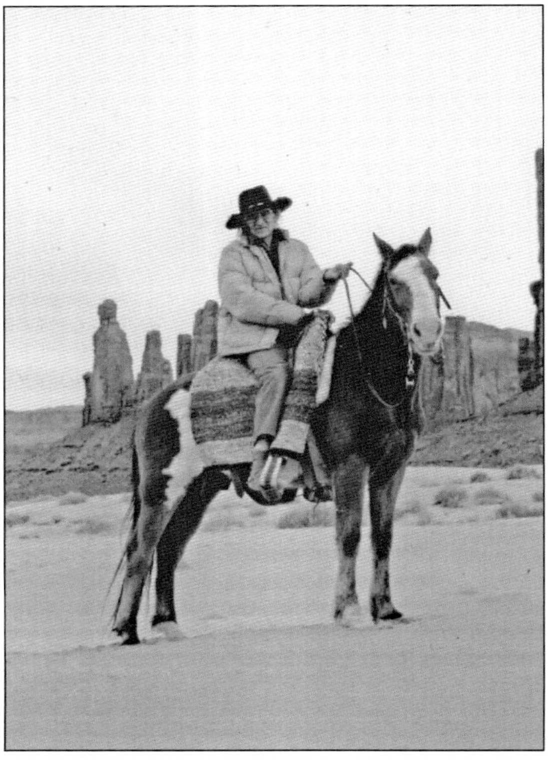

Billy Yellow, shown here on his horse about 1960, lived in Monument Valley and appeared in many western films. He was a Blessingway singer and a medicine man. The Blessingway is an important Navajo ceremony. (Courtesy of Billy Crawley.)

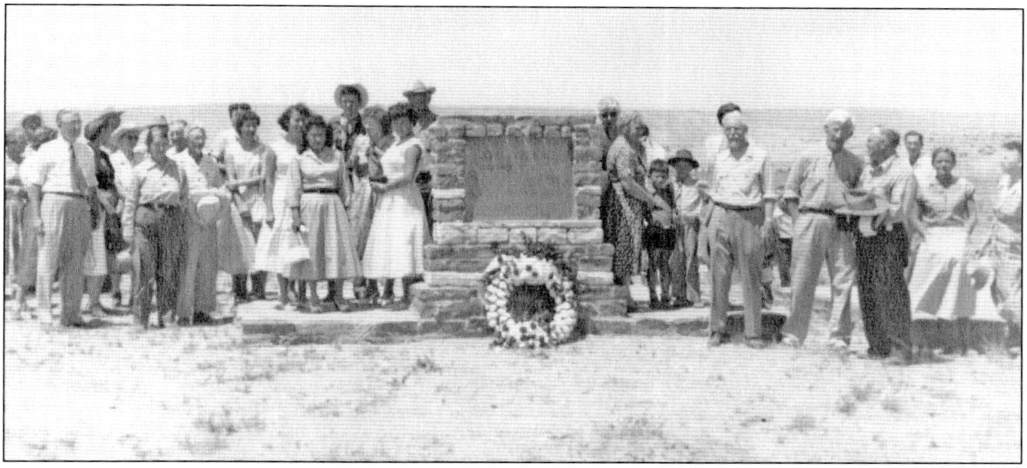

In honor of the pioneering work done by John and Louisa Wetherill to establish Kayenta, a monument was built at the site of their graves on a hill overlooking the town. John and Louisa Wetherill, Clyde Colville, and the Wetherills' son Benjamin, who died in 1946, are all buried in the hilltop site. A memorial service was held at the grave site on July 31, 1954.

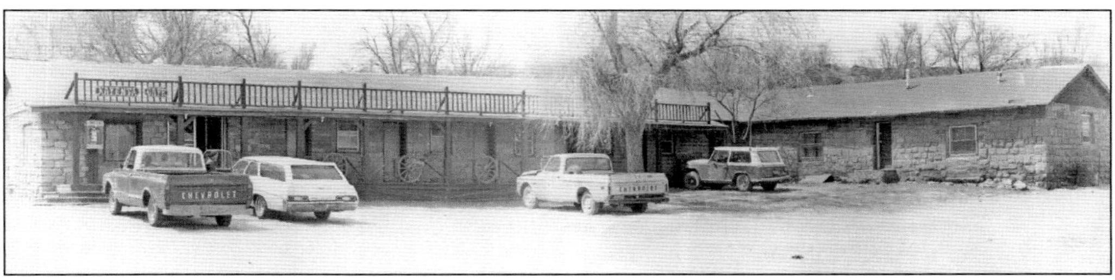

After 1945, when Louisa Wetherill sold the trading post to the Babbitts, the store had a series of owners. In addition to the store, there was an inn and café, shown in this 1973 photograph. The building burned in 1976, and there is no trace today of the home and trading post where the Wetherills lived for 35 years.

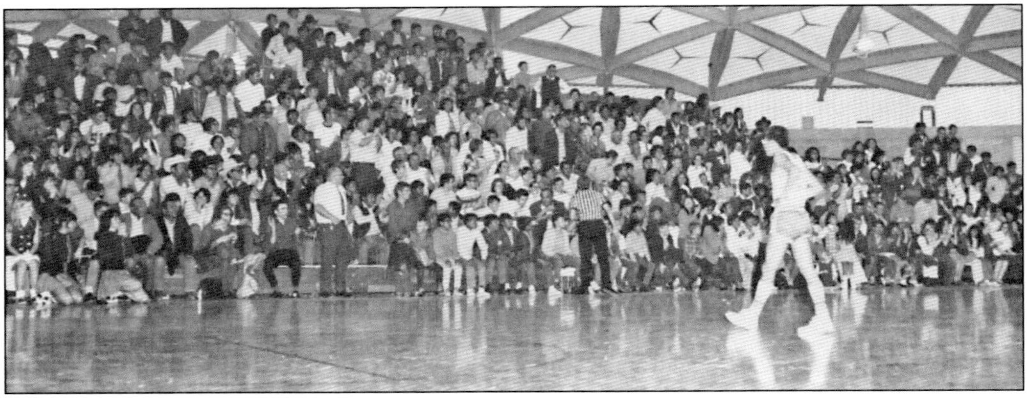

The Monument Valley High School was built in the early 1960s. It was a dome-shaped structure built to represent the shape of a traditional Navajo hogan. As the school population expanded, rooms were added, encircling the main building. In the photograph above showing the packed bleachers during a basketball game, the dome-shaped ceiling arches over the gymnasium. The Monument Valley High School band practices on the field in the 1960s photograph below. (Both, courtesy of Andrew Singer.)

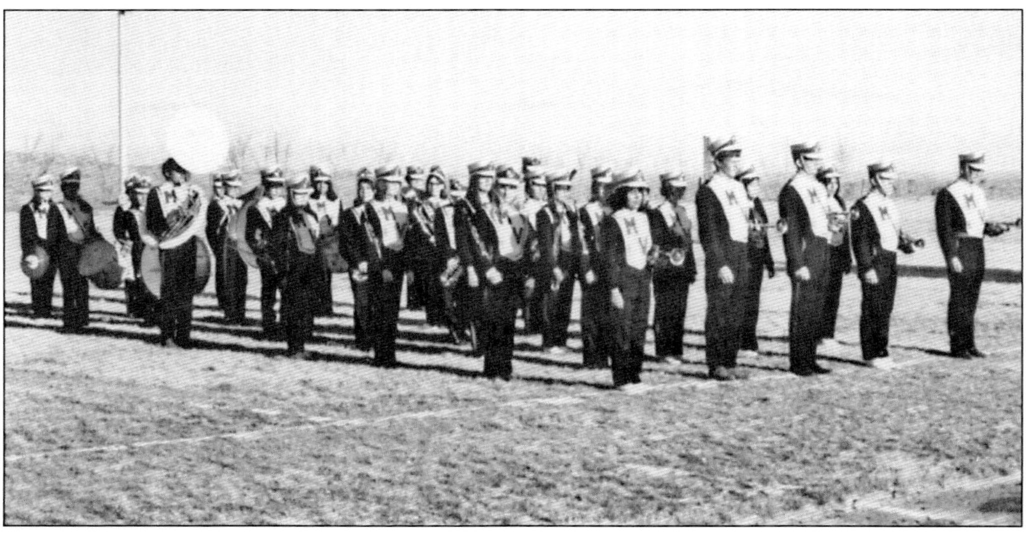

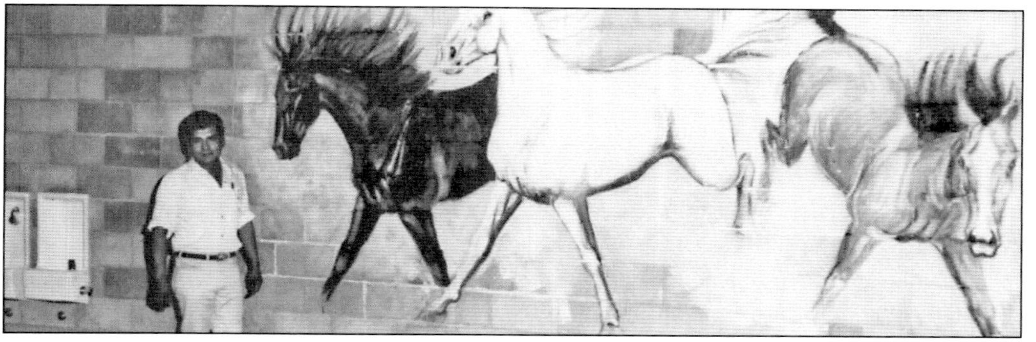

Navajo artist and Kayenta resident Shonie Keith stands in front of the mural he painted for the Monument Valley High School. The original hogan-shaped high school building, along with the running horse mural, burned in 1978. (Courtesy of Andrew Singer.)

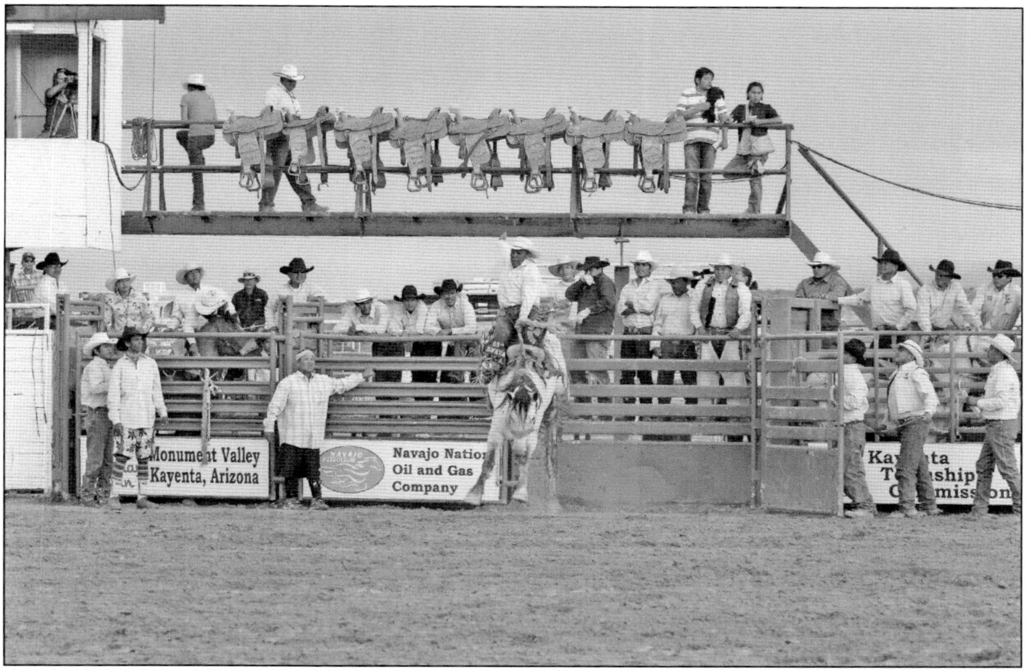

The annual Kayenta Fourth of July Rodeo is a great attraction for locals and tourists. It has been recognized seven times as the Rodeo of the Year and twice as Outstanding Rodeo by the All Indian Rodeo Cowboy's Association. Note the row of commemorative saddles across the top railing. (Courtesy of Mario Dominguez.)

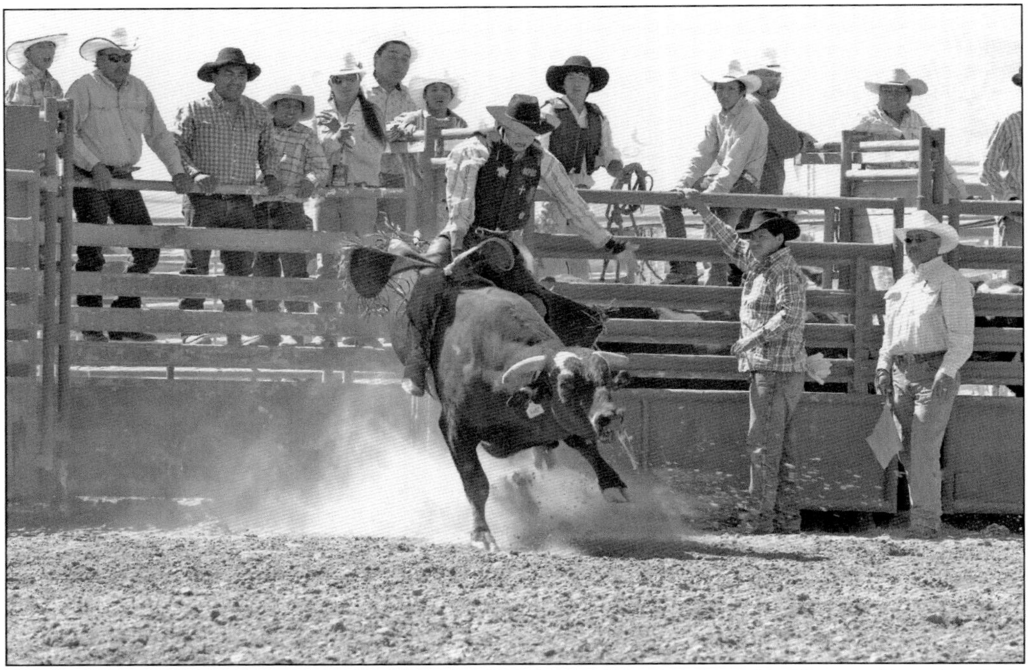

A bull rider has just come out of the chute in the above photograph of the Kayenta Fourth of July Rodeo. The contestant must stay on the animal for eight seconds, and then a pick-up rider will help him safely dismount away from the bull. A young woman, below, races around the barrels placed in the arena in a competition with other riders to complete the course in the shortest time. The Kayenta rodeo has been described as one of the premier rodeos in the Southwest. (Both, courtesy of Mario Dominguez.)

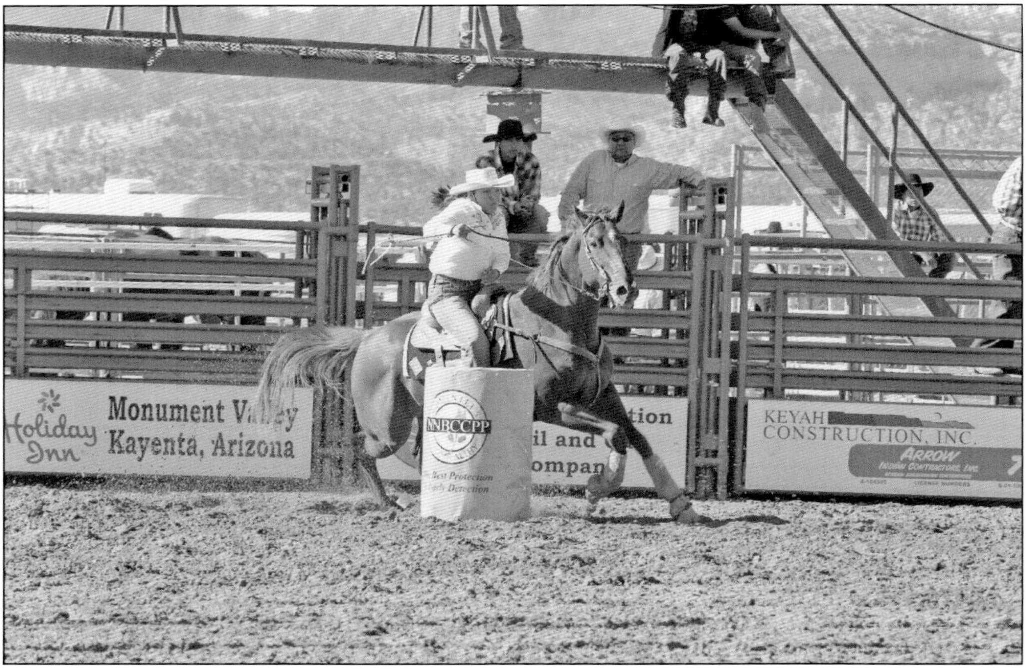

Bibliography

Christenson, Andrew L. "The Last of the Great Expeditions: The Rainbow Bridge/Monument Valley Expedition 1933–38." *Plateau* 58, no. 4 (1987), Museum of Northern Arizona.

Correll, J. Lee. "Navajo Frontiers in Utah and Troublous Times in Monument Valley." *Utah Historical Quarterly* 39, no. 2 (Spring 1971).

Cummings, Bryon. *Indians I Have Known*. Tucson: Arizona Silhouettes, 1952.

Dixon, Winifred Hawkridge. *Westward Hoboes*. New York: Charles Scribner's Sons, 1921.

Gillmor, Frances, and Louisa Wade Wetherill. *Traders to the Navajo: The Story of the Wetherills of Kayenta*. Albuquerque: The University of New Mexico Press, 1934.

Judd, Neil M. *Men Met along the Trail: Adventures in Archaeology*. Norman: University of Oklahoma Press, 1968.

Kawano, Kenji. *Warriors: Navajo Code Talkers*. Flagstaff: Northland Publishing Company, 1990.

La Farge, Oliver. *Raw Material: An Artist's Journey*. Boston: Houghton Mifflin, 1945.

Linford, Laurance D. *Navajo Places History, Legend, Landscape*. Salt Lake City: The University of Utah Press, 2000.

Pyle, Ernie. *Ernie Pyle's Southwest*. Palm Desert, CA: Desert-Southwest, Inc., 1965.

Reilly, P. T. *Lee's Ferry from Mormon Crossing to National Park*. Logan: Utah State University Press, 1999.

Reinhold, Ruth M. *Sky Pioneering: Arizona in Aviation History*. Tucson: The University of Arizona Press, 1982.

Roosevelt, Theodore. *A Book-Lover's Holidays in the Open*. New York: Charles Scribner's Sons, 1916.

Sayle, W. D. *A Trip to the Rainbow Arch*. Privately printed. 1920.

Zahn, Curtis. "The Automobile is Here to Stay." *Arizona Highways*, June 1946.